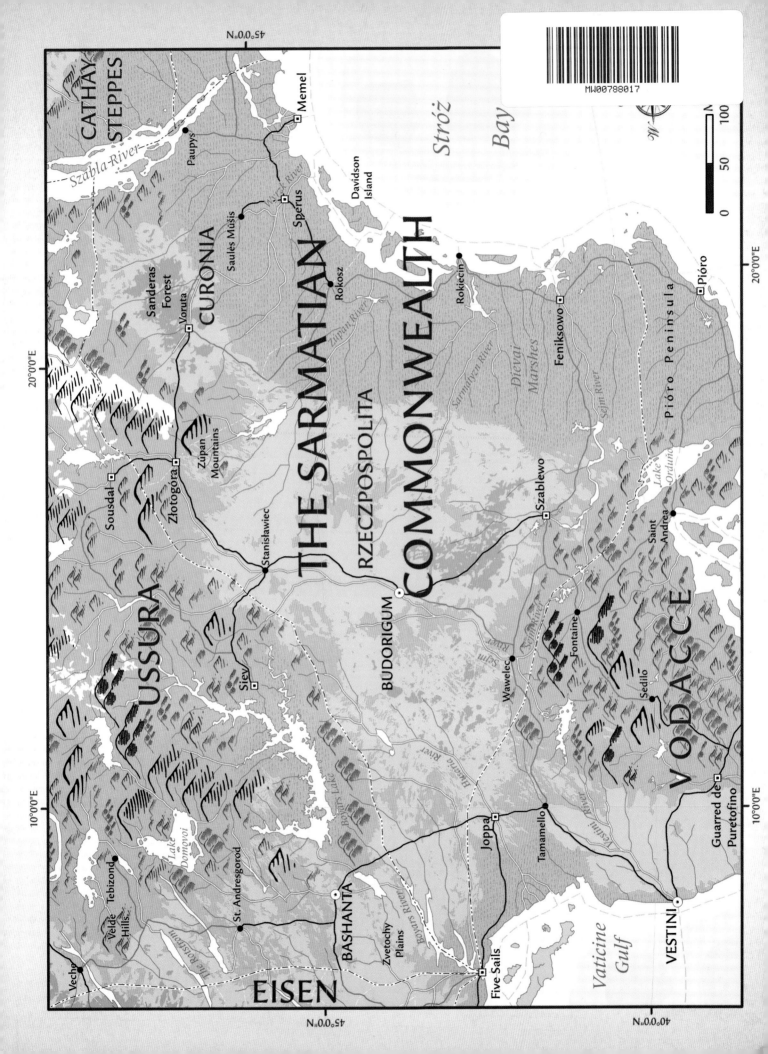

CATHAY STEPPES

Szabla River

Memel

Paupys

Stróż Bay

Davidson Island

Wark River

Sperus

CURONIA

Saulés Mūšis

Rokosz

Rokiecin

Pióro

Sanderas Forest

Voruta

THE SARMATIAN COMMONWEALTH

Żupan River

Sarmatbyzn River

Dievai Marshes

Feniksowo

Sejm River

Pióro Peninsula

Żupan Mountains

RZECZPOSPOLITA

Sousdal

Złotogora

Stanisławiec

Lake Ordun

Szablewo

Saint Andrea

USSURA

BUDORIGUM

Sejm River

Wawelec

Sejm River

Fontaine

Sedilo

Siev

VODACCE

Lake Domovoi

Boyars Lake

Husarz River

Trebizond

Velde Hills

St. Andresgorod

Guarred de Puretofino

The Rolstrom

BASHANTA

Zvetochy Plains

Boyars River

Joppa

Tamamello

Vestini River

Veche

EISEN

Five Sails

Vaticine Gulf

VESTINI

45°0'0"N

20°00'E

20°00'E

20°00'E

10°00'E

10°00'E

45°0'0"N

40°0'0"N

40°0'0"N

100
50
0

# 7TH SEA
## Nations of Théah
### Volume 2

JOHN WICK PRESENTS A SOURCEBOOK FOR 7TH SEA: SECOND EDITION "NATIONS OF THÉAH: VOLUME 2"

LEAD DEVELOPER DANIELLE LAUZON    CREATIVE DIRECTOR LEONARD BALSERA    SYSTEM LEAD MICHAEL CURRY

WRITING BY ADRIAN ARROYO    FABIEN BADILLA    CHRISTINE BEARD    JEREMY ELDER    MEGHAN FITZGERALD

JAMES MENDEZ HODES    BETSY ISSACSON    SHOSHANA KESSOCK    ERICKA SKIRPAN    BRETT ZEILER    TARA ZUBER

ADDITIONAL WRITING BY DANIELLE LAUZON    ANDRÉ LA ROCHE    STEPHEN SKIDMORE    DAN WASZKIEWICZ    NICOLE WINCHESTER

"KEEP CLOSE TO THE ROAD" BY JENNIFER MAHR    SENIOR ART DIRECTION BY MARISSA KELLY    ART DIRECTION BY ANDRÉ LA ROCHE

ART BY ZULKARNAEN HASAN BASRI    CHARLOTTE CREBER    SHEN FEI    YONG YI LI    DIEGO RODRIGUEZ

LANGUAGE SUPPORT BY OLESIA BAGINSKI    CARLO FEDERICONI    MONIKA HORTNAGL    ADAM "ADEXO" MALINOWSKI    JEANENE THOMPSON

GEOGRAPHY DESIGN AND MAP BY MARK RICHARDSON    GRAPHIC DESIGN AND LAYOUT BY THOMAS DEENY

EDITED BY MONTE LIN    PROOFING BY SHELLEY HARLAN    STAFF SUPPORT BY J. DERRICK KAPCHINSKY    MARK DIAZ TRUMAN

7TH SEA: SECOND EDITION DEVELOPED BY MICHAEL CURRY    ROB JUSTICE    MARK DIAZ TRUMAN    JOHN WICK

BASED ON 7TH SEA: FIRST EDITION BY JOHN WICK    JENNIFER MAHR

# A note from John...

When we began redesigning Théah for the second edition, the Nations that underwent the biggest changes were the Eastern Nations. Ussura needed an overhaul and I wanted Eisen to be terrifying. Vodacce escaped relatively unscathed, but the differences are there if you know how to look. And then there was adding the Sarmatian Commonwealth, a promise I made on my first visit to Poland to a friend who is no longer with us. I named one of its primary villains after him—a fact his friends and loved ones told me he would have enjoyed beyond measure. Goodbye, Magic. I miss you.

While the Western Nations of Montaigne, Castille and Avalon have much in common, the Eastern Nations stand alone. They are so very different from each other in more than just language and costume. Also, they are our link to lands even further East, giving us hints of what is to come. If you stand on a tall hill in the Commonwealth or in the eastern part of Ussura, and you squint, you can almost see the Crescent Empire...

Soon, my friends. Soon.

—John Wick

# Special Thanks

In *Nations of Théah: Volume 1*, I started a story about working on the Nations of Theah project. Here is how I joined the JWP team. I had just decided to start working part-time at the day job and wanted to expand myself as a writer and developer. I saw an all-call come across my desk for full-time writers for **7th Sea: Second Edition**. Of course, I had backed the book, this was my favorite game of all time. When Mark and John contacted me for an interview, we chatted about larp and development. After the meeting, I knew for sure I wasn't going to be a full-time writer. I thought maybe I'd be a freelancer, but I certainly wasn't expecting an offer to become a staff developer. I'm pretty sure I made noises that might only be interpreted by dolphins.

Mostly, I want to thank Mark for encouraging me to apply to JWP in the first place. Without your vote of confidence, I might have hesitated and missed this chance. Thank you to John for letting me take your baby and expand upon it. Thank you to the writers for really knocking this book out of the park. These nations are probably the hardest to represent correctly, and I'm overjoyed with how well you took what I was thinking and put it to page. Getting a book from a concept to a final print is a herculean task and takes a team, no matter how big or small, of dedicated people. I'm happy to say I've worked with one of the best teams ever in developing the *Nations of Théah* books.

And as always, I reserve a very special thanks to my husband, Weston Harper.

—Danielle Lauzon

# Table of Contents

# Keep Close to the Road

*by Jennifer Mahr*

The traveling party wasn't large—the Vesten merchant and his niece, his bookkeeper, two guards and a swordsman for defense, plus a sturdy pair of squires to tend their horses and belongings. They'd been on the road for more than three months, following business interests in Montaigne, Castille, and most recently Vodacce. In all those places they'd garnered little notice in the busy cities and sparkling capitals. That changed sharply when they reached the tiny port of Memel on the south coast of Sarmatia.

They disembarked their chartered sailing vessel to the open curiosity of the locals. Fishermen, packs of children, women at the market all stopped to watch them unload their things and make their way to the largest inn, which was still pressed to find space for them all.

The people they met in Memel were friendly, if a bit provincial. The serving girls at the inn were eager to speak to the merchant's niece about her clothes, which were grander and of a different style from their own. The local men shared local drinks, and compared blades with the guards—proudly showing off their own szabla, the curved swords favored in the region.

Their eventual destination was the Ussuran capital where the merchant had business interests and trade partners who would give them a warm welcome. But Ussura lacked warm-water seaports of her own, depending on her eastern neighbor for access to trade ships, and the merchant wanted to see first-hand the routes his goods would be traveling. In the brisk chill of early morning they left Memel and set off on the road north.

As the sun began to wane on their third night, they looked for a place to make camp. The road had brought them to the outskirts of a forest where the trees were tall and their thick canopies brought the darkness on that much earlier.

"I think we've got a good spot just up ahead," called one of the guards, who'd ridden ahead as a scout. "There's enough of a clearing that we can get up a pair of tents, and a brook not too far off."

The swordsman stretched. "A tent would be good, but I'll settle for a fire. The warmth's gone with the sun." There was a mumble of general agreement from the rest of the group. It was still early autumn, but they'd learned quickly that the weather here was harsher than in the other countries they'd travelled in. They were grateful to have avoided rain so far, but the clouds stayed densely gathered through most of the days.

It didn't take long to raise the camp. With the horses brushed and secure they gathered around the warmth of a cheerful fire and the large pot of fragrant stew simmering there.

They all startled when the guardsman keeping watch called out, "Who's that? Hold where you are and give a name!" There was a faint rustling further out in the forest, and the swordsman and the other guard both had their blades drawn, when the reply came, too muffled to hear in the camp. Then a stranger came into view at the edge of the firelight.

He was tall, and probably big, though it was hard to tell under the thick clothes and heavy furs he wore. He didn't carry a sword, but a blade too thick and long to be called a knife hung from his belt. He looked weathered and his long hair was coarse, the bulk of it pulled back, but braids of it dangled forward, woven with bright bits of fabric, incongruous with his otherwise grim appearance. Between the gray-purple of twilight and shadows from the

dancing flames, it was impossible to tell his age.

"My name's Jurgis," he repeated for the group gathered there, voice a low rumble. "But perhaps I should be the one asking all of you who you are since you're here in my forest."

"Your forest?" asked the swordsman with skepticism.

"Mine as much as anyone's," agreed the newcomer. "More so than most since I live here."

"You live here?" asked the merchant's niece, surprise and interest in her voice. She'd come along to see more of the world, and this was something new.

"I do," he answered with a hint of amusement.

"Do you have a house in the forest?"

"I do, of a sort. But it's nowhere near here," he answered. "What brings you all out so late at night? This isn't a road that sees many travelers."

"We're headed north, to the Ussura border," the merchant answered, puffing himself up a bit. "Why does this road get so little use? It seems the most direct way, but the locals we've met say that most people use the route west of here, even though it looks further on the map."

"You took this road because you were in a hurry?" asked Jurgis.

"We're looking for the best road to use to move goods," explained the merchant. "I expect to send shipments through regularly, and I wanted to see the way they'd be traveling."

"Ah. Well then you're on the wrong road," Jurgis said with certainty. "You should have taken the westerly one."

"Why?" asked the merchant, growing frustrated. "This way is faster."

"This way goes through the forest."

"Yes certainly, but a few trees can be cleared to widen the way," said the merchant confidently. He was always confident where commerce was concerned.

"You can't clear trees here," said the newcomer firmly. "Not here. This is Sandaras forest."

"Yes, I've seen the map." The merchant spoke with exaggerated patience, but the other man seemed not to mind. He just smiled faintly.

"You've seen the map. You don't know the forest. Next time you find someone from here, you ask them about the forest. Then ask the person you meet after that. And the one after them." He looked around. "I should be going. You all should keep close to the road."

"Wait!" said the girl as he started to go. She tugged her uncle's sleeve, speaking to him urgently until he sighed and nodded.

"Jurgis, would you like to join us for dinner?" he asked. "We're about to eat, and you're welcome to share our fire and our food."

"I wouldn't feel right taking your hospitality for nothing," he said, looking hesitant for the first time since he arrived. "And I doubt I have anything to pay you with that you'd value."

"A story!" The girl looked around with bright eyes. "You could trade us a story about this place." Her uncle gave her a look of indulgent amusement.

"All right," agreed the stranger with a chuckle. "That seems a fair offer."

With the guards still looking faintly uneasy, he joined them at the fire. One of the squires lifted the lid on the stew pot to stir, the savory aroma filling the air. Abruptly the man still on watch gave another cry, this one startled and inarticulate.

"What is it?" called the other guard, leaping up.

"In Theus's name, I don't know," shouted the other. "Something moved out there. It was huge."

"No need to worry," assured Jurgis. "Just my hound."

All eyes turned to him. "It was enormous," insisted the guard from where he still stood deeper in the tree line.

"Yes, but she won't give you any trouble," Jurgis told him. "So long as you leave her be."

Now the rest of the group was staring out into the trees as well. The light of the fire made the shadows further out even darker, but they could see, now and again, something moving in the trees. The girl gave a gasp. It was large, but unexpectedly graceful, moving fluidly at the edge of the light. Her eye caught Jurgis's and he smiled reassuringly. "I still don't know your name, lady," he said.

She blushed. "Asny. Asny Thranddatter. And this is my uncle Ketil Haak."

Jurgis inclined his head to her. "Very good to make your acquaintance, Asny Thranddatter. And now, here is your story."

***

The winters in Curonia are harsh, no question. But about once in every score of years comes a winter that whips the limbs from trees, hurls snow like stones, and scours the earth with its frost. My story comes just at the end of one of those.

In a village an old man died from age and sickness, and maybe the cold. He left a grandson who was alone in the world—parents long under the earth, and no other kin. No one else in the village was in a position to feed another mouth, and the boy knew he couldn't keep the little house they'd shared on his own, so he packed up his meager things and set off into the woods to find his fortune.

He was a smart boy, and he'd grown up learning to trap and hunt, and at another time, he'd have been able to take care of himself without much trouble. But at the tail of a winter like the one they'd had, the first in his eleven years, he found himself hard pressed to find food. Shelter he had to share or fight for with bears and badgers. He knew if he walked long enough he'd come to the road. And from the road he could travel to anywhere and do anything. It was as good a plan as any for a boy his age who'd been nowhere and seen nothing.

He got by for a few days, scraping along, but he was hungry and tired, and thinner than when he'd started. One day he heard shuffling sounds nearby, smaller than a bear, but bigger than a rabbit, and he thought maybe his luck had turned very good and he'd come across a deer. He readied his slingshot, and started for the noise. There were no tracks to follow with the snow mostly melted but the ground still frozen, so he had to use his ears and his wits. In a small clearing he found the source of the rustling, but it wasn't a deer. It was a girl.

She was thinner and hungrier than he was, and she had a feral look about her. He guessed she was about his age. Her clothes were rags, and whatever hue they'd started, they were the color of mud now. Her hair was pale under the dirt and tangled like a briar patch. And her eyes were the blue-purple of the sky before the last light goes.

*** 

Jurgis paused in his story. He looked as though he was seeing something further away and more real than the camp in that moment. Then he shook his head. "I think your stew might be done," he said with a nod at the pot, which was beginning to bubble over.

With a start, the steward who'd been tending it hurried to lift the pot from the fire, and set about ladling food into wooden bowls. The rest of the party shifted in their seats, settling down with their food. They'd all been intent on Jurgis's story. When they were back in their places, and everyone had their dinner, Asny spoke. "Will you go on?" she asked.

"Of course," Jurgis agreed, tasting his stew. "This is very good." Letting his gaze drift again, he continued.

***

The boy did his best to talk to the girl, but if she had words, she didn't use them. He thought she might be dumb, but not deaf. He learned quickly that her hearing was much better than his own. They traveled together from then on, and she was always quick to lay a hand on his arm, or tug at his sleeve and point out a squirrel or a bird that might become their supper. She was clever too, and found them places to sleep that he'd have missed on his own—little shelters and cubbies that kept off the wind.

He tried to convince her to talk, because the silence was lonely, and she picked up a few of his words, finding the meanings quickly. They fell into a routine where he would talk to himself as they went, and she would listen, and at the end of each day she knew a few more words than the day before. It was still hard going, though. Food was scarce, especially split between the two of them. The boy had been walking in the woods for more than a week, and he had no idea how long the girl had been out there, but it was certainly longer. So when they came upon a hunter's snare with three fat rabbits in it, he didn't think twice about taking two of them.

That night they found a small cave, made a tidy fire, and ate cooked rabbit. He sang songs he'd learned from his grandfather, and the girl hummed wordlessly but beautifully along.

A little before dawn they learned their mistake. They woke to angry shouts and the sound of something beating the tree branches. It was the hunter they'd stolen from, and he was looking for them. They stayed in their cave, listening to his bellows and threats, and for the first time, the boy was glad of the cold ground that made it hard to track.

When the hunter was further off, they snuck from their cave and headed away. They couldn't keep going in the direction of the road, because their pursuer was between them and it, so they turned back deeper into the forest. They tried to keep a course parallel to the one they'd had, so they could circle back in the direction of the road. The boy guessed it was only a couple of days off by then, but the hunter didn't give up his pursuit, and they had to turn further and further into the trees.

After two more days, they'd come to a place where the trees were taller, and the forest was darker than the boy had ever seen. All the stories his grandfather had told him about the heart of the forest, and the things that lived there—neither man nor beast—played through his thoughts. He heard sounds of things moving more often now, but he didn't dare hunt them. The things that moved in the trees here were bigger and harder to identify, and he wasn't confident his slingshot and stones would bring them down. And however deep they went, the hunter was never far behind them.

The only good thing was that the harshest cold had spared this place, and his companion seemed more familiar here. She found them berries and plants to eat, and the deeper they went the more certainly she moved.

They spent a night in a thicket where the branches reached out and around so that they made a little cove, out of sight and out of the wind. The boy argued that they should keep walking, to get as much distance as they could between them and the hunter. Nature said the man had to sleep, but he seemed to edge closer to them all the time. But the girl took his arm and tugged him into the hollow. They were both tired enough to be stumbling.

The place was dry, and even without a fire it quickly warmed with the heat of their bodies. He drifted off in a bed of dried leaves even while he was straining to listen for any sounds of pursuit. Maybe he slept for hours. Maybe it was minutes. He heard rustling which turned into whispers, then the whispers turned into a song—quiet like the sound you get if you cup your hand over your ear.

He opened his eyes and he could see shadows moving outside the shelter, shifting on the other side of the branches as though they were dancing to that song he could almost hear. Some of them went on four legs, some on two, but try as he might he couldn't see what cast the shadows.

Dimly amazed at his own lack of alarm, he watched as some of the shapes scuttled, small and close against the ground, but moving together like they were one larger creature. Others slipped in and out amongst the trees and each other as fine as flowers on long stems shifting on a spring breeze. Still others moved with awkward grace, long limbs bending at unexpected angles like men made of sticks joined carelessly together. One rose up taller than the others and he thought that it lifted its arms toward the sky; then he thought those weren't arms but horns that reached upward as it lifted its head.

The whispering song picked up a deeper sound underneath it, like a moan that made his bones vibrate even while his ears still strained to make it out, as though maybe it wasn't a real sound at all, just something inside of him, except that the shadows still danced to it. He was dreaming. He knew that. He looked to his companion to see if it was a dream she shared, but he was alone in the shelter.

Sometime after that he fell properly asleep and in the morning woke to the clearer and familiar song of birds overhead. His companion was where she'd gone to sleep the night before.

As they prepared to leave he remembered his dream and the tracker in him had to stop and examine the forest floor. The leaves were unbroken, the earth undisturbed. There was no trace of the shapes he'd seen in the night, no hint of a grand dance of shadows. As he followed the girl into the thicker woods he looked back at the cove of

branches where they'd taken shelter, and there was no sign of that either.

There came a day when they were running, the hunter close enough that they could hear him breaking through branches behind them and hear the vivid descriptions of what he'd do when he found them. Listening to him rant, the boy knew just how long a pot of soup made from two children would last, and how quickly the hunter could hang them up and strip them and smoke them into jerky. If he'd been less concerned with what was just behind them, the boy might have paid more attention to what was in front.

They came up against a wall of rock so suddenly there was no warning. The trees were so dense, the boy hadn't seen it coming, and now he scrambled to find a way up or around. The trees here were so thick, four big men standing close together still wouldn't match their girth, and they were tight enough that they made a kind of corridor that the children were caught in now. Thinking quick as he could, the boy hustled the girl into a space between the trees and the rock, and tried his best to explain that she needed to stay there and be very still. He readied his slingshot and tucked his little knife in his belt, close at hand, and he walked into the middle of that corridor to meet the hunter.

I don't suppose he really expected to win that fight. But there were few enough options, and he thought about those blue-purple eyes, and he thought, if he could hurt the hunter, the girl could still get away. In a few minutes the man chasing him came into view. He slowed down and took his time when he saw the boy. He had a bow on his back, and a great long knife, but it was an axe he took from a sling at his side, big and sharp enough to cut through a tree. No doubt it'd go through bone easy as you please. He was large and rangy, and he looked to be about half man and half madness, and he grinned with a dark kind of joy as he stalked closer.

The boy knew that even if he made his best shot with his slingshot, he'd have no better chance stopping the man coming for him than he would a rampaging bear. Some things are so angry and hungry they're too far gone to know when they've been hit, but he got ready anyhow. He raised his slingshot and the hunter raised his axe, and then there was a growl like if a mountain ground itself against another mountain, and something pale and lean and full of sharp teeth leapt from the trees and hurled into the hunter.

It hit him so hard he lost his axe. Then his hand. Then his throat.

The boy stood with his slingshot still drawn back, his legs frozen, his feet rooted where they stood. What looked back at him was no animal he'd ever seen. It had four legs, a long body that moved like muscle in silk, teeth—so many teeth—sharp and bloody, and blue-purple eyes.

*\*\**

Jurgis's voice trailed off, his gaze still far away.

"Did he shoot it?" asked one of the squires, his voice a bit breathless.

"He did not," answered Jurgis, taking a sip from a canteen by his side.

"Did he get away?" asked Asny, leaning forward, eyes shining.

"He didn't do that either," Jurgis replied with a shake of his head.

"So then..." the swordsman hesitated. He'd been studiously trying to look bored all along, but he'd given it up. "What did happen?"

Jurgis raised his bowl to his lips and drained the last of his stew. "The boy stayed in the forest," he said. "He found the road eventually. More than once. But he never took it."

"And the girl?" asked Asny.

"Oh, she stayed too," he said with a fond smile. "They had some harsh winters after that, but the worst weather never reached all the way into the heart of the forest. Even storms know better than to go there." He set his bowl down and stood up. "And now I think I'd better be on my way. I thank you for your hospitality." The others all stood as well, the merchant looking uncertain.

"That was a very fine story," he said courteously. "A bit of local folklore?"

"Something like that," Jurgis said with a nod.

"Is it meant to be a particular forest? The one in your story?"

"Oh yes. It's this one of course, the Sandaras. The heart of the forest is very, very old you see. But sometimes, the things that live in it wander further afield. Which is why you won't find anyone from these parts who will help you cut down trees here. Or travel with your caravans." He shifted his heavy cloak, adjusting the great axe that hung across his back on a leather strap. "Take my word for it," he said. "Use the westerly road."

With a nod to the group and a deeper one for Asny, he turned and headed back into the woods, now shrouded in full dark. As he went he gave a low whistle, and something much too large to be a dog bounded through the trees and to his side, giving a low rumble that made the horses whinny nervously. The two of them walked into the dark together.

Introduction

This book is the second of a two-volume set detailing the Nations of Théah. For the purposes of these books, we have split the nations into west and east, with Eisen, the Sarmatian Commonwealth, Ussura and Vodacce as our eastern ones. Within these pages, you will find an inside look at each of these lands.

# The State of Things

The eastern countries have gone past the flux the western countries currently suffer under and have come out the other side. In a few places, this means the Nation is battered—but not quite broken—and in others, a person's entire way of life has been upended.

A common citizen in the eastern nations in a better place than those in her neighboring countries. While class systems often still remain in place, she has more to hope for and more room for innovation. Many of the eastern nations teeter just at the brink of change, or have changed in recent history. That change has the potential to bring greatness, or tragedy, to each Nation. While war may be on the horizon for many of the Nations, the people are hopeful instead of downtrodden. The nobility and commoners alike work in tandem to solve the problems of the nation, instead of being divided wholly along class lines.

The resounding theme among all the Nations is hope in the face of turmoil. Even in places with little to hope for, the people grow and adapt into their new environments. Eisen slowly rebuilds after the ravages of the War of the Cross, and now they seek a new Imperator to guide them. Ussura stands at a precipice of a new Czar (or Czarina), or a savage civil war. The Sarmatian Commonwealth grows into a new democracy, yet the future of its leadership is uncertain. Vodacce sits at the brink of revolution as Princes maneuver, and those who oppose their unjust rule gain strength.

Unlike in the west, where each Nation's problems influence the others, in the east, each Nation's successes influence their neighbors. Ussura finds strength in Eisen innovation. The Commonwealth finds duty in the strong leadership of Ussura. Vodacce finds honor in the new nobility of the Commonwealth. And Eisen finds hope in the faces of all her neighbors.

## Eisen

Eisen struggles in a near shambles after the War of the Cross. Even after twenty years have passed, the Nation's population remains small. The chief reason for this is the Horrors that cover the landscape. Travel in Eisen is a dangerous prospect, and travel at night is a suicide mission.

Despite those truths, the people have bonded together in a stronger national identity than ever before. The people of Eisen help their brothers and sisters, regardless of Vaticine or Objectionist beliefs, all in the name of turning back the Horrors.

The Eisenfürsten rally the people, and the thought of a unified Nation under one rule brings hope. The young are motivated to enact change and are made strong by surviving the Horrors of the land. The old still remember the War and strive to make Eisen a better home than it was before. Through all this, the people prosper, despite the odds, and the Nation is on its way to a strong comeback in the greater politics of Théah.

## The Sarmatian Commonwealth

The Sarmatian Commonwealth has just recently gained the status of true democracy. Every person has a vote in the Sejm, regardless of birth or wealth. Though this does little to change a peasant's day-to-day life, he exercises that right while learning that the will of the people can be more powerful than the will of the nobles. A common person is in a position to make real changes in her Nation, if she can simply organize with others. A noble finds himself beholden to the commoners in a way he never was before.

The Sarmatian people identify strongly as one Nation, but age-old grudges between the Rzeplitan and Curonian peoples still color interactions. Beyond that, the people finally have a choice in who their next Monarch could be. Many support the King's son, Aleksy Nowak, and already call him Stanisław II. Yet, anything could change, and not a few other contenders to the throne have made themselves known, forcing a conflict in loyalties and an uptick in politics amongst the common people.

## Ussura

Ussura stands at the brink of something great, with no one true path to guide it. The government is in a state of arrest as two valid rulers vie for the title of Czar: Czarina Ketheryna, wife of the former Czar, and Prince Ilya, the Czar's disowned son. The people, the government and even the Nation's capital city remain split between the two. Each attempts to prove their worthiness, making it even harder for people to decide.

A citizen of Ussura leads a simple life and follows simple rules set by the spirits of the land, the Leshiye. She often seeks guidance from these sources, yet her Nation's patron, Matushka, has not spoken on the subject of her leader.

Now, the people must decide on their own, but in the meantime, little moves forward. In the absence of a true government, a military might has arisen and threatens to bring Ussura to the brink of war. Of course, if neither Ketheryna nor Ilya can solidify their right to rule, the Nation may simply fall to civil war.

## Vodacce

Vodacce, the most traditional of all the eastern nations, has no single ruler. Instead, seven Princes in seven districts rule and scheme against each other and their own people. Of the seven Princes, three families have enough power to make a move towards taking over the Nation and declaring themselves Emperor. The very power that each holds, though, is what keeps the others at bay.

It wouldn't take much to upset that balance, sending Vodacce into a civil war of its own or a neat and clean coup leading to a single ruling family. Despite the lines that divide the Nation, people from Vodacce are fiercely national.

The people chomp at the bit against the rule of the Princes. The women seek a way to break free of their bonds, and the peasantry simply seeks a way to make a living. In Vodacce, rules are made to be broken. The rules and laws that govern the lives of the nobles and the commoners alike are ready to break, and that may end in a revolution rather than a war between Princes.

## What's Inside

Inside this book, you will find four chapters, one for each of the eastern nations. The chapters are broken down into setting information and new Hero mechanics for Heroes originating in the nation.

### Chapter One: Eisen

The Eisen chapter contains detailed information on the Eisenfürsten of Eisen as well as the military might of the Iron Guard and the Drachenblut Söldners. We take a look at major players across the Nation, as well as give some examples of common people with big destinies.

We examine each of the Secret Societies, and how they operate in Eisen, as well as introduce the Kinder von Morgen, a highly organized group of Rilasciare who seek democracy for Eisen. Hexenwerk is expanded to include a group of Monster hunters who seek out creatures other than Horrors and use their parts to make different Unguents.

We examine dueling in Eisen, and how Duelists serve as de facto judges, as well as introduce the Verzweiflung Duelist Style. Finally, we take an in-depth look at the various Horrors found in Eisen.

### Chapter Two: The Sarmatian Commonwealth

The Sarmatian Commonwealth chapter contains information on the royal family and the major political players in the Nation now that it is a democracy.

We examine each of the Secret Societies, and how they operate in the Commonwealth, as well as introduce the Most Noble and Honorable Order of Post, a faction of the Knights of the Rose & Cross concerned with reviving chivalry in the Nation. We expand on the concepts of Sanderis and detail the various factions among the *losejai* and the *Ratas*, as well as expand upon the Seventh Deal.

We examine dueling in the Sarmatian Commonwealth and the advent of various different Chivalric Orders, as well as introduce the Szybować Duelist Style. The legends of the Sarmatian Commonwealth include the famous *dievai*, the hanging tree, knights in silver armor and a weeklong celebration of the rusalka.

## Chapter Three: Ussura

In Ussura we offer detailed write-ups of both Ilya and Ketheryna, our contenders to the throne, as well as the various other important members of the Ussuran government.

We examine each of the Secret Societies, and how they operate in Ussura, as well as introduce the Ushkuiniks, the river-faring branch of the Brotherhood of the Coast. The chapter contains information on Tură, the spirit of storms who offers his blessing to people in the guise of Chernobog.

We examine dueling in Ussura, where grappling and bare-fisted fighting is the order of the day, as well as introduce the Kulachniy Boy Duelist Style. The legends of Ussura include enchanted flowers, Leshiye, domovoi, rusalki, vodyanoi and upir.

## Chapter Four: Vodacce

The Vodacce chapter describes major players across all of Vodacce, from the Princes to important courtesans and Heroes who try to make their way in a land of Villainy.

We examine each of the Secret Societies and how they operate in Vodacce, as well as introduce the Philosophi Sanguinis, a group of Invisible College members devoted to experimentation with occult resources. We discuss Sorte, how new *Streghe* receive training and what happens when a Fate Witch manifests her powers without proper tutelage.

We examine dueling in Vodacce, and how Vodacce Duelists rarely fight legally, as well as introduce the Le Strade Duelist Style. The legends of Vodacce include creatures who seek to punish the bad and reward the good, and various Monsters who haunt the Vodacce landscape.

## Appendix

Here we introduce new Advantages available to any character, and new Backgrounds for each of the four Nations presented in this book.

# How to Use This Book

This book is supplemental to the 7TH SEA CORE RULEBOOK. As such, you need access to that book to make the most of NATIONS OF THÉAH, VOLUME TWO. The information presented here is supposed to help both players and Game Masters better understand the game world. Each Nation offers setting information to help ensure rich character backgrounds and stories. The people of the Nations are approachable, and a Game Master can use these people as presented in her game or tweak them to fit her story.

This information in this book provides an insider's view of the Nation, though anyone could know what is in these pages. Each chapter contains secrets about the people and locations therein, and the Game Master should decide how much of that information is widely known outside the Nation, and within.

The new mechanics presented in each chapter are meant to give additional choices to Heroes and are completely optional to use in your game. The Game Master is the final arbiter on which options are allowed.

Chapter 1

Eisen

# EISEN

*"We were once a land of drachen and Heroes riding shining steeds to fight monsters. We were once prosperous and full of promise. We were once a lot of things. Now we are this. But I will tell you one thing. We are still proud. And there are still monsters to fight."*
—Unknown veteran of the War of the Cross, Freiburg

Mention the name Eisen anywhere across Théah and people tell tales of horrifying beasts, mountains where drachen once roamed and stretches of land soaked deep with the blood of armies long since gone.

Nearly twenty years ago, the War of the Cross ravaged an entire generation of Théans, killing and traumatizing the Eisen people and marring the countryside. The nation collapsed, its monarchy destroyed and all industry driven to a halt. In its place, monsters roam with impunity and former soldiers fight to keep people alive against nightmares other Théans could only imagine.

Eisen struggles to unify and rebuild in an ever-modernizing world. A new generation has come into adulthood since the War, and an Eisen youth chafes under the constant reminders of a war she never fought. The respect she has for her elders mixes with frustration over the country's focus on its past when the future seems so uncertain. The Nation looks to the seven Eisenfürsten to lead them to a better tomorrow. Too bad none of them can agree on what that tomorrow should look like, or who should rule.

And then, there are the Horrors. From every corner of Eisen, the darkest shadows give up terrifying beasts, ready to savage, corrupt and destroy. To be a child of Eisen means being born to fight, to survive the Horrors and to keep the people safe, one day at a time.

# Rebuilding a Nation

It has been a full twenty years since the War of the Cross, and Eisen still struggles to find its feet. The largest hindrance to rebuilding the Nation may be the Horrors, which ravage the countryside, but the lack of a single ruler doesn't help. On top of that, the population of Eisen is markedly decreased, leaving land untilled and work undone. Emigration is a huge problem as the Horrors send people fleeing to safer nations, and few newcomers stay for very long.

The one thing Eisen does not lack is funding. Even the poorest Bauern has more wealth than the peasants in many other nations. The Adel have riches untold, with little to spend it on. Labor is a hard commodity to come by, though a worker who serves an Adel to maintain her lands can expect a handsome payment. Many Eisenfürsten do all they can to entice people to come live under their protection, often offering great rewards just to till a small plot of Horror ridden land.

Other Théans recognize the potential of Eisen's people and land, and try to help as best they can. The Vendel League hopes to give support to the people, but only a few Eisenfürsten bother to deal with them, making it hard for their help to make much of an impact.

Most of Eisen remains Objectionist with a few Vaticine holdouts remaining in pockets here and there. Mostly, the people of Eisen are so exhausted of religion that many of them have forsaken Theus all together.

The people who remain in Eisen are fiercely loyal to their Nation and strive to make it a safe place again, or at least to carve out islands of security for the people to live. Each and every person living in Eisen trains as a warrior by necessity. Few native-born Eisen die to Horrors after the age of ten, as by then they are fully versed in how to most efficiently kill the creatures. Their dedication and prowess could be enough to beat back the Horrors, if only they organized.

Recognizing this truth, several factions have sprung up throughout Eisen, each proposing a new Imperator to lead them to stability and safety. Unfortunately, no one can agree on the best options, and some of the candidates want nothing to do with the position.

Additionally, some Eisenfürsten are happy to continue ruling with little oversight or laws. These do all they can to prevent a new Imperator from rising, or possibly seek to take the position for themselves.

# Important People in Eisen

## The Eisenfürsten

Before the War of the Cross, Eisen had a ruler whose blood went back countless generations. When Imperator Riefenstahl died, he left a power vacuum which politicians have struggled to fill for the last twenty years. Devoid of a ruler, the country split into seven königreiche, ruled by the former barons of the land. These new Eisenfürsten have since solidified their territories, and rule their portion of the country as they see fit. With the people looking for more stable leadership, each Eisenfürst presents a possible new leader.

The Eisenfürsten set the tone for their königreiche, from their political views to the way they manage the land. The people of Eisen are fiercely dedicated and stand behind their leaders, despite any qualms they may have with them. The Eisenfürsten also maintain a court of advisors around them, each with their own needs for their business and the people they represent.

A person seeking aid, information or trade of favors finds the courts of the Iron Princes the place to get what she needs. Heroes can find the Eisenfürsten embroiled in their political plays and always looking for new allies, hirelings or even enemies to push along their own agendas.

## Niklas Träge

The most enigmatic of the Eisenfürsten is also perhaps the most popular. Niklas Träge did not begin life as a baron, but the discovery of a hidden cache of dracheneisen deep in a mountain cave during the War allowed the former commoner to buy his way to a title under the Imperator. Everyone forgets to mention that Träge only found the weapons and armor after he lost his unit on the battlefield and went wandering, but the power of money and prestige can bury any dishonor in the public eye. Träge, however, never forgave himself for the loss and carries the scars of his time at war to this day.

Once the War ended, the other Eisenfürsten and the people expected Träge to care for the königreich under his domain. Instead, he spent over a decade slogging through the desecrated battlefields fighting Horrors and trying to forget his mistakes during the War. He eventually ran out of funds and returned to the wreck of a königreich to pick up the pieces. The result is Freiburg, the "Free City." All within Träge's territory live with no centralized law in his grand social experiment, which he watches from the top of his Watchtower with a bottle of wine and his memories to keep him company.

Träge, a solitary man, remains haunted by his feelings of unworthiness and the tragedies he witnessed during the War. Of all the Eisenfürsten, Träge has no interest in higher political aspirations, instead focusing his time on maintaining Freiburg for its people and keeping the other Eisenfürsten from poaching resources or power. While Träge is aware many see him as a great candidate for chancellor or perhaps even a crowned leader, almost nothing on all of Terra could move him to take the position.

The management of Freiburg is about as much responsibility as Träge wants and he relies heavily on his right-hand woman, Wilma Probst, to keep the barely controlled "Free City" and the rest of the königreich from burning to the ground. A lover of poetry and learning, Träge surrounds himself with books in a library. His most prized possession is the gauntlet of the Imperator, a reminder of their great leader, tragically lost.

## Roswitha von Wirsche

Roswitha von Wirsche was a young baron's wife when the War began, and her husband Reinhard rode off to war with her sons Edgar, Frederick and Siegrud. A beauty with Vestenmennavenjar blood, Roswitha's world shattered when her husband and sons died in battle. Roswitha went into seclusion and many believed her husband's brother would take over the barony. But it was Roswitha who arrived for the first meeting of the Eisenfürsten. Her husband's brother was incidentally never heard from again. And Roswitha emerged from seclusion a different woman. Her beauty and strength returned, after the War she took up management of her lands with vigor.

In the twenty years that followed, Countess Roswitha worked tirelessly to rebuild her territory until the land once more bloomed. Wirsche became a success story for all of Eisen to see, a land protected by a division of the Iron Guard desperately loyal to their Countess. Wirsche's success helps the rest of Eisen ignore the rumors about servants and travelers going missing at Roswitha's manor in Siegburg, rumors that point to Roswitha as the cause.

The few bodies that do turn up are mysteriously short on blood. Moreover, many have begun to notice the Countess has not aged a day in twenty years. And anyone who knows about the monsters of Eisen whispers only one possibility in hushed tones: *blood drinker*. Still, without clear evidence, pointing a finger at one of the most powerful women in Eisen would be impossible, so even her growing group of detractors remains silent. Meanwhile, Roswitha keeps Wirsche growing through a healthy application of carrot and stick, offering incentives to those who work hard and threatening those who fall behind on her standard of productivity with visits by her Iron Guard.

To the world, the Countess is a ruthless, efficient ruler, dedicated to the prosperous growth of her königreich. With her territory's growth, she leads as a frontrunner to take control of the country, a position supported by Heinrich Dray, leader of the Iron Guard in Wirsche and her passionate lover. Dray publicly issued a challenge to Niklas Träge of Freiburg: hand over the gauntlet of the Imperator so that Roswitha might wear it and rule. Whether the message came from the Countess herself, no one knows. One thing is for sure: Roswitha has been annexing territory slowly from other königreiche around her with the help of her Iron Guard, and no one seems prepared to stop her.

## Elsa Pösen

Set against the northern sea, the territory of Pösen survived the War mostly unscathed, leaving the young baroness in charge of one of the last intact homes of Eisen's pre-War culture. The sense of peace did not stop the brave Elsa from marching south with her father's best warriors to lend the Pösen armies to the war effort. Elsa distinguished herself as a great leader and heroic fighter, and once her father died, she was the obvious choice to take up leadership of her königreich. Then the real troubles began.

Once the War ended, Horrors besieged Pösen, climbing up out of the swamps that dot the landscape. Warriors returning from war found themselves without respite, driven into a pitched battle to rescue family and home from all manner of monsters. Elsa set to work immediately bringing her Iron Guard to order and recruiting ex-soldiers to patrol her borders. A brilliant tactician, Elsa turned the rise of the Horrors into an opportunity, organizing military bands to sell their services to traveling merchants for protection traveling south from Vestenmennavenjar. With the cut she got from the endeavor, she renovated her ports to put Pösen in place to control the import and export of goods into Eisen and solidified herself and her city as paragons for the rebirth of the country.

The baroness remains a proud and arrogant warrior, at home fighting Horrors as much as arguing with the other Eisenfürsten. Below the arrogance lies a canny mind, however. Elsa has begun secretly supporting the flagging Fischler and thrown her support behind the Drachenblut in the hopes their young commander Rosamund Roth might be the Hero Eisen truly needs to pull itself back into a single, united country.

## Stefan Heilgrund

Of all the Eisenfürsten, only Stefan Heilgrund never saw the horrors of the War of the Cross firsthand. Born at the end of the War, Stefan is the youngest of Eisen's leaders and a brash believer in setting aside the past to fight for a new, more energetic future. Stefan was the only son of the old Baron Peter Heilgrund, born in the golden years of the former military commander's life. Young Stefan wrestled control of the barony from his elder uncles almost as soon as his father died and set about leading the territory by force of youthful energy and aggressive reform.

Stefan himself cares little for the everyday difficulties of ruling his königreich. Instead, he sets his sights a great deal higher: on leadership of Eisen itself.

Stefan believes he is the perfect man to unite Eisen and lead it into the future, a fact he has not bothered to keep secret from anyone, including the rest of the Eisenfürsten. Largely disliked and derided by the rest of the Iron Princes, Stefan seeks new and more radical displays of power to gain footing among his peers.

The baron splits his time between riding out with his Iron Guard in great displays of "military leadership" and studying all manner of the occult in a massive library of tombs bursting with knowledge collected from all over Terra. Stefan believes the key to winning leadership of Eisen is to discover a magical solution for the Horrors. To that end, he has funded numerous expeditions all over Eisen and the world in search of Syrneth relics and drachen bones, a combination he believes hold the key to untold power for the wielder. If he can only unlock their secrets.

## Falk Fischler

Falk Fischler represents a cautionary tale of the mistakes of youth. This fifty-two year old Eisenfürst started from humble beginnings, the second son of a struggling merchant, and ended up marrying a poor Ussuran traveler. Despite their lack of money, Falk lived happily with his wife Olga.

When War came to their town, both Falk's father and brother, Dieter, went to fight while Falk stayed behind due to failing health. He never imagined their bravery would earn them a barony. Though Dieter died, the Fischler family received a title and land carved from Sieger and Hainzl territory. When Falk's father died soon after, Falk inherited the title.

Falk was overwhelmed by the duties of an Eisenfürst. In one of his first decisions, he moved his family to a newly purchased villa in the mountains, something befitting a new baron. Yet, tragedy struck as Horrors attacked. Falk survived with his young daughter, Ketheryna, but the Horrors slaughtered Olga.

Fischler, intent on presenting Ketheryna with every opportunity to make up for their former poverty, wanted to build her a barony she could be proud of. Obsessed with keeping her safe, Falk seized on the opportunity to send her to foster in the court of Ussura, where she grew to catch the eye of the Czar. Excited by the prospect of his daughter becoming a queen one day, he accepted the marriage proposal without asking her permission. The decision drove a wedge between them, and the two have not spoken since.

Separated from his beloved daughter, Falk watches his königreich struggle. The fishing industry falls to near ruin, as each haul out of the Südsee grows leaner and more sickly. The nobles have divided up power among them and maneuver themselves with impunity, disrespecting his rule. Far away in Ussura, Ketheryna is now a contender to become the new Czarina—a fact that would overjoy her father if she would just speak to him.

And worse, even his own Iron Guard seems to have turned against him, taking bribes to protect the nobility over the commoners. Only the Drachenblut, a new organization out to protect Eisen, seems intent on helping defend his territory from their place in the mountains to the west. Their stirring call to the old days of Eisen pride and power is the only thing wresting the melancholy baron to action, inspiring him to heroic deeds for the first time in his life.

## Erich Sieger

Erich Sieger's desperation has warped him into a singularly driven and ferocious man. Erich has ruled Sieger since he was a young man during the War. The young Erich started off as an idealistic and passionate follower of the Imperator and a staunch Objectionist. He believed his service to his Nation and to his ruler would earn him the Imperator's thanks. Instead, Erich watched helplessly as Riefenstahl carved off a piece of Sieger land to make the Fischler barony.

Sieger originally stretched to the south and west, making it prime territory for invasion forces from Montaigne and Castille. Many of the worst battles of the War hopelessly ravaged the population and razed entire cities to the ground. Erich's hope lay in peace finally restoring his land, but the Imperator had other ideas. The ruler had decided in his final days to carve off the southern edge of Sieger land to give to Castille should peace negotiations become possible, a decision honored in the Treaty of Weissburg at the end of the War.

Intent on keeping what little land he had left, Erich ordered his farmers to salt the fields to stymie invaders. Between the ruined fields and the Horrors, nobody wanted anything to do with Sieger land, even its own tenants. In the last twenty years, people have fled Sieger to all corners of Théah and across the Seas to find new lives. Only Erich and his most dedicated followers remain, eager to keep what little they have left.

Sieger is old, exhausted and out of sorts. He flies into rages and dangerous paranoia plagues him, consumed with the notion that others want to take the last of his land away. The fact that Wirsche has made overtures to annex parts of his land have not made this any better.

## Georg Hainzl

During hard times, some prefer to embrace the grim reality around them. Others choose to ignore the difficult reality. Georg Hainzl, baron of Hainzl lands in the northwest, is one of the latter. A generous and gregarious man, Georg Hainzl refuses to accept Eisen's decrepitude and instead calls others to recognize the country for what it could be: a place of wild beauty and grand adventures. Some like his charming view of Eisen; most believe him simply delusional.

Georg Hainzl's rule is based on mining the forbidding Dracheneisen Mountains. The historic mountains were the source of dracheneisen, the country's

famous iron forged into terrific weapons and armor. Though the veins of dracheneisen have long since gone dry, the mountains also possess rich deposits of silver, ore and gems which flow right into Hainzl's coffers. Georg has used that money to spruce up his part of the Nation. While the invading armies marched west into Wirsche or east into Sieger, Hainzl remained relatively untouched in the mountains, and stockpiled wealth and welcomed refugees.

Many believe Hainzl's focus on beauty comes from the tragedies in his life. It is no secret Georg lost his family in the War. Most believe his lost love Kurt, a musician killed by Horrors while traveling to a festival in Freiburg, drove Hainzl to his isolation. Left alone to rule with no loved ones around him, advisors whisper, Hainzl could not handle the stress of Eisen as it is now.

Instead, Hainzl buries himself in music and beauty, all in tribute to his lost Kurt and the family he struggles to honor. Only Hainzl's Iron Guard and the Drachenblut, headquartered in the mountains, keep the monsters lurking in Eisen from swallowing the königreich whole. The other Eisenfürsten, especially Elsa Pösen, caution Hainzl to be wary, but Georg can hardly be bothered. Too busy spending his money on lavish parties, town beautifications and concerts, he fails to notice the dangers around him.

## The Drachenblut

Once, Eisen was a land of warring tribes and monstrous creatures called drachen, who prowled the land and slept beneath what became known as the Dracheneisen Mountains. No one knows exactly what happened to them, but the legend of the Heroes who slew drachen in ancient days resonates across Eisen into the current difficult times. The people see the drachen as an important icon, the image of a sleeping power waiting to be reawakened in the land. In the years after the War, with no leader to bring the country together, the people of Eisen needed such a symbol to unite behind.

Enter the Drachenblut. Made up largely of errant knights, disenchanted Iron Guards and former soldiers, the Drachenblut are an organization born out of the idea that to heal Eisen, warriors must become as great and as strong as the drachen. A potential recruit travels across Eisen and braves the dangerous climb through the Horror-infested mountain passes to Burg Wachesherz, the home of the Drachenblut. There he trains for three years before being initiated into the organization.

Underneath the banner of a gold drachen with outstretched wings, the knights ride to protect the people of Eisen from all dangers, Horrors or otherwise. The image of these powerful warriors riding into town to save the day has inspired many to claim the Drachenblut the true saviors of Eisen and perhaps the ones to lead Eisen into the future.

They point to the organization's leader, war veteran Rosamund Roth, as a powerful contender for chancellorship or even Imperator. Rosamund has never publicly denied interest in leading, but instead focuses her dedication on the Drachenblut and the suppression of monstrous threats across the country. The group otherwise takes no position or stance on politics, instead serving the greater good of all the people of Eisen.

The Drachenblut are not without their detractors. The Iron Guard bristles over what they perceive as a direct threat to their military and policing powers, and groups of Iron Guard have clashed with Drachenblut warriors over jurisdiction in several königreiche. And they are not wrong; the Drachenblut claim allegiance to Eisen as a whole and travel to any land within it to enact justice.

People are unnerved by rumors about Drachenblut initiations. Stories in which a recruit bathes in the blood of monsters, eats the hearts of animals or maybe bites into living animals with her bare teeth, just like a drachen did. Whether these are rumors to turn the people against the organization or a sinister truth, no one is certain. Burg Wachesherz is so secluded, few visit without the Drachenblut's permission and live to tell the tale. While people question their methods and intentions, everyone agrees the Drachenblut are a Heroic, powerful force for good in a weary and barely recovering Eisen.

And they are recruiting. With the ever-present problems in Eisen, the Drachenblut spread the message far and wide: join the blood of the drachen, and become a force for change to shake the foundations of the world. A new member must only make pilgrimage to Burg Wachesherz after getting a member of the Drachenblut to vouch for him and survive the grueling trials before he can ride beneath the golden drachen banner.

They sometimes work with die Kruezritter, though their methods are less savory to the group of Horror hunters. Die Kruezritter fear that the Drachenblut are in danger of falling to Villainy. They also openly accept hexe into their ranks whenever they find them. Recently, the Drachenblut have announced a search for more dracheneisen weapons, an announcement met with derision and rage from the Iron Princes and their Iron Guard.

## The Iron Guard

Few fighting forces in Théah command as much fear and respect as Eisen's Iron Guard. These loyal guardians have existed as far back as the Nation's inception under Stefan the Great and have served the ruler and the people of Eisen ever since. Now with the leadership of Eisen in question, the Iron Guard has been split into seven small private armies, each loyal to an Eisenfürst. Still, each unit protects its königreich under their rallying oath: *Geschmiedet aus Eisen, Gehärtet in Blut.* "Forged from Iron, Tempered in Blood."

The Eisenfürsten take warriors from all across Eisen. A recruit can come from common or noble stock alike, with the prospect of setting aside her entire life to seek out a position in the Guard. A recruit must already know how to track, fight with a sword and ride even before entering training, which is some of the most rigorous anywhere. She must also secure a letter of introduction from a person of note from her home königreich before even being seen by the head of recruitment and division's leaders for consideration.

Many prospects never make it through training to take the oath, but those who do are some of the most formidable fighters in the entire country. The secret to their superior fighting capability lies in their ability to work seamlessly as a unit. Iron Guard units, made up of twenty soldiers, operate as one, trained to anticipate their fellows' movements and able to move in concert without the need for words. Iron Guard members train to protect one another or risk leaving their flanks exposed. For this reason, units historically experience a low turnover rate, with every death mourned like the loss of a limb.

In previous generations, the Iron Guard stood united under the banner of a single commander who served at the side of the Imperator. Now, each of the seven individual Iron Guard units have formidable leaders, living legends whose reputations precede them all across Eisen. The most notable leaders of Iron Guard units are Kurt Valrund, a powerful but older bull of a man leading the Swamp Dogs in Pösen, as well as Selena von Hoff, a savvy and sneaky younger woman in command of the Wachhunde serving Niklas Träge. The most famous is Heinrich Dray, an Adel's son who gave up his position of nobility and wealth to serve as commander of the Roaring Drachen under Roswitha von Wirsche.

The lack of centralized leadership has unsettled much of Eisen, and the Iron Guard have fought, bled and died to keep everything from falling to pieces. Despite supposedly being apolitical, the seven divisions find staying out of the political fray swirling around the Eisenfürsten impossible. A young recruit comes to see the other divisions of the Guard as his enemy rather than compatriots, and the groups have more often than not come to blows as the militant enforcers of their Eisenfürst rather than protectors of the people. This has led to a few defections from the Iron Guard when a jaded member chooses to uphold her oath to the people of Eisen alone, joining small independent bands or as a solitary mercenary. Still others have left to join the Drachenblut, seeing the new organization as a throwback to what the Iron Guard once was and should become once more: an elite fighting force, guarding Eisen with its very lives.

# Perchta

Long before Stefan the Great named Eisen for the iron found in its mountains, a powerful spirit walked the land and protected its people from harm. Perchta, a powerful fæ expelled from Avalon by her fellow Sidhe in ancient days, settled in Eisen when drachen still flew the skies.

Revered as a goddess by local tribes, she was transformed by their stories about her into a benevolent, if often capricious, nurturer. She remained a force for good in Eisen, until the coming of the Vaticine Church. As their influence spread, their denouncement of magic forced Perchta into hiding, ceding her many followers to the Church. Eventually she settled into the Angenehme Wald where she swore to make the Wald a haven for magic and a safe place for those in need.

All magic has its price, even for an immortal. Cut off from the Sidhe's ancient homeland, Perchta strove to maintain her power. A person who wishes to settle in the Angenehme must swear never to leave, tying his life force to Perchta, feeding her strength to keep her magic.

To her credit, Perchta hates this arrangement. She yearns for the days when Eisen stood proud and accepting of all magic. To that end, she has set about a plan to help find a leader who might accept magic. She chose Rosamund Roth, leader of the Drachenblut, as the woman to lead Eisen ahead into the future, and appeared to the warrior to prophesy her rise to greatness.

## Portraying Perchta

Perchta is an immortal being. She knows secrets that could destroy or raise kingdoms. She often acts the part of an ancient witch, gifting her protection to those who seek her out.

Perchta's greatest secret is that despite her inhuman origins, she spent so long pretending to care about Eisen's fate that the feelings may now be genuine. She knows one thing for certain: she is not content to be an invisible force in history.

### Story Hook

+ Perchta would like to see herself untethered from feeding on mortals, and seeks other avenues to replenish her magic. She charges the Heroes to help her find a new source of magic, in return for allowing them to leave the forest.

## Kevistoph "Two Stripes Jack" Braun

Kevistoph Braun was born near Wirsche shortly before the end of the War of the Cross. Like most children his age in Eisen, he ended up an orphan. His parents were both soldiers in the War, and though they both survived the next few years, they were eventually overcome by Horrors.

Braun grew up with other Waisen, but instead of letting the shock of war and the Horrors cow him, he learned to fight and defend himself. His large size and superior strength gave him an advantage against the other children, and he learned to use this to his advantage in most things.

Braun never liked the sea, though he grew up in a port city. He preferred standing on solid ground and the reassuring way it did not rock back and forth. For most of his life, he made his way as a mercenary. Life was good, he got paid to fight, and he spent his money drinking and spending time with jennys.

That is, until one morning, still drunk from the night before, and woefully disoriented he bargained his time for a pair of pants. He didn't realize that his time was going to be spent on the schooner the Shoal Seeker. The first day in, and he was already arguing with the boatswain, earning him a night in the brig and eight lashes the next day. Braun was determined to prove he was tough enough to take the lashes, and remained silent through the first, which impressed the crew. Unfortunately, he passed out soundlessly after the second, earning him the nickname "Two Stripes Jack."

Despite the rocky start, Two Stripes thrived on the ship, making his way to midshipman before the crew of the Shoal Seeker ran afoul of Roswitha von Wirsche. The Countess tapped the ship to bring goods for sale to Gottkirchen, but when they arrived, the people there had little to pay with. The captain, a pragmatic man, sold them what they could afford and brought the rest back.

The Countess, expecting the ship to simply leave the rest of the goods, grew furious and tried to imprison the entire crew. Two Stripes and a few others escaped, but not before the Iron Guard ransacked the Shoal Seeker, making it impossible to sail.

Now, Two Stripes Jack and the few remaining crew members from the Shoal Seeker are trying to find a way to rescue their captain and crew. Roswitha's Iron Guard has warrants out for their arrest, but to this day none of them know what crime they are accused of committing.

## Portraying Two Stripes Jack

Kevistoph "Two Stripes Jack" Braun is a big man with a kind heart. He has dark hair, cut short, and keeps himself clean shaven and presentable, even when out at sea. He enjoys a good drink and a good brawl just as much.

He's a land lover at heart, and though he wants to help the crew of the Shoal Seeker, he isn't much for returning to a life at sea. Right now, his priority is finding out what Countess Wirsche is up to, and possibly stopping her.

The Heroes are likely to find a friend in Two Stripes Jack, as long as they don't ask him to get on a boat with them.

### Story Hook

+ Two Stripes Jack and the rest of the crew discovered a secret passage into the Countess's castle dungeon. They went into the dungeon in the early hours of the morning, but instead of finding their imprisoned crew members, they found a group of Horrors behind the bars. Now, the group is looking for help to both find out what happened to the rest of the crew, and to find out why the Countess has Horrors in her dungeon.

# Knight Inquisitor Friedrich

Knight Inquisitor Friedrich was born in Sieger to a devout Vaticine family. He was old enough to join the War, and fought for three years before it finally ended. Then came the Horrors. Friedrich, always devoted to the Church and fueled by hatred for Objectionists, believed that the Imperator's abandonment of the true faith had brought this blight onto his land.

Unlike many of the other Eisen knights who fought in the War, he did not remain to fight the Horrors, but instead traveled to Vaticine City in Castille to reaffirm his faith. There, he joined the priesthood and learned all he could to find a way to stop the Horrors in his homeland.

Quite on his own, he came to the conclusion that Hexenwerk must be the true culprit behind the Horrors, and decided Sorcery of all kinds were a blight. This line of thinking attracted Cardinal Verdugo's attention, and he initiated Friedrich into the Inquisition. Friedrich is one of Verdugo's staunchest supporters, and he helped as the Inquisition slowly took over leading the Vaticine Church.

Armed with a new hatred for Sorcery, monsters, and all things that hint at the unnatural, Inquisitor Friedrich returned to Eisen, hoping to defeat the scourge. In his way, he is fighting to cleanse his homeland, working diligently to root out and destroy Horrors wherever he finds them.

Now, Inquisitor Friedrich lives in Pösen and advises Elsa Pösen on dealing with the Horror threats. He has also turned her to cataloguing all the hexen in her königreiche, and possibly beyond.

## Portraying Inquisitor Friedrich

Willful, dedicated and completely driven, Knight Inquisitor Friedrich is a man who does the wrong things for the right reasons. He is dedicated to cleansing Eisen, but he doesn't care how many people have to die to bring around that reality.

For Friedrich, the War of the Cross is an ongoing threat to Eisen, and though it ended twenty years previously, the blight it caused is still a menace. He is committed to finally ending the war and bringing peace with a single-minded devotion that would terrify most sane people.

# Wilma Probst

In a free city with no rules like Freiburg, someone still has to keep the place running. If Freiburg survives the next morning, people in the know say a little prayer of thanks for Wilma Probst, second in command to Niklas Träge and de facto governor of Freiburg.

Wilma Probst grew up watching the War tear her country apart. Not a soldier but a common girl, Wilma learned to read at a young age. Because of that skill, she became a page to a young knight named Barhelm in service to the Imperator's court. Fascinated by the goings-on of government, she used her free time to study not only politics but the inner bureaucratic workings of Eisen. Her position as a page let her hear and see everything as she ran messages for the government and eventually from the barons under the Imperator himself. There she met Niklas Träge just as he purchased a title after he discovered the cache of dracheneisen in the Mountains.

She saw early on that Träge, while he meant well and had many great, radical ideas, had no idea how to manage his household or his new political position. One night, Probst presented herself to Träge and laid out in no uncertain terms why he needed her. To her surprise, Träge agreed and she became his head of household, maintaining it even when he went out to fight Horrors. When Träge established Freiburg, the "Free City," and stepped back for his hands-off approach, Wilma knew someone had to step up to manage what few rules the city did have. She has been doing the job ever since.

Wilma Probst knows everything going on in Freiburg. She has her finger on the pulse of the königreich and from Freiburg has watched Eisen struggle to find its identity again in the face of its near collapse and split. A devoted member of Sophia's Daughters, Probst supports the chance for a new leader to step up in Eisen and has been using her considerable political acumen to maneuver people into supporting a chancellorship with equal rights for all, much like in the Sarmatian Commonwealth.

## Portraying Wilma Probst

If something happens in Freiburg, Wilma Probst probably knows about it. Meticulous in recalling details and fastidious in appearance, Wilma remains calm in the face of even the most blustering Eisenfürst and rarely raises her voice. Her very presence cools the most heated exchanges, and many fear her anger, expressed in the most clipped, icy tones.

Get on Wilma's bad side and someone can find himself frozen out of all business and social activity in Freiburg and beyond until he has made amends. Above all things, Probst is a dedicated daughter of Eisen, a staunch believer in women's equal rights and a believer in a strong, central government to secure her beloved country's future. She goes out of her way to ensure Freiburg provides a safe place for Vodacce Fate Witch refugees, a sticking point between herself and Träge.

## Story Hooks

- Wilma's political manipulations have brought Elsa Pösen to her side. The two secretly plan to push their support behind Eisen's young rising star, Rosamund Roth of the Drachenblut, to see her on the throne. Probst is concerned that if Roth takes the throne, the Iron Guard and the Drachenblut may come into conflict. Are the Heroes willing to help soothe egos and get involved in this political hotbed?

- Eisen holds a seat on the Vendel League's Council, a mostly ceremonial position that ensures continued economic and political support from Vesten. Eisen's representative, Joseph Volker, is old and needs a replacement. With no ruler, the Eisenfürsten cannot come to a consensus. If no new representative is selected, Eisen will lose the League's support. Wilma wishes to send someone without the counsel of the Eisenfürsten. But the other Eisenfürsten have their own ideas, and are willing to act against Probst. Can the Heroes help ensure Eisen has a seat on the League?

# Rosamund Roth

They say greatness comes from humble beginnings. Rosamund Roth was born in the small town of Grünfeld at the edge of the Wälder. Before she was born, Roth's family rose above their station when her father rescued an Adel's young son from being trampled by a cart. Her father asked that he be taken into the noble's household as his reward. The Adel, Lord Hans Dieter, agreed and the family moved into the lord's estate.

Roth's mother served in the house as a lady's maid. One night during a terrible storm, the Imperator, out traveling on a diplomatic mission, showed up on their doorstep in need of shelter from the weather. The storm lasted three days, during which the Imperator spent an inordinate amount of time with Rosamund's mother. Nine months later, she was born.

The circumstances of Roth's birth were a tightly guarded secret all her life, yet from an early age she received special treatement. When Rosamund showed aptitude as a warrior, she trained alongside Lord Dieter's fighters and became a squire at the age of twelve. Despite her family's concerns, she and her two elder brothers rode out with Lord Dieter to serve during the War.

Near the end of the War, she had earned her own command and rose steadily through the ranks under the watchful eye of the Imperator. His death hit her hard, and the fracture of Eisen's government into the hands of the squabbling Eisenfürsten made Roth furious. Her Nation struggled, and her fellow veterans returned home to Horrors with no leadership and no plan for the future. Spurred to action, Rosamund began the Drachenblut—knights dedicated to protecting the people of Eisen without any political allegiance or affiliation.

Twenty years later, with no end to the political strife in sight, Rosamund has become restless about the Nation's future. When the witch Perchta appeared to her and revealed Roth's true parentage, she came to accept that she might need to lead Eisen. News spread of Rosamund as a good political choice, and support swells among both the youth and veterans who respect her reputation.

Roth, not sure whether she wants to rule the Nation, would rather fight to keep it in one piece. She spends her days riding out at the head of Drachenblut to defend the land, surrounded by a cadre of her most loyal warriors.

## Portraying Rosamund Roth

Rosamund Roth is a fighter, leader and commander of the Drachenblut. She is a seasoned veteran with iron hair and a commanding yet kind voice. Roth has tried to stay out of politics her entire life. Instead, she dedicated herself to the belief that Eisen can be great through the strength of its people and the resurrection of ancient practices and values.

Rosamund is practical yet quietly a romantic, desperate for a time of grand Heroes like those in the legends. She has yet to embrace that perhaps she might be one of those Heroes, and secretly harbors the scars of being branded illegitimate.

### Story Hook

- The Drachenblut have heard rumors of corruption in Pösen's Iron Guard. A few younger members want to destroy the Guard and replace them. Roth knows that to do so would cast the Drachenblut in a bad light, removing her own credibility. She asks the Heroes to search for evidence of the corruption and show it to the Eisenfürst.

# Chaim Ledovid

The Yachidi are a religious and ethnic group whose homeland in the Crescent Empire could not be more different than Eisen. Chaim Ledovid, or Chaim ben Dovid ben Shimon of Tribe Binyomin, was born far from Eisen's shores, but traveled north to Théah with his parents. Along with ten other families, Chaim and his parents first settled in Castille to work with some of the finest universities to share leading medical techniques from the Crescent Empire. There, the Castillian court honored Chaim's parents for saving the daughter of a noble. They changed their name to Ledovid to appear more Castillian, and the honor included a title of land near San Cristóbal, where Chaim's aged parents and five brothers remain to this day.

Only ten when the War of the Cross ended, Chaim felt the devastation of the War's impact keenly. At age eighteen, he organized a group of Yachidi families from all over Théah to head to Eisen and bring aid to the wounded country. Settling in the tiny town of Heimstatt, Chaim became the founder of a small Yachidi population and brought his knowledge of medicine and healing to the renowned Heiligherz-Krankenhaus and local Eisengeist-Universität.

Soon Ledovid was the leading spokesperson for the local Yachidi population and their community in the neighborhood of Lodz on the west side of town. He helped navigate differences between the primarily Vaticine followers and atheist population of Heimstatt in learning more about the Yachidi, and soon Heimstatt became the major stopping point for any Yachidi after coming into Théah—a home away from home for the Yachidi, a tiny outpost of their culture far from the Crescent Empire.

Chaim's work to help integrate the Yachidi into Eisen society has not gone unnoticed. When the Eisenfürsten or any nobility needs to reach out to the Yachidi community, they seek out Ledovid in Heimstatt. When not serving as a physician or lecturing, he spends his days traveling through the country to spread knowledge from his community. He lives with his scientist wife, Batsheva, and their six children, with his son Mayron serving as his medical assistant. The two can be seen racing through the city on medical business with their Dinist associate, another transplant from the Crescent Empire, Amira.

## Portraying Chaim Ledovid

Chaim is a quiet and thoughtful man, well-spoken and eloquent in several different languages. A man devoted to peace, Ledovid abhors carrying weapons and instead prefers to settle any conflict through communication and sharing of knowledge. Still, though well sought by more militant members of the Yachidi community for his council, he stands in staunch defense of all life, not only those of his people.

Chaim abhors ignorance and though he tolerates the persecution of those who use magic on a larger scale, he uses every resource in his power to circumvent those organizations that harm sorcerers and openly spreads ideas of accepting magic and science side by side. Ledovid loves whiskey and long nights of deep discussion as much as he loves spending time with his family.

## Story Hooks

+ Recently, several Yachidi community members have disappeared from Heimstatt. Chaim has uncovered reports of Yachidi going missing from several communities without a trace. All signs point back to the Inquisition, though he has yet to gather any proof. Ledovid asks the Heroes to help him find his fellow Yachidi, before the Chavra, a more militant Yachidi neighborhood watch group, can get involved and stir up trouble.

+ The Yachidi have maintained a network of communities throughout Théah, coming upward through Castille from their home in the Crescent Empire. For that reason, Chaim is in the perfect position to smuggle those running from repressive communities and opens his home to refugees of repressive nations. This has brought him in direct conflict with the Inquisition, and he asks the Heroes to help find a new hiding spot for his refugees, before the Inquisition comes into his home and arrests them all.

# Heinrich Dray

Few military leaders command as much power or as much public fascination in Eisen as Heinrich Dray, captain of the Roaring Drachen division of the Iron Guard in Wirsche. Born the son of an Adel, Heinrich was the second child in a family that had far too many.

Heinrich's family remained poor after the War, often selling off priceless heirlooms to feed themselves and their servants. Heinrich's eldest sister Nadina intended to be the head of the household upon their parents' passing, a fact that enraged Heinrich. He believed he was the natural choice, being a man, and aimed to showcase his leadership talents by entering military service. This opinion did not sit well with his family and led to an eventual falling out.

His father disapproved of Heinrich's prejudices, but, happy to see his son dedicating himself to a cause, negotiated a commission in the Iron Guard for him based on his family name. Heinrich saw this as his father seeking to push him out of the spotlight and never forgave the slight, even staying away from his father's deathbed. When Nadina and her husband Konrad took over the family lands, Heinrich swore to never return.

Rededicating himself to his military training, Heinrich distinguished himself as a powerful fighter and quickly earned his spurs as a knight. He was assigned to the königreich of Wirsche after an incursion of undead Horrors wiped out nearly half their Iron Guard on the southern border, the worst the area had ever seen. Heinrich arrived to see the Roaring Drachen in disrepair, without a leader, and seized the opportunity to work his way up in the ranks. He led a successful campaign to crush the undead horde and save a number of endangered towns.

In celebration, he was invited to dine with the Countess von Wirsche. Upon seeing her, Heinrich Dray knew he would love no other woman alive. The brazen young knight even dared tell the Countess so that very night. She laughed in his face and told him to prove his worth to her and she would consider his advances. Dray took up the cause and spent one year slaying every Horror he could and whipping the Roaring Drachen into shape. He returned on the anniversary of their meeting with trophies of his conquests and declared his love once more. The two have been inseparable ever since.

## Portraying Heinrich Dray

Heinrich Dray is a terrifying figure in combat, a charming if ruthless man at court and utterly devoted to his beloved Roswitha von Wirsche. He knows more about her than anyone else, including the truth behind her connection to disappearances in her königreich and dead bodies found drained of all blood.

Heinrich doesn't care about what anyone says about Roswitha, but instead has helped put her name forward as the potential new leader of Eisen, citing the success the Countess has had rebuilding her königreich from its previous devastation. That he will become ruler at her side is a foregone conclusion to him, as he would rather die than be parted from her side.

## Story Hooks

+ Heinrich Dray has issued a challenge to Niklas Träge: either step up and declare intent to become leader, or hand over the Imperator's gauntlet, one of Träge's most prized possessions. Träge has responded by asking the Heroes to go and talk some sense into Dray, but Dray readies a host to take the gauntlet by force if necessary.

+ Heinrich is rising in the people's minds as the kind of man who could stand beside Roswitha von Wirsche as a new Imperator consort, or even Imperator himself. Still, rumors fly behind the scenes that Dray knows where all Roswitha's secrets—and more than a few bodies—are buried. Servants have spread rumors the man keeps a journal about his rise to glory, and his sister, Nadine, has quietly offered an incredible prize to anyone who can recover the diary and uncover the secrets Heinrich hides for his lady love.

## The Explorer's Society

Though common belief holds that the mines of the Dracheneisen Mountains played out long ago, the Eisenfürsten hope the mountains have yet to give up more veins of ore or secrets, and so they have turned to the Explorer's Society for aid. The country's leadership wants dracheneisen back in circulation and pays any Explorer handsomely for taking on the dangers of the mountains to find them their answers.

An Explorer has plenty otherwise to occupy herself in Eisen, however. With the Ausgewogene Ort Syrneth ruins rising up under the swamps in Pösen and the potential Syrneth relics underneath Freiburg, an Explorer sees Eisen as a treasure trove of relic hunting.

## The Rilasciare

Few places are as exciting for a member of the Rilasciare as Eisen now in the years after the War of the Cross. With no monarchy in place and the power of the Vaticine Church broken all over Eisen, the Rilasciare see Eisen as the perfect place to kindle a new revolution featuring the people as leaders in building a better tomorrow.

Agents of the Rilasciare are everywhere, recruiting disaffected veterans and headstrong Junges Blut alike in the hopes of empowering Eisen to rise up and claim its future before the nobility can establish another monarchy.

## Sophia's Daughters

The power of Eisen's women is without any doubt, and Sophia's Daughters have found powerful allies within the Nation. In the wake of the War, with so many veterans in need of a purpose, the Daughters have been hiring powerful women fighters and leaders from Eisen to help their Vodacce counterparts. They help rescue Fate Witches and remove them from their bonds, and teach women vital skills of self-defense and even how to read and write.

Many of Eisen's finest warriors now work for Sophia's Daughters both in Eisen and in Vodacce. Some act as guards, but many serve as instructors and confidants to rogue Fate Witches.

Within Eisen, the Daughters use the disconnection between the various königreiche to smuggle women on the run into safe communities where they can begin new lives. One of their largest camps is a tiny village called Mieben, deep in the Angenehme Wald, under the protection of the witch Perchta.

They are the only group capable of staying for long periods in her forest and still able to leave, though ten women must remain there for the rest of their lives to maintain the camp's protection by the witch.

# The Brotherhood of the Coast

Travel and trade between Vestenmennavenjar and Eisen has been the lifeblood keeping Eisen alive ever since before the War of the Cross. Now with the War over and the Nation in such dire straits, the Brotherhood recognizes Eisen deserves a break.

The pirates of Eisen have called an unofficial truce, halting all raiding and pillaging of Eisen's cities until such time as the Nation can get back on its feet. The Brotherhood honors this cessation of activities, and any Brotherhood ships sailing Eisen's waters enforce the ban on any ship that dares attack an Eisen town.

Many renegade raiding vessels still sail the Maw and even travel down the Nation's rivers despite the ban. Should they be spotted, the Brotherhood always executes swift and brutal retribution. Brotherhood members often take the cargo from said raiders and distribute it among the local villages most in need, turning over the raiders for trial and justice before sailing away.

Meanwhile, the Brotherhood recruits Eisen by the dozen ever since the War, with more ships full of sailors taking to the seas every year. Eisen make fine sailors and their strong military training makes them excellent pirates.

## Favor in Eisen

Heroes who are members of the Brotherhood of the Coast may earn Favor in Eisen in the following way:

+ Reporting a raiding vessel attacking Eisen ships is worth 3 Favor. Helping to dispatch such a ship can result in 2 Wealth from the Brotherhood.

Heroes who are members of the Brotherhood of the Coast may spend Favor in Eisen in the following way:

+ Gaining safe passage from Eisen to Vestenmennavenjar or vice versa costs 2 Favor.

# Los Vagabundos

Eisen has been without a leader for too long, or at least so says Los Vagabundos. The organization is adamant about finding a new ruler for the Eisen before the country falls even further into disrepair, or worse falls into civil war.

The people of Eisen need aid in recovering from the War and in twenty years, no one has stepped up, so Los Vagabundos has decided to just intercede. The organization has selected three front-running candidates: Niklas Träge of Freiburg, Elsa Pösen of Pösen and Rosamund Roth, leader of the Drachenblut. Though each leader has support from different members of Los Vagabundos, the entire society knows each leader must be tested and retested to make them worthy of leading Eisen into the future.

In the end, the Society will support any worthy leader who finds him- or herself at the head of the Nation, but until such a time, they do what they can to support their three candidates. The true test is not only getting one of them to step up, but to protect them from enemies while they unify the Nation.

## Favor in Eisen

Heroes who are members of Los Vagabundos in Eisen can earn Favor in the following ways:

+ Presenting definitive evidence either for or against one of their chosen leaders is worth 3 Favor, especially if the evidence is related to Träge or Roth's direct actions.
+ Assisting Roth, Träge or Pösen in their eventual climb to the leadership of Eisen is worth 5 Favor. The assistance should be something substantial, such as helping form alliances between the Eisenfürsten or undermining the efforts of the Rilasciare in Eisen.

# Kinder von Morgen

Though the agents of the Rilasciare operate all across Théah, they long ago targeted Eisen as the tinder to spark a new revolution to do away with the Church, monarchies and all subjugation. While the rest of the organization is spread thin, a smaller group has broken away from the Rilasciare proper in the face of the establishment of the Sarmatian Commonwealth.

This new group, calling themselves the Kinder von Morgen or "Children of Tomorrow," has set the Commonwealth as a blueprint for how to establish a new and free Eisen. Many members, former Rilasciare members from the Commonwealth, have brought their experience in their own country to teach and mentor the hot-blooded young Eisen.

The Kinder are highly organized, with a functional hierarch and members organizing under a common banner. They stage rallies and speeches in every königreiche, they print pamphlets and have criers at every city corner informing the common people about a hope of taking leadership into their own hands.

Agents also execute more daring, covert actions to hinder the rise of any new potential monarch in the country. Their main targets for action are the various Eisenfürsten, though they focus more on the Iron Princes who mistreat or ignore the needs of their people. Many hold Niklas Träge as an almost ironic figure of reverence and wish to convince him to support transforming Eisen into a Commonwealth alongside Sarmatia.

The Kinder recruit only from the disaffected and the commoners, abjuring the assistance of nobility, and rage against the Iron Guard as the militarized arm of the old leadership. Recently their eyes have also turned towards the Vaticine Church in an effort to make sure no organizations, such as the Inquisition, gain a foothold once more in the country. Their sign, the clenched fist around a drachen's throat, symbolizes the stranglehold the nobility has maintained on their people for far too long.

They keep a headquarters in a converted noble's household-turned-tavern in Freiburg called the Amber Eye. The place is maintained by jennys, all members of the organization and experts at gathering and trading information.

## Favor with the Kinder von Morgen

The Kinder von Morgen concern themselves with convincing the people that a democracy is the best way to restore Eisen. A member mostly holds rallies and demonstrations, but she keeps her eyes on those who may declare themselves as the new Imperator. While she is not fond of murder, public embarrassment is right up her alley.

Heroes who belong to the Kinder von Morgen may earn Favor in the following ways:

+ Organizing a rally or demonstration is worth 3 Favor, especially if the event is well-attended or gains government notice.
+ Destabilizing an Eisenfürst's rule is worth 7 Favor. If that königreich ends up adopting a more democratic rule as a result it is worth 10 Favor instead.
+ Publicly humiliating an Eisenfürst, or anyone else who may declare as Imperator, is worth 5 Favor.

Heroes who belong to the Kinder von Morgen may spend Favor in the following ways:

+ Gaining access to the Kinder von Morgen's libraries costs 2 Favor. The group is made up of scholars, politicians and academics, and they have amassed a huge library of scholarly works in just a short period of time.
+ Requesting aid from a Kinder costs 3 Favor. A generic member is typically Strength 6, but also possesses the Academy, Lyceum or University Advantage. For each additional 2 Favor you spend, the Kinder you recruit can have an additional 4 points in one or more Advantages of your choice.

## Die Kreuzritter

The call has gone up across Eisen: now is the time to destroy the Horrors once and for all. Too long has die Kreuzritter relied on individual members and their allies wiping out monsters across the country. Now the Society prepares for a massive campaign to sweep the Horrors from Eisen, vowing to eliminate entrenched threats, such as the creatures of Rücken Island and Viktor Franzeller's Changed in Höhenlage. They only need the support to do so.

They created *die Eisensänger*, or "Iron Singers," a messenger service to carry information from one side of the country to the other. A member of die Kreuzritter carries these messages as he travels, leaving them on bulletin boards marked with the words "The Song of Eisen" at the top. He carries information about Horror attacks, successful monster hunts, political information and news of the day, in hopes of garnering support. So far, the successes against the Horrors and the organizational efforts has done the most to bring Eisen together.

## Knights of the Rose & Cross

If any country needs the Knights of the Rose & Cross, it is Eisen. The heroic Knights have seen their ranks in the country decimated by the never-ending waves of Horrors and have kept hope alive in many of the most hard-pressed areas.

After the War, the Knights saw a swelling in the ranks from Eisen veterans looking to dedicate their lives to a higher cause. But when financial support and armed assistance were slow to come to outlying areas from the Knights, many new recruits became jaded and broke off to form a new organization, the Drachenblut.

Relations between the Drachenblut and the Knights of the Rose & Cross remain strained, with the Knights seeing the Drachenblut as an upstart new organization almost sure to flame out, and the Drachenblut seeing the Knights as largely ineffectual.

## The Invisible College

Eisen is the hottest place to study monsters in all of Théah, and the members of the Invisible College have been fascinated enough to descend on the country in droves. The membership has been challenged to discover why Eisen draws so many monsters, with a member expected to share information with others while he races for an answer.

The challenge is as much about glory for the one who discovers an answer as an incentive to members to aid Eisen in its most desperate time. In fact, some members have begun circulating an alarming theory: the Horrors are not decreasing in number despite all the fighting, but in fact may be increasing.

To that end, College members embed themselves in places of learning all across Eisen to further research into the Horrors, and have become some of the leading researchers into the different kinds of Horrors out there. They often work with die Kreuzritter to share information with their monster hunters to better equip them for fighting the Horrors at hand.

## Močiutės Skara

With so much horror going on all across Eisen, the Shawl is all but swamped gathering supplies and aiding ailing communities. The organization has facilitated plenty of shipments of everything from medical supplies to food and weapons to hard-pressed communities from allies in the Sarmatian Commonwealth and Ussura.

Most recently they have reached out to the Yachidi population settling in Eisen in towns like Heimstatt to establish trade further into the Crescent Empire with a great deal of success, as the Yachidi consider helping those in need a cardinal part of their religious and cultural ideals. Still, the roads from so far away into the heart of Eisen have many dangers and a member of the Shawl finds herself picking up a sword as often as she feeds the hungry these days.

They also watch the growing movements supporting the various personalities for leader, hoping no one is stupid enough to start another war over who gets to rule. The members of the Shawl are ready and willing to stop such a war before it could begin.

*Places*

## Freiburg

No city in Eisen captures its beating, complicated, wounded heart as much as Freiburg, the Free City. Born as a social experiment by the newest Eisenfürst, Niklas Träge, Freiburg is a city with few rules and a mostly disinterested government to keep it functioning. Träge saw the horrors of the War and dreamt of a city where a person could live without a yoke around her neck, without the burden of authority, and used what power he had to establish Freiburg before sitting back to watch what happened. And what came about was perhaps the most brilliant, impossible city in all of Théah.

Freiburg existed before the War of the Cross as Güldentor, one of the Imperator's palaces. During the war, it fell into disrepair and disfavor due to the ruling Baron's poor choices. During the war, the Imperator stripped the Adel of his title and he died soon after, leaving the city with no one to rule. Towards the end of the War, Träge's new title included the city, but he mostly ignored it. Flooded with veterans and refugees of the conflict, the city nearly fell in upon itself without a leader.

Years later, Träge finally returned to the city, which had fallen into near ruin. With Wilma Probst's help, he laid the foundation for merchants, architects, thinkers, scholars, organizers and powerful individuals to carve the city out amongst themselves, without any religious influence.

He named his experiment Freiburg. Many imagined Freiburg would implode within a year as organizations vied for power in the vacuum. Instead, the city has remained afloat for four years, with conflicts resolved by a cobbled-together series of understood rules that are half arbitration, half street justice. Most believe the rules, known as the Freiburg code or just "the Free code," survived as long as they have because a citizen of Freiburg understands his city is all that stands between him and destruction. Outside Freiburg's walls lurks a country full of monsters, and the city may be a chance at growing something great in a time of such darkness.

## City Proper

To a traveler and local alike, Freiburg has everything. The city is separated into six quarters all radiating outward from the Wachtturm, an ancient edifice held up by the power of Syrneth crystals, which once served as headquarters for the Imperator and now houses Niklas Träge in the top floor apartments. Each quarter is separated by main roads, almost like the spokes of a wheel, heading out from the center to bridges over the rivers that surround the city on all sides, and out through the main gates to the countryside beyond.

The first quarter, the Griffon, centers on the gorgeous open-aired Griffon Park. The most cosmopolitan of districts, Griffon boasts shops with wares imported from all over Théah. Inns and drinking holes of all kinds dot the landscape, and travelers head here to find lodgings. Most of the population is transient, so Griffon remains one of the most dangerous areas in Freiburg at night.

Cross the High Road and you arrive in the High Quarter, where the most powerful members of the town live and work. The Vendel League has a suite of houses here where they conduct business freely, and their guards protect the High Quarter from any "undesirable" influences from other parts of town. Anyone looking to seek out aristocrats and diplomats visiting Freiburg finds them in the High Quarter.

To the west of the High Quarter is the Reinhagen, named after the massive amphitheater there. The amphitheater serves as home to performances, religious holiday celebrations and any kind of large public gatherings, and can be rented by any organizations. The most recent and controversial events have been gladiatorial-style combat games, run by a group called Lonely Streets. They invite all who wish to show their martial prowess to enter and hold all-day competitions. The rest of the quarter serves as an artistic center, with the Sylvester Playhouse run by the Montaigne philosopher, revolutionary and playwright, Jean Lemaire, acting as its creative heart. A creator looking for patrons lives in flats over the workshops, seeking nobles from the High Quarter to support his work.

Just below the Reinhagen is the Stein. This quarter is the eldest part of the city, built around the old military fortress. Nearly decimated during the War, the Stein itself has been rebuilt and serves as headquarters for all military troops operating in Freiburg, including Träge's Iron Guard. Many fighting academies and dueling schools have sprung up in the area as well, and anyone seeking good military weapons could find them along one long street run by the Weaponsmith's Guild, the Iron Arm.

Just south and east of the Stein is the Institutional Quarter. It is home to groups, organizations and institutions of Freiburg, like the Freiburg gaol, the town's newspaper offices for the *Freiburger Gazette* and the beautiful Drachen Cathedral. This district houses all the administrative offices trying to maintain any order in the city, including the headquarters of the Eisenfürst's staff led by Wilma Probst. Seekers of knowledge can visit Freiburg University, which boasts the freest exchange of ideas in all of Eisen, where students often explain, "All is welcomed for knowledge's sake." Their library is second to none, with a quarterly pamphlet called the *Wahrheitspapiere*, "The Truth Papers," circulated with new and often heretical ideas by anonymous contributors printed for all to read.

Snug between the Institutional and the Griffon quarters is the Goldviertel, the Gold Quarter. This section serves as the hub of all commerce in Freiburg, home of its robust Marktplatz and the trade yards, where all cargo brought into Freiburg comes in off the riverboats. The Freiburg Marktplatz is a wild, uncontrolled place, and though the Iron Guard try to keep the peace, hired muscle from every organization control different sections of the quarter. Criminal organizations make their home all over the Goldviertel, as do mercenaries looking for work down at the Drachen's Toe Tavern. Recent inroads from the Atabean Trading Company to bring merchandise, including slaves, through the Goldviertel has thrown the whole quarter into an uproar, and even the Iron Guard has been having trouble keeping outrage from boiling over.

## The Politics of Freiburg

The beauty of Freiburg lies in the heights it can reach, as well as the lows it can muster. Powerful figures in Freiburg can influence everything from trade in the region to religious and intellectual thought from the university, to criminal enterprises across Théah from the Goldviertel. But more important than anything else, Freiburg sits at the crossroads for all thought about Eisen's political future. Everyone from diplomats to criminal cartels to the Eisenfürsten want to help choose who will lead Eisen into the future, and every secret society in Théah has its fingers on the pulse of this brewing tempest. The most powerful are the Rilasciare, who have pledged not to allow Freiburg and therefore Eisen to fall beneath the hands of another monarch. An offshoot of their organization, called the Kinder von Morgen, have promised to do whatever they must to see Eisen become a Commonwealth like Sarmatia, and the ferocious battles over the country's future have already led to blood in the streets.

Meanwhile, many others believe Eisen's future lies in understanding its past. Many believe that, as one of the country's oldest cities, Freiburg holds the key to power long since lost in Eisen. The Explorer's Society has the largest presence and a huge chapter house on the east side of town near the Conservatory, dedicated to exploring one of the city's worst kept secrets: Freiburg is built on a wealth of Syrneth ruins.

## Nachtblut Cemetery

No one knows exactly how deep down the Syrneth ruins beneath Freiburg lie, but every year, people become hopelessly lost sneaking into catacombs beneath the old Nachtblut Cemetery to seek out the ruins themselves. Syrneth crystals and relics can be found all across the city, including a large and ancient statue in the middle of Conservatory Gardens. A Syrneth crystal, whose power keeps the tower from toppling down, in fact holds up the Wachtturm, the current offices of Niklas Träge himself. As if all the Syrneth relics didn't make the city odd enough, the cemetery grounds are strewn with drachen bones, leading many to believe the city was built on an ancient drachen burial ground. Quarry Lake on the south side of the city is just shallow enough that treasure seekers often dive to the bottom in search of crystals or bones, only to be pulled down below by Horrors in the depths.

In fact, though crime contributes to a lot of the dangers in Freiburg, the Horrors that walk, swim and fly through the night make Freiburg an exciting place to visit. Whether searching the Marktplatz for illegal Hexenwerk components, or visiting the Bone Bridge at the end of High Road to explore the floating contraband market operated by the orphan-run street gang the Children of the Drachen, every person in Freiburg knows one inescapable truth: the city doesn't just belong to them. In every shadow lurks a monster. That is the way of Eisen. But in the Free City, a citizen dedicates himself to living every day like his last, until the Horrors have disappeared or wild old Freiburg falls into ruin. So far, neither has happened, and so the great experiment of the Free City goes on.

# The Dracheneisen Mountains

Some call the Dracheneisen Mountains the backbone of Eisen itself, and they are not far off. In a country dominated by rocky cliffs and mountains, the Dracheneisen are a forbidding presence on the landscape, a long ridge separating Fischler, Wirsche and Hainzl and cutting off northwest Eisen from easy access. But these mountains are more than a geological travel impediment. Once they held one of the richest prizes in all of Théah, the dracheneisen mines. While those mines have long since stopped producing the famed metal, many still stake their claim in the hopes of discovering such treasures once more.

## Hidden Treasures

The Dracheneisen, so named for the ore they produced, served as the roosting places of drachen themselves in ancient history. Legendary Heroes rode out to defeat drachen in their aeries high above the mountain peaks, and ancient caves dotting the mountains still hold the massive bones of drachen long gone. Some of those same caves revealed other treasures, like the hoard of dracheneisen weapons and armor discovered by Niklas Träge during the War of the Cross. That priceless find bought Träge his place as one of the Eisenfürsten. When a bard at the end of the War popularized the new baron's rise to power in song, many treasure seekers took to the mountains in the hopes of earning a new fortune. Most were swallowed up by the deadly Dracheneisen, never to be seen again. But over twenty years later, their descendants and the inhabitants of the mountains have established permanent homes in the high altitudes, and developed new ways of surviving in the harsh environment.

## Mountain Bandits

Just like every other part of Eisen, the Dracheneisen Mountains are thick with Horrors. Monsters live deep in some of the caves and haunt the passes at night to pick off travelers. A particular winged species of ghoul, capable of gliding on leathery membranes under their arms, drop down from cliff faces and rock outcroppings onto unsuspecting people, and others dig their way out of loose earth graves to pop up unexpected from below.

Cut off from any aid, an inhabitant of the Dracheneisen mining towns had to adapt quickly to her surroundings. She usually turned to banditry, stealing what she could to arm herself. She became a ruthless and swift mountaineer, capable of rappelling down the rocks to surround caravans and strip them of their goods in no time.

Still others turned to enslavement, turning tiny mining towns into chain-gang camps, kidnapping travelers and pressing them into seeking out dracheneisen deep underground. No one has yet reported finding such a treasure, but the gems and minerals brought up from the mines keep these towns in service. Most recently, they have begun unearthing the strange glowing crystals often found under Freiburg and in Syrneth ruins across Théah.

When asked about such terrible towns, the Eisenfürsten deny anyone keeps any slave towns in their königreiche. Both Fischler and Hainzl have launched multiple expeditions to investigate these allegations, prompted by concerned relatives of missing travelers, but every time they turn up nothing. Curious in her silence, however, is Roswitha von Wirsche, who consistently scoffs at the idea and refuses to send her own Iron Guard to look into the matter. The fact that her summer manor house, Klarhimmel, sits not too far north of the alleged slave towns has many wondering just how much she does know and condone.

## Höhenlage

As if the dangers of bandits, Horrors and chain-gang servitude were not enough, a new nightmare has grown in the Dracheneisen over the last fifteen years. The large mountain town of Höhenlage used to be a major meeting place for small villages dotting the mountains and served as the only place to catch a caravan heading either north to Wirsche and the coast beyond or south to the city of Atemlos and further down to Montaigne.

Before the War, the town was a thriving community set on a flat steppe nestled in the crook of two mountains. But, once the Horrors rose, life in the town became a nightmare with constant attacks winnowing down the population and driving away travelers. Calls for aid from the Eisenfürsten fell on deaf ears. While those who could flee left, those who remained despaired of any way to turn back the tide. Then one day, a young nobleman arrived with a solution to the problem. His name was Viktor Franzeller, a scientist but also a hexe. He swore to the people of Höhenlage they could survive alongside the Horrors peacefully. All they needed was to listen to his every word.

A generation later, Viktor has completely transformed the people, using them as his personal experimentation pool, grafting pieces of Horrors onto the townspeople to make them stronger. He created Leibewerke Horrors, undead creatures with various limbs grafted together. Eventually, he learned how to keep the people alive after the grafts. Franzeller has adjusted nearly everyone in some way. The Changed, as they call themselves, vastly outnumber those who refused the grafting process. Obsessed with creating the perfect blend of person and Horror, Viktor's grotesque experiments have yielded a little success. The townsfolk remain largely invisible to some Horrors, though whether due to the grafts or Franzeller's Hexenwerk is anyone's guess. Because of his success the townsfolk are nearly all fantastically devoted to him, and those who are not keep their opinions to themselves. Those still resisting Franzeller warn an outsider traveling through Höhenlage to keep his head down and his mouth shut if he doesn't want any trouble, or risk facing the terror of the Changed.

Of every danger in the mountains, it is the Changed that may bring down the wrath of the outside world fastest. Rumors about Franzeller's work have reached die Kreuzritter, and they have set their sights on ending his work once and for all. If they want him, however, they need to get into the mountains and survive its perils, no easy feat for anyone looking to challenge the dangers of the Dracheneisen.

# The Wälder

The Wälder technically falls into three separate königreichen: Freiburg, Fischler and Sieger, and covers nearly a third of southern Eisen. Anyone traveling from east to west in Eisen finds it almost impossible to do so without traversing the forest, and many trails and roads carve through the deep woods. However, most of those roads remain unguarded, as neither Sieger nor Fischler have the resources to patrol such a volatile and dangerous territory.

Only Freiburg has the money to even consider such an undertaking and so far, Niklas Träge seems more intent on leaving the forest alone. Instead, a merchant or caravan traveling through the territory brings his own mercenaries and hired guardians if he wishes to come out unscathed. It is not unusual to hear of entire parties entering the forest never to come out the other side. Whether from the blood drinkers to the northeast, the shapeshifting creatures seen racing through the night or the terrifying Schattenmann himself, the Wälder takes its due from Eisen's population.

The Wälder is full of monsters, each more terrifying than the last. Horrors, including many kinds of undead, tremendous and blighted animals, life-sucking mists, witches, ghouls and monstrous twisted creatures all call the Wälder home. These roving nightmares are only the simplest of the dangers in the woods, however. Travelers report ghosts of long-dead soldiers roaming in units along the borders of the forest, ready to reenact moments from their last battles with any unsuspecting people in their path.

Those who sleep in the forest find themselves waking up to the sound of sobbing ghosts in their camp.

Should travelers not come prepared with Hexenwerk unguents or a good exorcist, those same ghosts may possess a member of their party, draining the life from the host as it goes. The possessed person's companions can only rescue their unfortunate associate by helping the ghost resolve its unfinished business or risk seeing their friend lost forever.

Men and women have settled in the forests along with the monsters, many just as monstrous as the rest of the denizens. Many go to the Wälder with nothing left in their lives and turn to theft as the only way to survive. Only the hardiest of these desperate people survive to become dangerous bandits; most simply fall prey to the Horrors.

Those who do survive long enough are a breed set apart from most Eisen. Some become what the locals call Wilde Kinder, a roving band ripping apart anyone they come upon in an attempt to cull the "herds" of people entering the forest. Survivors of their attacks report the Wilde Kinder are more than just forest folks: they are shapeshifters, taking on the forms of human-animal hybrids to track and hunt their prey.

Between the Horrors and the people lurking in the Wälder, few travelers make it through the forbidding forest unscathed. Most merchants refuse to make camp for the night, preferring to travel many long hours to avoid such a prospect. Others band together, making huge temporary settlements in the forest, and hope that their numbers deter creatures and bandits from attacking. Of course, it doesn't stop the Horrors, but at least with a large group, the fight ends quickly.

## Waldemar Estate

An equally terrifying threat resides in the northwest part of the forest. Under the canopy of the Wälder, built deep into an ancient set of Syrneth ruins, a crumbling manor molders. A traveler who strays off the beaten path can find herself drawn to the supposed safety of the house, only to become the guest of the Waldemar family. And while the family may seem hospitable, their appetite for drinking the blood of their guests has transformed so many grateful Eisen lives into waking nightmares.

## Schattenmann

Schattenmann, "the Shade Man," walks the forest with a tremendous pair of shears in his long, stick-like arms, ready to cut anyone to pieces who crosses his path. His plans are his own and while some believe him a simple Horror, survivors of encounters with the Schattenmann speak about a haunting, terrible intelligence behind his black, pit-like eyes.

Perhaps he protects the rumored prize of the Wälder, the Imperator's Grove at the very center of the woods. Named for the first Imperator of Eisen, Stefan, a grove of bone-white trees surrounds a fountain purportedly able to cure any illness or repair any injury. Old stories say Imperator Stefan negotiated for use of the woods from the guardian of Eisen, a powerful spirit who wished to remain out of the king's mortal disputes. She removed her protection from the Wälder, leaving behind her magical fountain in the rapidly darkening territory.

## Kummerholt

Tiny hamlets dot the outer ring of the Wälder, as woodcutters, miners, hunters and many more face certain peril to live in the forest. Kummerholt is the largest of these towns. Run by Alwin Rainer, a seventh generation son of the Wälder, this smattering of huts and cottages clustered in the outer ring of the southwest side of the Wälder is the closest to a safe haven for travelers.

The people of Kummerholt treat outsiders with weary humor, finding anyone traveling through the Wälder in the face of such obvious danger to be an arrogant fool. Anyone who survives his first trip through the forest can expect a drink at the Rosswind Inn on the house, a standing offer from the innkeeper Rolf Barkhaus and his wife, Romilde.

# Angenehme Wald

If the Wälder is the terrifying heart of Eisen, then the Angenehme Wald is a haven from the dangers of the monster-infested land. The dense forest ranges across a large section of the northeastern side of Eisen, a countryside full of trees so tall and foliage so thick it is impossible to penetrate in spots. If not for the three main roads going through the Angenehme towards the Ussura border, a person might never venture into the woods. And she would be missing a wondrous sight. There is a reason why people call the forest Angenehme, meaning pleasant, because this forest is pure magic.

Unlike the blighted lands surrounding it, the Angenehme is an almost fairytale forest, full of giant trees, beautiful flowers and healthy animals. Birds sing under the towering firs that never seem to lose their greenery, and woodland creatures of every variety travel through mossy overgrowth amid thick ferns.

Even the roads themselves seem to stay in near perfect condition, despite the fact no one has sent a repair crew to maintain them in years. Those living on the outskirts of the Angenehme have a saying for the near perfect stasis in the woods, *Der Wald dauert fort.* "The forest will go on." Those who remain outside the woods keep a suspicious eye on it with a mix of wonder, wistfulness and hearty worry. Those who live in the Angenehme Wald choose to never leave, though many travel the roads through the Angenehme to Ussura and back again.

The magical perfection of the Angenehme has been a reality for as long as anyone can remember, going all the way back to the time before the War. Old stories abound about someone escaping to the Angenehme, running from one circumstance or another, only to find the very land itself welcoming her and protecting her from her enemies. Those stories always end with the Villains destroyed and the rescuing Heroes settling down to live in the beautiful forest, happily ever after. Sometimes a soldier, demoralized by the War, passed around legends about the Angenehme Wald and the life of beauty he could have there.

Many deserters tried to reach the forest, only to be caught and executed, but sometimes one did reach the Angenehme's shelter. There he found others living in isolated hamlet communities under the tall canopy who welcomed him in. Some of these people were other displaced soldiers, running from Horrors, and sometimes an Ussuran hopping from her side of the border into Eisen. All newcomers are welcomed, but told the same thing. Perchta, the witch of the woods, protects the Angenehme. And woe to anyone who tries to upset the peace of her forest.

The people of the Angenehme lead happy, protected lives. There is only one caveat: once they settle there, they may never leave.

## Perchta's Cottage

Though the Angenehme falls partially under the governance of both Pösen and Freiburg, neither königreich rules the forest. Instead, those in need of aid go to a single cottage at the very heart of the forest and ask the collection of happy children, women and youths there for Perchta. Depending on her mood, the woman who emerges either looks like an old crone, stooped and bent over a cane, or a gorgeous dark-haired young woman in a simple homespun dress.

Perchta makes no attempt to conceal her power or hide the fact she is not human, and scorns any who speak out against magic in her woods. She has lived as the forest's protector for as long as the Angenehme has existed and pledges to remain that way until the stars fall from the heavens. To listen to her tell it, she has been the protector of Eisen for longer than the land had a name. Now, she concentrates her power within the single forest and has since left the rest of the country largely to its fate. Her immortal power keeps the Angenehme always in spring and protects any who live on her land.

The forest, a virtual paradise in the middle of a nightmare, attracts many. Much like Freiburg to the south, the area is fairly lawless save the following: anything taken must be repaid, and no one leaves without Perchta's express approval. Every bit of firewood must have a return to the forest in some form; every deal made under the forest branches must be completed.

Anyone trying to take without repayment in the Angenehme quickly discovers that Perchta's power extends through every blade of grass and every living thing in the woods. Animals, trees, the very ground can turn against anyone who does not trade fairly and equally within the woods, with deadly consequences. The bones of rule-breakers can be found along the sides of the road.

Perchta is also an avid negotiator, and the price of exploring her forest is a favor. Should a person wish to visit the forest temporarily, he must do favors or trade with Perchta. The better the deal, the longer he will be allowed to stay. A person who impresses Perchta can find himself with an ally more powerful than almost anyone in all of Eisen, with knowledge going back centuries. Anger her, and the entire forest becomes a deadly enemy. A traveler who wishes to leave the forest may also try to negotiate with Perchta for her freedom, but the price for leaving her protection can be steep and even deadly.

Once a visitor has gained Perchta's permission to explore, he discovers the Angenehme is much more than a simple hiding place for refugees. Inside its boundaries lies a venerable treasure trove of flora and fauna not seen in such abundance anywhere in Eisen. Plants and animals long since destroyed by the years of War thrive there, especially plants known for their medicinal qualities. Extremely rare ingredients for Hexenwerk can be harvested there, and there are rumors of magical relics of different ages, including Syrneth relics hidden deep in troves beneath the earth.

Rumors abound among the inhabitants about caves to the north of the Angenehme said to hold a labyrinth of tunnels holding an underground magical river that leads to strange and wondrous lands. More than anything, the Angenehme hosts all kinds of strange magical creatures, drawn by Perchta's power, glorious creatures almost out of storybooks. Whether real or just Perchta's powers given form, no one entirely knows for sure.

Perchta has also involved herself directly in the politics of the country, covertly backing Rosamund Roth's bid for future government control. From her cottage, she reaches out with her emissaries, loyal residents of the forest, who carry her messages to push along support for the Drachenblut commander in the ever-evolving political drama for Eisen's leadership.

## Kreuzweg

Anyone traveling the Angenehme's roads must pay a toll or offer tribute to the forest, which can be paid at the crossroads at the Wald's western border. A small town has grown up around that crossroad just inside the forest's boundaries called Kreuzweg, where a traveler might resupply and rest on her journey.

An inn at the heart of the town, the Skipping Stone, serves as a warm and pleasant rest, and often hosts an Ussuran on his way west, merchants heading into Ussura and travelers between Pösen and Freiburg. Explorers looking for Syrneth artifacts in the woods, in which there are several relic sites, use the inn as a base of operations.

Though the woods are peaceful and idyllic, many over the years have found the clearly magical nature of the Wald, and its protector Perchta, disturbing. When armies loyal to the Vaticine Church marched on the woods during the War to purge it of its magical taint, they found themselves facing a battle unlike anything they had ever seen. The woods themselves ripped the troops to shreds.

A young Captain, Jakob Berlitz, sent to lead the charge, returned to his commanding officer and refused to destroy the forest, even on penalty of death. Before he could be hanged for disobeying a direct order, he escaped into the woods with his surviving soldiers, where he lives to this day as the mayor of the Kreutzung.

With the country in such dire straits, many have sought out refuge in the woods, swelling the number of people living under Perchta's protection. When emissaries from the Eisenfürsten tried to speak with the people, they remained tight-lipped about their conditions, and instead sent the emissaries on to Perchta.

Whatever they saw apparently intrigued Niklas Träge enough that he took a special trip to visit the witch of the woods herself. Rumor says the two struck up an understanding. Perchta has since made the roads through the woods the safest way to travel to Ussura unmolested and trade has become very lucrative, provided all involved follow the laws of the Angenehme.

## Burg Wachesherz

The Castle of the Vigilant Heart lies at the foot of the Tiefstrabe Mountain deep in the Dracheneisen range. An ancient relic from before the War of the Cross, the hulking mountain stronghold fell long ago into disrepair, claimed by the elements, its history lost to time.

Legends about the castle say ancient sorcerers created the place to study the drachen who once made Eisen their home, but no one can be certain if this is true. By the time the castle was rediscovered during the last days of the War of the Cross, it had already turned into a half-collapsed heap. Only its outer walls stood unaffected, sealing the castle into a niche between two steep cliffs.

Soldiers on the run during the War discovered the castle when seeking refuge from terrible winter storms. Led by Rosamund Roth, the unit found the castle's interior completely overrun by Horrors. They boiled up from the depths of the keep and slaughtered many of the soldiers before Roth led an excursion to seal the lower levels. The survivors left the castle when the weather cleared, but not before Rosamund swore to return and clear out the Horrors and restore Wachesherz to its former glory. She came back from the lower levels changed, as though she had discovered something both terrible and wondrous.

It took years for Rosamund Roth to return to Tiefstrabe Mountain. When she did, it was at the head of a column of warriors dedicated to a new organization known as the Drachenblut. The warriors, led by Roth, had committed themselves to becoming a new force for good in the troubled Eisen, a battle-ready small army not held back by politics and with only one goal: protect the people of Eisen from everything and anything.

For that, however, they needed a headquarters. The first major battle of the Drachenblut took place in Burg Wachesherz's halls as they fought to retake the castle from its monstrous tenants. When they finished, Roth planted the flag of the Drachenblut above the castle ramparts and set about the task of rebuilding the stronghold to its former glory.

## The Fortress

Burg Wachesherz is now a true mountain fortress. Set with its back to the Tiefstrabe Mountain's face and hugged on both sides by its cliffs, the castle only has one narrow mountain pass. Its towering walls allow guards to stand watch and see anyone approaching, and archers stay on the battlements at all times. The forces inside Wachesherz might be small, but they are regimented and disciplined, well-staffed by crafts-people and servants who have seen the good done by the Drachenblut and made the long trek into the mountains to help the organization survive.

Where once the Drachenblut were more secretive, Rosamund has recently opened the castle up amid accusations of strange blood rituals and dark magic going on underneath. The organization has nothing to hide, and they greet guests and share their ideas with anyone who listens. They eagerly entertain anyone interested in supporting their cause with coin, weapons, favors or military might.

Trustworthy visitors to the castle may be invited to see the Drachenblut's strategy academy, a training center teaching its finest young recruits the art of tactical action and military history, or train in the lists with the organization's fierce warriors.

One of the castle's greatest treasures is its growing library in the northern towers, being restored by a defrocked Vaticine priest turned historian named Diego Monsancino. The library is known to hold texts about everything from history to magic going back as far as the days of Stefan the Wise.

Anyone who wishes to stay and learn must first ride out with the Drachenblut and prove himself a worthy ally. Those who survive are counted as *Blutsgeschwister*, "blood-sibling," and may stay. All who stay at the castle share the same kind of living quarters and eat together in a giant communal feasting hall. There is no head table and Rosamund Roth eats among soldiers and guests alike under a giant banner of the golden dragon.

The trip to the castle is not an easy one, as Horrors in the mountains and dangerous weather hazards take many lives before they ever reach Wachesherz. Enemies interested in curtailing the Drachenblut's power ambush travelers on their way to the castle. Meanwhile the remoteness of the castle has served the Drachenblut well, keeping their enemies far away and their resources and secrets far away from prying eyes.

## The Iron Caves

Strange stories have come down from the mountain about the initiation ceremonies of new Drachenblut recruits and what Rosamund Roth might have hiding in the lower levels of the castle keep. Loose lips and the Eisenfürsten's spies carry stories about a hooded ritual where new warriors receive a goblet full of drachen blood to drink. Of course, most do not believe the organization actually has drachen blood, as the legendary creatures have not existed in Eisen for thousands of years. Still, many wonder if somewhere deep beneath Wachesherz lies a cavern holding a terrible and amazing secret.

If Rosamund Roth and the Drachenblut do indeed have a drachen in their fortress, nobody is talking.

## The Village of Wachesherz

Along with its knights, commanders and visitors, the castle has a population of nearly two hundred, from servants to hostlers and weaponsmiths, with more arriving every year. Every day, construction continues on the castle, renovating old sections and adding new places to house the burgeoning population.

A small village, named after the castle itself, has sprung up outside of the citadel's walls, boasting artisans and merchants from all across Théah. Those who stay outside the city barter and bargain from those uninterested in becoming blutgeschwister, and a sprawling marketplace lies in the shadow of the castle's towers.

The most lucrative trade item is Hexenwerk parts, and merchants in the know spread rumors of Hexenwerk ingredients found at Wachesherz that can't be found anywhere else. The town's chief civilian, nominally its mayor, a woman named Kiva Hollitz, not only supports and sympathizes with hexe but also with many sorcerers. She even works to bring those in danger of ostracization or being hunted into her remote little village, far from prying eyes.

In the face of maintaining costly renovations to Wachesherz, the Drachenblut have solicited many noble supporters, who they entertain at the castle. Those noticing Rosamund Roth's rise to power have also chosen to visit the castle, and an expensive and well-appointed inn has only recently opened up, protected by castle walls. Called the Drachen's Jewel, it is run by a Vesten couple, Gertrude and Sigrun Jarlsmann. The two, known associates with the Vendel League, serve as hosts to all those higher class clientele visiting the mountain fortress.

The Burg Wachesherz, a growing power in Eisen, draws much political ire from both foreign dignitaries and the Eisenfürsten. A recent influx of weapons to the fortress also has many sitting up to take notice, as an anonymous donor gifted the organization with extremely rare dracheneisen weapons and armor.

Many point the finger at Niklas Träge, who denies the accusation. Still, the arrival of these powerful weapons continues to expand the legend of Wachesherz as the center of a great new adventure beginning in the heart of Eisen.

# Starkbrunn

On the border between Castille and Eisen lies the high-walled city of Starkbrunn. Unlike many of the older cities in Eisen, Starkbrunn is a city revitalized after the War. Ravaged by constant attacks and overrun early in the conflict, Starkbrunn suffered Castillian occupation for much of the War of the Cross until retaken in the final push by the Imperator and his troops.

During this push, the Imperator lost nearly a thousand soldiers taking the high walls around the city, earning it the nickname the Crown's Graveyard. Outside the wall, the flower of Eisen's youth perished by the tens of thousands in the shadow of the Dracheneisen Mountains over the course of seven days. The open ground between the Starkbrunn walls and the mountains became known as *die Heulenden Ebenen*, the Howling Grounds, because they say the blood of Eisen and Castille soaked through every inch of earth.

In the shadow of Starkbrunn's walls, the two nations declared a cessation of hostilities. The battle on die Heulenden Ebenen began the road to peace, and Castille returned Starkbrunn to Eisen as a gesture of goodwill. The veterans of the battle swore an oath to guard against a return to war and many settled in Starkbrunn to rebuild. Despite their efforts, the remnants of the city fell into disrepair and remained occupied mostly by this remaining military force.

## Die Heulenden Ebenen

The Howling Grounds outside the walled city is a blighted, wretched stretch of land spawning some of the most dangerous Horrors seen in Eisen. These creatures do not hide but instead often crawl from crags in the rocky ground to brazenly attack a traveler on her way to the city.

The last few miles to Starkbrunn are a mad dash across the flat open ground to reach the safety of the garrisons who patrol just under the walls. Anyone caught on open ground after nightfall surely faces attack. Fatalities were common when only the elder veterans held Starkbrunn, but a new generation of fighters has taken up the call to make the city strong.

## The Junges Blut

When the garrison's elder commander, Bruno Elkhardt, died fighting off a pack of ghouls while protecting a merchant caravan, his daughter and second-in-command Elmina Elkhardt put out the call across Eisen. She urged those young and old to take up the new war for Eisen's future, the war against monsters who stole their Nation's chance for prosperity. Bards and messengers carried the letter to every corner of the country.

Soon, a fresh crop of young Eisen arrived. Though too young to have fought in the War, they have cut their teeth fighting Horrors all their lives. Tough and scrappy, these young fighters took to the task of protecting and rebuilding Starkbrunn, turning it into the leading military base in all of Eisen. Under Elmina Elkhardt's command, these new fighters styled themselves the Junges Blut, "young bloods," of Eisen, a new breed of monster-slayers ready to fight and die to protect their families against harm.

Though tensions run high between the elder veterans and the Junges Blut, the two groups have come together under Elkhardt's command to become the major power in the region. The town has become so powerful many families send their young people to take a turn as a Junge Blut in Starkbrunn as a point of pride, so their children might learn what it is to truly fight for Eisen.

The surprise came when Starkbrunn declared themselves a part of the königreich of Fischler rather than original barony of Hainzl. Falk Fischler was the only Eisenfürst to respond to Starkbrunn's call for aid, sending down supplies despite political advice to the contrary. When Commander Elkhardt sent him a letter of thanks, Fischler shocked her when he came south to meet her and tour the famous battlefields.

The Eisenfürst uncharacteristically charmed both the Junges Blut with his support and the veterans by paying tribute on the battlefield to those who fell. Since then, the city is fanatically devoted to Fischler and its Eisenfürst and follows him come what may.

With the support of Fischler and other benefactors, Starkbrunn has been rebuilt. Behind its towering walls now lies a fairly modern city, a layer of strong new fortifications over the crumbled and nearly destroyed infrastructure of the ancient citadel.

Still, old scars run deep. Any travelers coming up from Castille must travel through Starkbrunn for safety, and though the War ended long ago, tensions still run high should any Castillians come north.

## Jägerviertel

Starkbrunn has become a haven for fighting men and women from all across Eisen looking for a new cause, a new home or a place to belong. Those who do not fall in with the garrison often become private soldiers, and many mercenary companies find their home in Starkbrunn. And since the War, many an Eisen has turned his martial capabilities to hunting and destroying the one thing Eisen has plenty of: monsters.

A new class of wandering monster hunter called the ungetümjäger has emerged from veteran fighters well-versed in eradicating all classes of Horrors. A person seeking work as a hired monster hunter makes her home in the southern part of the city known as the Jägerviertel, the Hunter's Quarter. People with a particular kind of Horror problem can find specialists in local taverns, where innkeepers keep rosters of hunters looking for work.

Additionally, the Himmel Licht Hospital at the center of the town is world renowned for treating odd afflictions contracted from monster attacks. Their head researcher, Doctor Yedidya Neiman, specializes in gathering knowledge about all magical maladies, continuing the work of his Yachidi parents whose healing knowledge and skills brought them all the way from the Crescent Empire. Doctor Neiman works closely with his husband, Samir al-Rabbah, to network with other Yachidi institutions of learning to help expand knowledge of the anatomy of monsters, as well as the uses of Hexenwerk to help those in need.

## The Magic Trade

Starkbrunn also serves as one of the leading centers for the trade of Hexenwerk components. Considering the city's need for resources against Horrors, most fighters turn a blind eye to concerns over using Hexenwerk, taking on a more "whatever works" mindset.

For that reason, shopkeepers across Starkbrunn sell Hexenwerk ingredients on the sly while the local constables pretend not to notice. Unlike the shops at Wachesherz, whose wares are just as likely rumor as real, the shops in Starkbrunn hold fresh ingredients at reasonable prices. A hexe can find many hard-to-locate materials in the shops, and if the shops don't carry them, they can probably harvest the monster parts from the Horrors in die Heulenden Ebenen.

Additionally, Starkbrunn is a vital stop on the underground smuggling routes for sorcerers escaping from places of persecution. Many hexe, seeking to avoid signing up on Elsa Pösen's list, make their home in the city. No one really knows how many sorcerers the city harbors, though if you are looking for someone to teach or help with a specific problem, they aren't hard to find.

It is an open secret that Donatella Rossi, a Vodacce immigrant who serves as the best seamstress in Starkbrunn, is also a Fate Witch allied with the Junges Blut. The seamstress is rumored to know the location of every hidden sorcerer in the city, but no one has been foolish enough to try to make her talk. She has survived three assassination attempts already. Each time, the her would-be murderers found mysteriously outside the city walls after dark, where they met a gruesome fate. So is the end of anyone who stands against the rising power of Starkbrunn and its new generation of Eisen Heroes.

# The Ausgeglichene Platz

Until recently, no one knew about the strange, twisted ruins of the Ausgeglichene Platz. The Salzsumpf swamplands in the north of Eisen, deep inside Pösen, were always considered a horrible place, with thick bogs full of sinking mud, crawling Horrors and an awful infestation of sirens come down from the coast to settle in the shallows.

Before the War, people traveled carefully through the region and could largely come through unscathed, though probably miserable from the experience. In the years during the rise of the Horrors across Eisen, the Salzsumpf faced a geological shift. Strange noises escaped up from under the sucking mud and swamp, vibrating the ground and causing massive shifts in the landscape. From underneath a complex series of ruins rose to the surface, scattered for miles in every direction.

When explorers came upon the new find, they were shocked to find the ruins only represented the top portions of larger structures still buried deep beneath the earth. From openings in the towers, explorers could enter the underground to discover and map the complex's many rooms and passages.

They found the structures each to be enormous, with multiple levels full of beautiful, if waterlogged, mosaics and carvings along the walls and ceilings. But it was the discovery of Syrneth relics and crystals glowing purple in the dark that put the new and mysterious ruins on the map. The first visitors named the place the Ausgeglichene Platz, or "the Balanced Place," because the structures look precariously balanced, even while under the earth. Hallways and entire towers lie buried at an angle and in strange configurations, leading even the canniest of adventurers to get lost or injured. That does not stop a member of the Explorer's Society or a fortune seeker from testing her luck inside the Balanced Place.

With so many adventurers seeking the mystery of the Ausgeglichene Platz, Elsa Pösen sent a tax collector to levy a small fee from anyone who brought out treasure from the complex. Yet like the rest of Eisen, the Ausgeglichene Platz is full of undead. Attacks increased with such alarming frequency that Pösen declared the area off limits. Since then, only the bravest has taken to entering the Ausgeglichene Platz, armed to protect herself as she takes on the challenge of searching the buried palace.

# Gottkirchen and Rücken Island

Rücken Island lies off the northern coast of the königreich of Wirsche, a chilled and forbidding island, which changed hands many times over the centuries. The island once served as a depot for ships coming down from Vestenmennavenjar and hosted a small resupply station by the Vendel League, infrastructure which was destroyed during the War of the Cross.

During the War, pirates proclaimed it home until Castillian forces chased them off, and then Roswitha von Wirsche sent her best Iron Guard to repel the landing. Once the War ended, Wirsche hatched a plan to use the island to house excess population left landless during the War.

Called the Rücken Endeavor, Wirsche advertised free land to whomever settled this Horror-free new paradise by the sea. All told, five hundred families and almost two hundred orphans boarded boats to travel to Rücken Island, most of them Vaticine, bringing with them their meager possessions and the drive to create a new and safer home for themselves. What they found upon arrival was a wind-blasted barren land, barely arable for crops and vulnerable to attack.

Instead of creating new settlements, the people wanted to leave the island. Unfortunately, the boats that brought them there had abandoned them. The settlers sought shelter in the old Vesten town of Gottkirchen, and they might have all died out if not for a terrible pact made with the island's sole previous inhabitants: blood drinkers.

## The First Year

Roswitha von Wirsche proposed the Rücken Endeavor to free herself and the other Eisenfürsten of displaced populations, old veterans and refugees from Horror attacks. She, as well as Eisenfürsten Sieger, Hainzl and Pösen, promised support, including Iron Guard troops, to help the settlers create their own militia upon landing. Most were unaware of the vulnerabilities of the island.

When they learned how bad the land was, they all swore to help rebuild Gottkirchen, a burnt-out husk on the northwest coast, far from aid. Yet the Endeavor broke down almost immediately. Hainzl and Sieger withdrew the lion's share of their funding and supplies, and Wirsche's Iron Guard left after only three months without leaving behind enough weapons for the militia to defend themselves. As soon as the Iron Guard pulled out, raiders landed on the northern coast. Desperate for help, the settlers sent messages to Wirsche, but received only silence in return.

And still, more families arrived, seduced by the promise of safety, with no idea what a nightmare the Endeavor had become. The settlers tried to eke out what living they could, but the crops they planted performed poorly. Then, the unthinkable happened: Horrors appeared on Rücken, drawn by the influx of people. Gottkirchen became the only safe haven, and even those who had attempted to farm the land pulled back into the relative safety of the ruined city.

## The Blood Pact

The people of Rücken might have not have survived the first year, if not for the actions of Salomon Zeller, the island's magistrate. Zeller, selected by Wirsche to manage the island, quickly became Gottkirchen's de facto mayor, military commander and administrator.

One day, covered in blood, Zeller returned from hunting Horrors, the sole survivor of his party. He promised the people of Gottkirchen they no longer needed to fear Horror attacks thanks to new protectors. And though many were suspicious, true to his word, the Horror attacks stopped.

Soon, Gottkirchen reemerged as a fishing and trading village, a refuge against the nightmares of Eisen as it was meant to be. No Horrors attacked the city, and even criminal activity dropped to almost nothing after the first few criminals met swift and bloody ends in the night. People questioned just what kind of guardians protected them so viciously, but Zeller kept it to himself.

Another year later, a carriage pulled up into Gottkirchen square. It came from a small, dilapidated manor house on the far side of Rücken, high above the eastern cliffs. Zeller met the carriage, escorting his own brother, a sickly man near to death. Zeller's brother entered the carriage and was never seen alive again. The carriage delivered his body back, draped in a white shroud, three days later. Zeller then told everyone about the deal he had made. And after a great debate, reluctantly, the town accepted the blood pact.

Now, over fifteen years have passed and Gottkirchen remains under the protection of blood drinkers. They slaughter any Horrors who arise on the island and stalk the night to deal with any criminals in the town proper. No one knows just how many live at the old manor house across the island, and no one who has gone to challenge them has ever returned. Only Zeller speaks with them, and he is not telling.

Villagers warn merchants who land at Gottkirchen about the brutal rule of law, and so crime is nearly nonexistent. Most traders know to stay away during the summer solstice, however, when the sacrifice occurs. During the funeral for the sacrifice, the next volunteer steps up. So far, there has always been a volunteer, who spends a full year as an honored hero of the community, given anything he wishes until he steps into the carriage for his last ride. The village then takes care of the sacrifice's family for the rest of their lives. This makes it an attractive solution for the poorest, the ill or the lost.

Everyone knows they have made a deal with the very Horrors they fled Eisen to escape. But the alternative, returning to a life haunted by monsters on the mainland, has kept the pact going.

## St. Eugenia's and the Resistance

Few question the town's yearly sacrifice to the blood drinkers of the cliffs. The few adversaries of the blood pact are led by Father Alonzo Gonzalez, a Castillian priest who settled on Gottkirchen to reopen St. Eugenia's church on the west side of town.

He believes Gottkirchen must defend itself and root out the blood drinkers of Rücken. Still, he knows the townspeople live because of the willing sacrifices made by one of their own each year.

He upkeeps a stone memorial in the town square, a tall obelisk inscribed only with the names of those who sacrificed themselves in years past. The last few years, due perhaps to his sermons, fewer and fewer people express interest in volunteering for the sacrifice and instead grumble about overthrowing Zeller as magistrate and driving out the blood drinkers once and for all.

Recently, the Resistance has sent messengers back to the mainland in search of help. Gottkirchen survives under a pall as a tiny, wind-swept town clinging to a rocky cliffside. If the Resistance managed to fight back against the blood drinkers, raiders would have easy access to the village. The town has little of its own protection, with no walls and only a small militia, and depends wholly on the blood drinkers to keep the raiders at bay.

What it does have is an abundance of people living in poor housing—shanties all built up against one another with corrals for livestock and a robust if ramshackle marketplace in the middle of the city square. Even St. Eugenia's is a half-collapsing old relic of the ancient city. With no money for better infrastructure, and no aid to destroy the blood drinkers, the Resistance needs help from outside or will remain under the pact forever.

# Heimstatt

Just east of Freiburg near the Ussuran border lies the bustling town of Heimstatt. Once a farming and agrarian village, the tiny hamlet found itself growing by leaps and bounds when the road from Ussura leading up through the Angenehme Wald expanded to head past their town.

Soon, traders and travelers from all across Théah headed through Heimstatt, turning it into a surprisingly cosmopolitan stopover to anyone heading north to Vestenmennavenjar or further east. During the War, Heimstatt served as a refuge for those in need of medical care and a major army hospital annexed several farms on the outskirts of town to create a ramshackle facility to care for the wounded.

While the people of Heimstatt first resented the seizure of their land, they pitched in and soon became integral in treating so many veterans. The villagers saved thousands of lives through their hard work and dedication to their fellow Eisen.

For their service, the Imperator granted Heimstatt the title of "the home of heroes" and promised a portion of the budget raised by the government to turn the army hospital into a permanent facility for medical service and research. Upon his death, the promise would have been forgotten if not for Eisenfürst Träge. Supported by Pösen and Fischler, Träge threw the full weight of Freiburg behind building sleepy little Heimstatt into a city known for its training hospital and the small scientific Eisengeist-Universität.

Now, the little town is a bustling and productive place amid all the terrors that plague the rest of Eisen. It might be the proximity to Ussura, or just the fact that little fighting happened nearby, but the area is blessedly free of Horrors. The hospital and the Universität attract some of the best minds in Eisen.

Heimstatt now sits as a beacon of hope for the rest of Eisen. The land around the city is still lush and full of life, the people prosper through trade and the city is one of few with an influx of immigrants seeking to settle in Eisen. This spotlight of what Eisen could be like if the Horrors were finally removed lends a great deal of strength to the Eisen people.

## Hospital and University

Heimstatt has retained its charming small town appeal, growing around the university and hospital to serve their needs. Moreover, the town has attracted some of the greatest minds in medicine and scientific thought to what might be considered the middle of nowhere.

Heiligherz-Krankenhaus not only retains its capacity for accepting mass traumas for aid, but trains some of the best field medics anywhere. Their surgical wing is second to none, and they have received aid from medical institutions all over Théah to expand their library. The Vaticine Church saw the good work done by the hospital and extended financial support, and helped send doctors from as far off as Vodacce and Castille to join the teaching staff.

The peaceful city has drawn other groups to join the community. A large contingent of Yachidi, moving north from the Crescent Empire for the purposes of business and learning, settled in Heimstatt only ten years ago. In that time, the Yachidi population has exploded, with the religious minority taking over the small neighborhood of Lodz almost entirely.

At first, the local Eisen weren't sure what to make of the foreigners, but soon embraced the Yachidi's diligent dedication to helping others and bettering the community. The Yachidi organization known as the Chavra was instrumental in bringing up medical supplies from the Crescent Empire to tackle a plague threatening the countryside three years ago. Since then, the Yachidi have helped to build up Heiligherz-Krankenhaus and Eisengeist-Universität, fostering both institutions as places where science and magical knowledge could be explored side by side.

This radical approach to joint magical and scientific study for the purpose of healing has drawn the ire of some of the more militant branches of the Church. Recently, the Inquisition has made public statements against Heimstatt for welcoming the study of magic, and the townsfolk publicly expelled members of the Church for nearly coming to blows with the medical college faculty. Tensions have been running high for some time and it is only a matter of time until a crisis fully erupts.

# Hexenwerk

Eisen folklore tells of great Heroes who donned enchanted armor to defeat foes in great battles, gaining the praise of all of Théah. Reality reflects a much darker tale. One of loss and heartbreak, of witches and monsters. One where struggle brings forth a whisper that beckons you ever closer to a darkness you cannot escape.

No one person can tell you when or where Hexenwerk originated, but all can tell you why. Every story of Hexenwerk's beginnings is just that, a story, a rumor. Each tale, similar in that all Hexenwerk tales speak of sadness and heartbreak, ends with the blight of the land. One story tells of the original hexe who used Unguents to enchant armor and weapons. In an Unguent accident, the armor and weapons brought all of the fallen warriors who touched them back to life. The hexe repurposed the Unguents to fight against the new threat and so birthed modern Hexenwerk.

Another fable invokes the witch who watched her land get taken away. A military force making camp in a forest in Eisen started destroying the woods. This also destroyed the witch's wards and crops. After she came home to a house burnt down, she wanted to punish the interlopers. In doing so, she caused the spirits she summoned to ravage the land.

Yet another theory claims that during the War of the Cross, the Eisen military was losing in numbers. They needed reinforcements and food. Experimenting with sorcery, a few of the generals figured out a way to bring back the fallen troops. It worked, but they couldn't control them and the undead spread and devastated the land.

Hexenwerk is grotesque, an artform of using the undead against themselves. Eating undead hearts or making a paste of rotten eyes is not pretty. Many who practice it only do so to help their Nation. A hexe has to; Eisen is his home and the undead an unwelcome presence. It is a Sorcery of desperation. The War of the Cross drained Eisen's resources, but he still fights against a now-common enemy. He knows that someday this will be over. He just has to keep fighting.

Being a hexe is not easy. From rubbing a severed corpse tongue onto his own to eating a mix of ground liver and kidney, most cannot stomach it. Those who can, roam Eisen and clear the undead where they rise. Other Eisen fear and respect the hexe. The practice can alienate you from the ones you love while gaining you praise from those you do not know. However, a hexe believes that saving her country is a greater cause than any other. She is the reason why Eisen still prospers today.

To be a hexe you must find a mentor; very few can teach themselves this Sorcery. Learning and using the Sorcery is often shunned and in some places illegal, making finding such a mentor difficult. Most teachers insist that their students learn the proper skills for fighting the undead, and a novice hexe who attempts to teach himself does not fare well. Most hexe find the training difficult, leading to injury or death. If you do not ready your stomach for what you put in it, your Unguent can end up in a trash bin or with you in a casket.

A hexe inures herself by eating a few days old piece of meat. Then a week, then a month, and so on until she can eat year-old rotten meat without a problem. All that just to stomach the Unguents; getting the proportions just right takes months of practice. Each hexe requires a different amount of each ingredient since bodies react differently to each component. Unfortunately, hexe find trial and error the best way to find the right proportions, which is why you learn to stomach the ingredients first.

A mentor looks for a student proud of Eisen. One that would do anything for her country and is also ambitious. You have to be willing to learn even when that means doing repugnant tasks. A common task for an aspiring student is to find an animal corpse and properly dispose of the body without tools. This means removing all the organs, destroying each of them and then burning the rest of the body. Learning to completely destroy a corpse is a very important piece of knowledge for a hexe. Doing it without tools can be tough for a new student, especially those sensitive to smells.

## The Apostat

Elsa Pösen has tasked a group called the *Hexenjäger* (Witch Hunters) with registering all hexe. Elsa's goal is to send untethered hexe to the Drachenblut to help fight Horrors. If a hexe does not register, the Hexenjäger banishes or kills him, because according to the Witch Hunters, only an enemy of Eisen refuses to sign. Many hexe do not trust Pösen's list and fear she has something terrible planned for them. A hexe may even leave Eisen rather than risk running afoul of the Hexenjäger. If the Hexenjäger finds a hexe in hiding, he brands her with a symbol, a circle with an "X" in it, thus marking her an Apostat. If she continues to use Sorcery within Eisen, he hunts and kills her.

When a hexe leaves Eisen, she usually struggles to put her skills to use. Undead wander everywhere in Théah, but nowhere near as concentrated as in Eisen. Though free from the Horrors and from persecution, a hexe paradoxically finds herself abandoning Hexenwerk from lack of use or modifying and changing her knowledge. A struggling hexe hears of ways to adapt by taking Hexenwerk and converting it to affect monsters other than the undead.

## HEXENJÄGER

In the interest of creating a registry of hexe to keep tabs on who could possibly create—and thereby fight—undead horrors, Elsa Pösen created the Hexenjäger, a subset of her Iron Guard. She hopes to focus the hexe by placing them within military units, and eliminate those who act outside of the command structure.

Elsa believes that a Witch Hunter must have an understanding of Sorcery to register hexe; if one of her Iron Guard shows any sort of magical capability, he begins training as a Hexenjäger. After training, a Hexenjäger receives a sword and a registry book. Once he fills his 26-page book, with each page representing a hexe, he reports back to Elsa. After this initial mission, Pösen sends him out again or returns him to the Iron Guard.

An Apostat uses similar techniques to a normal hexe—instead of undead brain matter, he eats a Monster's brain and instead of an undead eye, he smears paste made from Monsters' eyes. You have to be careful though; Hexenwerk used on Monsters can be easier to swallow. Monster parts taste better overall than rotten and undead flesh, and an Apostat, susceptible to overeating, can fall into madness or contract a strange illness. An Apostat may be lured into thinking that fighting Monsters is a better path, but he would be wrong.

Outside of Eisen, it can be difficult to find tutelage. Apostaten created a way to contact each other. It isn't perfect, but it works. They have repurposed the symbol used to banish them into one of shelter and community. Apostaten find creative uses for this symbol, marking territory, offering or asking for help or just letting people know they are there. Some carve it into trees for a more permanent symbol or get it tattooed somewhere visible. This can help when trying to find a mentor or to help a hexe fine-tune techniques. She has to be careful, however; the symbol can be emulated. There have been instances where a hexe walked into a trap, because she thought herself safe in another Apostat's territory. In some cases, intelligent Monsters have used this symbol against their own hunters.

## How It Works

An Apostat's Hexenwerk works exactly like normal Hexenwerk. Each time you purchase the Sorcery, you learn the recipe for one Major Unguent and two Minor Unguents. You can choose from either the Hexenwerk or the Apostat lists when choosing Unguents.

Creating an Unguent requires time (at least an hour) and a workspace (a kitchen or a lab). A hexe spends a Hero Point, combining the Materials to create 1 Major Unguent for which she has the recipe. In addition, she also creates 1 Minor Unguent for each time she has purchased the Sorcery Advantage. These can be multiple doses of the same Minor Unguent or single doses of different ones.

Once created, an Unguent can be used by anyone. Activating an Unguent costs a single Raise if during an Action Sequence, but requires nothing otherwise. Unguents are unstable; each Hero can only keep one unused Major Unguent or one unused Minor Unguent at the end of each Episode—all others spoil, melt through their containers or become otherwise unusable.

## Major Unguents

A major Unguent's effects last until the end of the Scene, unless otherwise noted. Many of the Major Unguents from the Hexenwerk list can justifiably be used on Monsters, with some ingredient changes. For example, with *Dead Man's Blood*, by changing the fresh corpse blood to blood from a live Monster and poisons to sedatives, you can use this Unguent on a non-undead Monster. Talk with your Game Master about what Unguents she will allow to use on Monsters. Remember to think about good ways to change the ingredients (and the application of the Unguent if necessary) so it makes sense.

### Anosmia Oil

A clump of fur and a drop of urine from a Monster, boiled in herbs, essential oils and acid, then reduced to an oily paste. This oil can then be rubbed on a person's body, to prevent all Monsters—for a single Scene—from tracking that person through smell. A Monster must spend an extra Raise to try to find you.

### Ferocious Mobility

A Monster's tooth, a dried frog and a crow's feather ground into a powder and added to goat's milk. Once swallowed a person gains the ability to run and jump like a wild beast. A hexe can use this Unguent to complete an athletic task that he could not normally perform. An example would be using the Unguent to jump across a twenty-foot crevasse. It does not allow the hexe to complete a task the Monster wouldn't be able to perform itself.

### Fugue Powder

Demon horn, mushrooms and bone meal cooked dry, ground into a powder and added to a tea. When consumed can make the person forget everything about the last day. Fugue powder is very hard to procure as demon horns are not often found lying around. It takes a large amount of tea for this to work.

### Wild Sight

A sharpened blackwood branch, burnt, then rolled in berries, mud and something from the target Monster (fur, blood, etc.). Using the branch to scratch the target's own body—taking 1 Dramatic Wound—that person goes into a trance. In the trance, she sees what the target Monster sees. This may be out of context but can give the user a better idea of the Monster's location and what it is doing. This connection is very weak and can be lost easily. If the Monster goes to sleep or takes a Wound, the connection is lost. If the user takes a Wound, the connection is severed. Wild Sight only lasts one Scene. While in the Wild Sight state, a person can spend 1 Hero Point to then perform a Notice Risk to gain additional information about the Monster.

## Minor Unguents

Minor Unguents' effects last until the end of the Round unless otherwise noted. Just like with the Major Unguents, most of the Minor Unguents from the Hexenwerk list can be used on Monsters, with some ingredient changes. For example with *Red Thirst*, by replacing the rotten meat with fresh meat this can be used on non-undead Monsters. Make sure to talk to your Game Master about converting Minor Unguents.

# Dueling in Eisen

As a Nation which relies foremost on the strength and hardness of iron to protect them, the skill of the Eisen Duelist is paramount. Three of the four major military academies (Steil, Unabwendbar and Gelingen) feature Guildhouses prominently on their grounds. The Duelist Guild has only grown in strength since the end of the War of the Cross; the rising number of Söldner in the Nation has increased the number of possible members tenfold.

Though they have no legal standing or right of authority granted to them, it is not uncommon for Duelists in Eisen to be seen as de facto mediators and arbitrators in disputes. The Eisenfürsten and the Iron Guard may keep the peace and defend the people, but for more personal affronts, a Duelist is the first choice. The Eisen people believe that a person who defends his point with the most strength possesses the most dedication to his cause, transferring an inherent sense of rightness to the issue. People seek out Duelists to settle debates, personal affronts and even legal disputes. This is particularly true among the younger generations who increasingly chafe at the idea of having to seek out their elders for judgment.

## Council of Swords

The large number of Duelists in Eisen drove the Council of Swords to establish its headquarters in the city of Freiburg. The original Council consisted of the three founding members of the Guild and their closest students. Their goal was not to be a governing body, but an administrative one. The Council keeps records of all Duelists (living and dead), collects dues and in rare cases adjudicates disagreements that cannot be settled by the simplicity of a blade.

These rare occasions tend to be matters of business such as competing contracts, or matters of diplomacy where a duel could be seen as an act of war.

The presence of the Council, combined with a cultural tendency to cleave close to the rules, has made illegal duels almost unheard of in Eisen. Even the poorest Bauern would rather pay a Duelist than face the Council's wrath (and fines) over an illegal duel.

## Classes of Duelist

Three distinct types of Duelists in Eisen exist across the four social classes. To wear the pin is an honor, a symbol of recognition among one's peers. An Eisen Duelist, regardless of his place in society, always wears his pin proudly and visibly, and would take great offense at the idea of concealing it.

### Adel Duelist

Plenty of nobles keep a Duelist on retainer to officiate any duels that may be declared and to serve as teachers, but many Adel see it as weakness to have a Duelist fight on one's behalf. This does not stop a cautious (or perhaps cowardly) member of the nobility from inserting retained Duelists into his own arguments. "How dare you speak so rudely in the company of my honored vassal! I'm sure he is extremely offended!"

Adel Duelists tend to be quiet men and women on the edge of the courts. The Eisenfaust school is favored among Adel Duelists, making the panzerhand as much the mark of a Duelist as the pin on the lapel.

Actual duels among Adel Duelists tend to be public and somber affairs. A Duelist salutes offhand on her chest and raises her blade before beginning. The two operate in near silence, the only noise the clash of iron and grunts of effort. Duels are almost never to the death, even for the gravest of offenses. Too few Eisen remain for all but the most severe of wrongs to necessitate another death. Once the duel concludes, if possible, the two once again salute and exchange grips.

## Söldner Duelists

The highest concentration of Duelists in Eisen is within the Söldner class. Though by no means required, it is common for Söldner Duelists to be officers, due more to skill than any type of social pressure. This plays a role during disagreements between two or more groups of Iron Guard; if there are Duelists among the squads, the groups commonly choose them to resolve the dispute.

Unlike duels among the Adel, duels between the Söldner tend to be raucous events. The other Söldner form a ring and the duel begins with drawn steel. The predominance of the Drexel style means that such fights become a dance of point and counterpoint as the two shift between stances. The loser of such fights is almost always left alive but rarely standing.

## Waisen Duelists

The War of the Cross cost many everything. A Waisen Duelist typically returned home to find his town destroyed, his lands salted and his family killed out of hand or consumed by wasting disease. Worse still were the Horrors that followed. The War cost him everything, but not his honor. A Waisen Duelist might part with his sword or his armor to feed himself, but never his pin.

Duels are far less common among the Waisen for obvious reasons. These people struggle for their own survival. This has lead many to adopt the Kummerholt style. It requires little more than a knife and can be the difference between life and a shallow grave when a Horror attacks.

## Kummerholt

The people of Eisen have many stories of normal people fighting against real Monsters. More often than not, these stories tell of desperate, unlikely Heroes fighting against impossible odds—such as a mother defending her children from the thing howling in the night, with nothing but the knife from her kitchen table. The story of Adel Dietz ends with him beaten and broken, then defeating the *Blutiger Fürst* by stabbing him in the heart with his hunting knife as the noble gloated. If the stories are to be believed, hunters slayed drachen with broken swords shoved home as the Monsters crushed them.

Duelists disagree as to who first codified the Kummerholt style, but no one can deny its effectiveness. It is not so much a way of fighting as a state of mind. The Duelist fights without regard for his own safety or well-being, rushing and stabbing at a stronger opponent. In the final moments when all seems lost, the Duelist pushes his blade home, ending the fight with a single well-placed thrust.

## Style Bonus: Death Knell

When you wield a small blade in one hand (such as a dagger, a jagged piece of shrapnel or the remnants of a broken sword), you gain a special Maneuver called the Death Knell. Spend all your Raises. You deal a number of Wounds equal to your Ranks in Weaponry + the number of Raises you spent + your opponent's Strength (or your opponent's highest Trait, if not a Villain). These Wounds cannot be avoided or prevented in any way. A Hero can only perform Death Knell once per Scene.

## Legenden of Eisen

Eisen has always been a land of Horrors. Stories of dead soldiers and graveyards rising back to life form the basis of many of the oldest legends. Whether a few ancient hexe began Eisen's problem with undead, or people started studying Hexenwerk in response to the undead is not clear. Blame the War or Eisen's haunted past, one thing cannot be denied: Eisen is a land of undead Horrors unlike any seen in other parts of the world.

The War of the Cross brought a proliferation of modern Hexenwerk across all of Eisen. A hexe back then did not study out of a love of things macabre or a need for personal power, but in a desperate attempt to defend her home, her people and her beloved land. This did not make the work any less grotesque or powerful. The hexe created a wide plethora of creatures locked in life-beyond-life to help defend the lands. Most highly experienced hexe laid the Monsters back to rest after their use in the War—that is how it was supposed to be done. However, it did not always work that way. In times of desperation, many poorly trained, inexperienced hexe let loose all manner of beings still roaming the lands of Eisen without control.

### Zombies

Poorly held together by rotting sinew, broken bones and decaying flesh, zombies move barely faster than a stumble and seem drawn by the scent of living flesh without needing to see their prey. However, finding a single zombie is a rarity. Hexe took advantage of the freshly dead masses on the battlefields during the War of the Cross and often raised scores of these creatures at the same time. The plan was to throw them back against the enemies that killed them, giving the noble soldiers their last revenge. However, after winning the battles, many unskilled hexe found they had poured too much power into their creations. They lost control of their undead minions and packs of zombies began to roam the land.

Zombies are weak individually, but powerful in groups. Depending on the size of the group, zombies can range in Strength. An average Monster Squad of zombies is Strength 4 with the Unliving Monstrous Quality.

### Revenants

A zombie rarely kills a person unless he is alone or highly unlucky. Revenants, however, murder with savage speed and skill. A Revenant is still an undead creature—they have no breath, no moving blood and are creations of Hexenwerk—but they are many times faster, stronger and better put together than a zombie. Most Revenants still maintain their skin and the muscle structure beneath. The best identifying features of a Revenant are sunken, shriveled eye sockets and skin, which has sloughed off their fingertips. They kill and eat so viciously with their hands that, while the rest of their body maintains its form, a Revenant's palms are stripped down to nothing but skeleton and sinew. Still, that skeleton is dangerously strong, even to a trained Hero. It is not clear exactly what makes a Revenant—some say they are simply zombies which had a bit more power poured into them. Others believe that Revenants had been specifically created after the War by hexe who captured zombies and turned them into better killing machines. While Revenants do not have human thought processes, they do seem better at following orders and are able to focus on specific targets. They do not kill with the mindlessness of zombies—they are a targeted, dangerous threat.

The average Revenant is a Strength 5 Monster with the Monstrous Qualities Relentless and Swift.

## Leibewerke Horrors

Four impossibly muscular arms, six spindly legs like some sort of centipede, two heads (sewn on opposite directions), two torsos stacked atop each other to support the extra limbs—this Monster was one of the first Leibewerke creations to have roamed the lands. Originally created during the War of the Cross, a Leibewerke is a type of Horror created from the choicest parts of various dead to make one giant nearly unstoppable creature. Leibewerke Horrors are the result of a hexe who has fallen to the dark temptations of her work and wishes to push it to the absolute limits.

The increase in Hexenwerk acceptance towards the end of the War allowed less moral hexe to flourish. These creations are larger, stronger and more versatile than zombies or Revenants. A particularly skilled hexe could create Leibewerke geared for certain situations: an oddly long, thin, multi-limbed creature for climbing difficult places or a multi-bodied massive beast made to roll across battlefields. The people of Eisen rose up in protest when they learned of the creatures, but the work had already been done and Leibewerke joined the roaming Horrors.

Leibewerke range in Strength from 5 to 7, depending on the reason for creation, and have the Monstrous Qualities Fearsome and Powerful.

### Hexe's Artform

There are still hexe who specialize in making Leibewerke and even seem to get a great joy in each Horror they produce. Most of these hexe have gone underground since the War, but among some, it is still considered a unique art and they cannot give up their chosen form of expression. Viktor Franzeller is one of these infamous hexe; he has transformed the entire small town of Höhenlage into a test pool for his dark Henenwerk, calling them his Changed. He has learned how to keep his test subjects, townsfolk with grafts, alive, making sick copies of the Horrors.

A small section of die Kreuzritter have devoted themselves to seeking out hexe who still make these creatures, and Viktor's name is on the top of their list. Sadly, the hunt has become an arms race—every time die Kreuzritter attacks, Viktor creates something more horrid to fend them off. More than a few of these creatures have escaped their master and now roam the lands, leaving destruction in their wake.

## Blood Drinkers

In the greater lands of Eisen, there are creatures only known as the blood drinkers. A sect dwells on the cliffs of Rücken Island, helping protect the small territory in return for a blood sacrifice once a year. The life of a single, willing townsperson is worth the protection from the greater Horrors in the world. The town does not know exactly what the blood drinkers do with the sacrifice, only that they return him bloodless and dead three days later.

It is a common assumption that the Monsters on the cliffs drink him to death, hence the colloquial name. In other places, people find the dessicated husks of animals, and sometimes people, which they attribute to the blood drinkers, though no one has ever caught one in the act.

### The Truth: Vampir

The townsfolk are right about the assumption, but wrong that a death of a single mortal a year sustains any Vampir for such a time. The most frightening and most human of the undead, a Vampir can speak, act, think and go about life like any breathing mortal— but she does not breathe and her heart does not beat. The Vampir began when a single hexe dared to test the very limits of immortality, and succeeded, ages before the War of the Cross.

It seems the key to living forever is to not be alive; immensely powerful Hexenwerk and the sacrifice of one's mortality can lead to immortality in the brain and "soul." However, to sustain the Hexenwerk, the Vampir must steal ten gallons of human blood a month. The blood can be consumed, bathed in or even simply worn like make-up. The use of the blood actually powers the Hexenwerk that sustains the Vampir in his state. Vampir rarely make more of themselves as they highly dislike teaching the secrets of their lifestyle. However, they do dwell in little pockets across Eisen. Several are quite unhappy with the publicity of Rücken Island and—even as the mortals plot to do something—they discuss if they should remove their too well-known brethren.

A Vampir is a Monstrous Villain and has access to Influence and Advantages just as a human Villain does. They use their Influence to control lesser undead, such as zombie Monster Squads. Vampirs have the Monstrous Quality Nocturnal and always have access to Hexenwerk.

## Werwolf

There is one way to die in Eisen and return to life, but it is not a life that anyone wishes. Rumors of humans who turn into massive furred and clawed beasts at the height of the full moon have been around for centuries. While some wild storytellers spin tales of a Werwolf relenting to his human side when close to his near and dear, no one has ever seen proof of such actions. Everyone in Eisen, however, knows someone who witnessed one of these beasts on a full moon. This makes travel severely limited when the moon is full; a person needing to take a journey on such evenings often hires a highly skilled hunter to guard her for the perilous trip.

### The Truth

While injury by Werwolf bite is not automatically deadly, if the attack is lethal, the victim returns as one of these creatures. The only way to transmit the condition is through death and rebirth as a Monster. This factor leads some highly studied hexe to believe that the "curse" of the Werwolf is an ancient and early form of Hexenwerk, as it requires death as a trigger. However, this Monster is not undead, as she still breathes, eats, walks and talks as a mortal in her normal life. Only during the full moon does the other side of this transformation take over.

Werwölfe are vicious and can easily kill a lone Hero. They stand nearly twice the height of most humans but generally hunch over so they have easy use of both their front and hind legs. Their hands and feet transform into massive paws with lethally long claws. They carry more strength than any known, natural animal on the continent and heal at a rapid rate. Regular weapons only injure them for moments before their body heals to their regular, dangerous vitality. Dracheneisen seems entirely ineffective on Werwölfe. However, they do have weaknesses. Silver has been proven to injure them grievously. Not only can they not heal silver wounds, but it seems to be poisonous to their blood. They also only have an animal mentality when in Werwolf form and seem driven by nothing but a maddened bloodlust.

Outside of a full moon, the Werwolf is a normal person, with little knowledge of his alternate personality. During the full moon, a Werwolf has a Strength of 6 with Monstrous Qualities of Nocturnal, Powerful and Regenerating. It does not regenerate against silver.

## Grundylow

Since the War of the Cross, Grundylow sightings have dramatically increased throughout Eisen. The reason for this is unclear. Some believe that the Grundylows have always been numerous, but people had a harder time believing in them before the rest of the Horrors surfaced.

The legend of Grundylows is one as old as time in Eisen. They are creatures of swamps, marshes, bogs and low water lands. Originally, many thought the creatures old wives tales used to warn the young away from dangerous pools of water. No one can dismiss them any longer, as at least a dozen children and small animals have gone missing to the boney white arms and sunken faces in the last year alone. Legends say they feast on living flesh but prefer the young. No one knows why, since this seems true for animals as well. They are most prominently found in the Salzsumpf swamplands and the ruins they contain.

### The Proof

A team of highly adventurous Heroes investigated the Ausgeglichene Platz in an attempt to catalogue what Horrors lay in the depths of its ruins. Three of the team were lost to the Horrors. Before they decided to withdraw, they managed to capture one wailing, horrific creature for study. It survived six hours outside the murky depths of its swampy home and researchers confirmed it as an actual Grundylow.

The academic described it as if someone had taken a body and stretched it longer by a foot. Its arms were as long as its legs and the body nothing but skin and bones. The hands contained seven fingers on each elongated palm and extra joints for a tighter grasp. The mouth had a double row of jagged teeth, clearly meant for the rending of flesh from bones. It had hair like kelp, which began to dry and break off within an hour of being on land.

Grundylows have Strength 5 and the Aquatic Monstrous Quality.

## House Wights

Despite the often horrific nature of Eisen's history, not all legends are of monstrous beings. In a land of great darkness, light shines all the brighter. Many legends pre-date the War of the Cross, but were mostly considered folktales until Hexenwerk became a regular practice. Now, most of Eisen's citizens indulge in some show of respect for the old myths. These indulgences are seen most prevalently in the deference given to House Wights.

Across Eisen, a large swath of the populace call on spirits called Wights to keep their houses safe, clean and calm. The average person performs tiny acts to bring him in touch with the mythical elements of the land, and gain protection. Like many spirits, Wights gain power through belief, and now there are more Wights taking care of Eisen than ever before.

A family must leave small gifts out for the creatures to receive their protection. These gifts include minor bits of food, hand-written tales or handmade scarves. As long as a gift is from the heart, the House Wights accept it. Once active in a house, Wights give varied blessings, adapting to what the family needs. For example, they can keep a roof intact through a particularly rough winter, ensure the sickly child of a household does not catch the flu or prevent forgotten food crumbs from attracting plague-carrying rodents.

### Other Wights

The people of Eisen give homage to a wide variety of Wights for their varied, small blessings. Wights of the Land are often paid with a small patch of a garden or farm to do with as they please. The Wights watch over the rest of the farm and livestock in exchange. They keep vicious animals away from sheep and blight from the corn. Almost every type of lifestyle has its own little Wight unique to its protection.

Once a family invites a Wight into their lives, they are stuck with that spirit as long as they maintain the place. Wights are not reasonable creatures, however. Should the regular gifts stop, a nasty relative move into the house or the family turn their back on the creature, a Wight can curse as much as it blesses. Homes who anger their Wights often find their food routinely spoiling or things catching fire far too quickly. Farms who anger their Wights end up with mysteriously infertile soil come the next planting season. Needless to say, inviting a Wight into one's life is a decision not taken lightly.

## Weise Frauen

About the farthest northwest point of the Dracheneisen Mountains, a humble, tiny house stands. While it may seem unassuming on the outside and barely strong enough to withstand the violent mountain winters, it contains a vast and ancient amount of wisdom inside. The Weise Frauen live in this house and always have, as long as legends have existed in Eisen.

The three ancient crones, while seemingly aged, never actually manage to die. They have watched the history of Eisen over centuries, recorded it all and have given guidance like no others. They are considered the wisest people in the lands, and while the journey to their doorstep is a perilous one, it is also an incredibly worthy quest.

A Hero must cross mountains and survive bandits, Horrors and weather to reach the three crones. If she survives the journey, they invite her into the house for exactly three days. Often, the first day she spends recovering, the second day she spends learning how to ask the right questions and on the third day, the Hero actually finds answers. No Hero has ever said she took the perilous journey in vain.

### The Order of Wisdom

The Weise Frauen are considered magical people of legend. They have cultivated this reputation over a thousand years, and the perception has only deepened as Eisen returns to believing in magic. In truth, not a single bit of anything other than hard work and study goes into the Weise Frauen. They call themselves the Order of Wisdom; hundreds of women have pledged themselves to keep the eternal knowledge of the lands. While the small house remains publicly visible, built into the mountain beneath that dwelling is a great and ancient temple.

Dozens of women occupy the space, keeping up its library, the history of the lands, an indoor farming facility and training the next generation. Not every member of the Order of Wisdom becomes a Weise Frau, but they have all dedicated themselves to trying. A woman studies for all of her life, until her hair is white and skin wrinkled, before she can be elevated to living in The House. Then, as one of the other Weisen Frauen finally passes of age, she silently replaces her sister in the night, and the cycle continues.

# Chapter 2

## the Sarmatian Commonwealth

# THE SARMATIAN COMMONWEALTH

*"I've never seen a people more dedicated and ready to be a part of something. This is what true freedom looks like."*
—Domenica Vespucci

The Sarmatian Commonwealth, like many other nations in Théah, is ruled by a king or queen, but that is where all the similarities end. Since the two halves of the Commonwealth, Rzeczpospolita and Curonia, came together as one, the nobles of the Nation have voted for their leader. The voting power of the Sejm, the voting body of nobles, makes and passes laws including—until recently—a right to veto anything the ruler decreed.

That is until Golden Liberty, the final desperate act of a king who had been systematically stripped of his power. This gave the title of noble to everyone living in the Commonwealth, effectively removing the class divide and giving control of the Nation into the hands of the people.

Before Golden Liberty, three Vaticine priests and 13 *Książę* and *Księżna* ("Dukes" and "Duchesses"), rulers of *Księstwa* (Duchies, singular Księstwo), made up the Sejm and together administered to the Commonwealth.

Post-Golden Liberty, the Sejm became two houses: the Senat, or "upper house," where the 16 old Sejm members (also known as the old nobility) meet and vote, and the house of deputies, the Izba Poselska, "lower house," where the new nobility do the same.

The old nobles still have a fair bit of power. Most notably, the Książę and Księżna have retained administrative control over their Księstwa, which means they can pass laws unilaterally in their own lands. These laws can only be overruled by national laws, passed by the Sejm, which requires both houses to vote and pass the law.

## Biały and Czerwony

The King or Queen Consort—the person married to the monarch—shares none of the monarch's powers. She may not make laws and may not preside over the Sejm unless appointed as the monarch's proxy (which the Sejm must approve). She also suffers none of the restrictions that bind the monarch, however, which means she may rule a Księstwo, hold other titles or keep her seat on the Sejm if she previously had one.

The current king, Stanisław I, is married to Małgorzata Domagała, Księżna Drajewicz. They live separately, Stanisław in Budorigum, Małgorzata in her Księstwo's capital, Szablewo. Stanisław and his son, Aleksy, jointly declared Golden Liberty, and Małgorzata, seated as a Księżna in the Sejm, opposed it the loudest. Factionalism followed, and today there are two proto-political parties: the Biały (white) and the Czerwony (red).

A "Czerwony," stereotypically, favors Golden Liberty and fights to maintain an open franchise; she is populist, pro-Vaticine, moderately pacifist and suspicious of Sanderis. She supports King Stanisław and Prince Aleksy, whom she refers to as Stanisław II. To show loyalty, she wears scarlet, the color of the capital, and, if she can, the King's coat of arms.

A "Biały," meanwhile, displays the Drajewicz twelve-pointed star and wears white to represent the marble found in Szablewo; he dresses conservatively in the styles worn pre-Golden Liberty. He is hardly trendy and very unlike Czerwony, who have taken to the new Sarmatian garb with relish.

This factionalism has spread beyond normal politics. Szablewo's elite colleges are rife with rumors of Czerwony forced to transfer or retire; Budorigum's bars, meanwhile, host red-clad toughs looking to violently dye white coats.

The issue of class and new-versus-old nobility only compounds the problem. Stanisław and Aleksy command the majority within the Izba Poselska and have loyalists among the Senat's sixteen older nobility. Małgorzata commands the majority in the Senat but has won herself a passel of landowners, professionals and academics. These supporters come from conservative middle-class minds who like the idea of having the franchise but are not sure the privilege should be extended to everyone. It is lost on no one that once Stanisław I dies, the two most likely candidates for monarch are Aleksy and Małgorzata.

## PRONOUNCING THE RZEPLITAN LANGUAGE

The Rzeplitan language has several accents and letters unfamiliar to the rest of Théah. Here is a basic pronunciation guide that may help:

ą sounds like the on in bon when it comes at the end of a word or before most consonants, but sounds like om when before b or p.

c sounds like ts, and ć sounds like ch, when you read ch together, it makes a sound like a soft h.

ę sounds like ehn when in front of most consonants, but sounds like em when before b or p.

ł sounds like w

j sounds like y

ó sounds like u

ś sounds like sh

w sounds like v

ź sounds like the si in vision, but ż sounds like the g in mirage

cz together makes the sound tch

dź, dż, and rz together make a j sound, and dzi makes a jee sound.

So, a word like Książę and Księżna would sound like Kshon-jheh and Ksheh-zhna. And Księstwo and Księstwa would be Kshen-stvo and Kshen-stva. Stanisław is Stan-is-wav and Małgorzata Drajewicz is Maw-go-zhata Dra-ye-vitch.

Note: The Curonian language is quite a bit different from Rzeplitan, but few other than rural Curonians speak only that language. Most people speak Rzeplitan alone, or both languages. A Hero can get by with only knowing Rzeplitan in most places in the Commonwealth.

# A Democratic Nation

The people in the Sarmatian Commonwealth have a new focus. Even the poorest Curonian farmer has the hope of making a difference. This has led to a positive atmosphere all over the Nation.

Many of the people who were once considered peasants view the Golden Liberty as a sort of freedom. Some have picked up and left the farms and workstations they once toiled to seek better things. Others, unsure of what this new ability really means, continue to dwell in the dirt, often at the insistence of those who still rule them.

Democracy comes with its own slew of problems though, as the people of the Commonwealth are coming to find out. When everyone gets to voice their opinion about how to solve a problem, they find out that there are as many different opinions as there are different people. While the Senat, what used to simply be the Sejm, is now in full working order, the Izba Poselska is not. The old nobles finally spend time to create laws and pass bills instead of blocking each other, but each law passed by one part of the house must also go through a vote with the other.

The new nobility agree on one thing, that the old nobility have had their time in the sun. They often refuse to pass laws the Senat voted on, even if they don't understand their purpose, just to spite them.

In addition, coming up with new laws is exceedingly difficult for the Izba Poselska. First, they must be called into session by King Stanisław I, which is sometimes difficult due to his health issues. Second, they have a hard time agreeing on anything and proposed laws end up in tatters after only a single session in the house.

Many of the voters cannot read, and so proposals end up going through word of mouth. Depending on the complexity of the proposition, the language may get muddled. Beyond that, those who disagree with one or more points argue for their versions instead of the proposed one. It can take several weeks for the Izba Poselska to pass a single proposed law to send to the Senat.

In that time, the Senat proposes three times as many laws, and many of the new nobles reach a point of fatigue on voting and arguing. To say that the Sejm has ground to a halt is not true though. Quite a few dedicated people have taken it upon themselves to continue to try to direct the lesser house and propose meaningful laws. Some of these have even been passed all the way through the Senat, generally with promises to pass some Senat law that comes to vote in the near future.

## Important People in the Commonwealth

## King Stanisław I

Stanisław Gracjan was a scholar before he started going blind—first his night vision went, then peripheral, and finally, the day his mother died, his vision started to tunnel. He hired a Močiutės Skara member, Rugilė Savickė (pronounced: ROO-gil-ea sa-VIK-ea), to read to him, and soon all the other nobles whispered of his blindness. When he was elected king, the other nobles thought him easy to control, and for a while, he was.

Stanisław didn't want to be king, but he accepted the election. And when the Sejm told him he was to marry Małgorzata Domagała, the powerful scion of House Drajewicz, he accepted that too. Separation from his home, his ever-worsening vision and Budorigum's responsibilities all took a toll on him; he began leaning on Małgorzata, appointing her his proxy to the Sejm. After their son was born, she began implying his blindness made him useless; sunk into depression, he believed her. She isolated him socially from all but his son and Rugilė. When Małgorzata

started to strike him with her heavy signet ring (embossed with the Drajewicz twelve-pointed star), he accepted it as due. Rugilė and Aleksy brought him brief joy, but it seemed nothing could snap him out of his despair until Małgorzata overstepped.

It started when Rugilė lost her temper with the queen and struck her. This was treason, and the queen imprisoned Rugilė. Three days later, when the king brushed his hands over his son's face, he felt scabs, the blood dried into the shape of a twelve-pointed star.

Within a week, he banished the queen from the Palace on pain of imprisonment. Within a month, Rugilė had been pardoned, recalled from prison to retake her place in the palace (with Uppman's notebooks, no less). Suddenly, to the nobles' surprise, Stanisław changed into a King; a lion in winter, but no weak man, who administered Budorigum and presided over the Sejm even while blind. As he remarked to Rugilė afterward, he still doesn't like being king, but he realizes now it is not a burden—it is a responsibility. And among the commoners (now "New Nobles"), he enjoys an extreme popularity, though that effect has not yet fountained up to the Old Nobility.

Recently he has begun suffering from mysterious bouts of sickness, and when he is too ill to move, his son serves in the Sejm as his proxy.

## Portraying Stanisław I

In public, Stanisław speaks quietly, with precision and dignity, but he always seems weary and very rarely happy. In private he becomes more at ease, especially when being scholarly; he has a tremendous memory, knows all the books in his library and can quote verbatim anything Rugilė has read to him. His voice rings with pride when he speaks of his son, and Rugilė almost always stands by his side.

A patient man, he listens to the concerns of his people, and is the only one who can bring the lower house to order, which he does on a regular basis. He has a quick mind and is no one's fool. He might not be able to see well, but it does not hinder his ability to read people.

## Story Hooks

- Stanisław tries to be a strong king, but the years he spent not ruling have taken their toll. The Old Nobility, unused to his presence, resents his "interference," and in the many in the Royal Household suspect his sickness is caused by an Old Noble's poison. The Heroes must discover the truth, and if they find the sickness sinister, reveal how the sneak accesses the king!

- Even Stanisław's personal guard find themselves split between Biały and Czerwony, making his house look weak as disputes arise often. A few Biały are plotting to assassinate the king, to force a new election while Domagała still has the ear of most of the Senate. Some of his guards have been courted to help, but now they must choose between loyalty and political aspirations. Can the Heroes talk some sense into the guards and ensure they continue to do their jobs?

# Aleksy Gracjan Nowak (Stanisław II)

Aleksy Gracjan Nowak still feels shame when he thinks about his first twelve years. When he was young, his mother hurt his father and he felt helpless and did nothing, but the first time his mother thought to hurt him, his father became furious and banished her. Reflecting, he feels like he failed his father by not trying to protect him sooner. Rugilė and Stanisław tell him that is not the case, but that hardly helps.

After his mother left the palace, little Aleksy blossomed. He learned how to dance, wield a sword and became bubbly and charming. He was also a voracious learner, endlessly curious, but when Rugilė introduced him to Uppman's writings, he came into conflict with himself. He had enough of his mother's hauteur to want to be king after his father died—but enough intellectual fire (and personal experience with helplessness) to seriously consider that monarchy and hierarchy might be regressive.

At sixteen, he discovered Sophia's Daughters, a Rilasciare branch that smuggled persecuted women from Vodacce. Since that seemed uncomplicatedly good, he threw himself into smuggling, working under the codename *flaki*, "tripe soup" (he had hidden a lot in the kitchens in his youth), since it would have been awkward for a member of the Royal Family to commit espionage openly. He eventually met and married Domenica Vespucci through the organization, having smuggled her into the Commonwealth through the Society.

Vespucci's commentary on Uppman helped inspire Golden Liberty (the fact that Rilasciare activity inspired Golden Liberty is *not* public knowledge). He adopted the surname Nowak to show his unequivocal support of the new nobility. The resulting popularity gained Aleksy the nickname "Stanisław II" and made him the favorite to succeed his father as monarch, with the only other obvious contender for the position being his mother. And with Stanisław I frequently crippled by sickness, he stands as his father's proxy in the Sejm, facing off against her.

Aleksy seriously contemplates not standing for election. After all, in a country where the people rule, what is a king but a figurehead? And a figurehead Nowak would not mind being—if he were not already going blind. He is losing his vision as his father before him, and much has been made of his father's blindness as weakness. If Aleksy stands against his mother for election, will he have to bluff away his blindness?

## Portraying Aleksy Gracjan Nowak

Aleksy Nowak looks like his mother, all high cheekbones and pale skin, but where she appears impassive, he overbrims with expression. He displays a palpable joy to the way he lives, though in private moments, care stoops him like his father. Overall, he is a picture of youth, energy and health. His new wife's magic may be a bit to blame, but the work he does to make his Nation the best in Théah gives him its own kind of energy.

He is thoughtful and careful. Years avoiding his mother's ire have given him a wealth of patience. He thinks before he speaks and takes care to say the most politic of things. In private, he is more open and opinionated, discussing his feelings on topics as complicated as revolution and as basic as which meat pies are the best.

Aleksy is deeply involved with the running of the Commonwealth and has a vested interest in seeing this new democracy prosper. He does what he can to help the new nobility, while always trying to find new ways to appease the old.

### Story Hooks

- Someone has been killing Biały in Budorigum and carving their faces with Aleksy's personal seal. Małgorzata has been making the most of it, and Nowak needs the Heroes to find the killers before he can no longer keep peace in his city.
- Aleksy thinks he inherited his blindness from his father, but Domenica believes a curse affects his failing sight. Can the Heroes confirm or refute Domenica's suspicions and find a way to cure Aleksy?

# Domenica Vespucci

Domenica Vespucci was born a Fate Witch, twinned to her brother Ennio, and from early days, her father's plan for the pair was clear: Ennio would inherit Carlo Vespucci's shipping conglomerate, and Domenica would be his companion, his constant support, the silent Fate Witch by his side, protecting and keeping him free to marry a non-Fate Witch ally.

Ennio, though, had no ambition—Domenica, it seems, had gotten his share—and from an early age the twins cared more for each others' desires than their father's plans. As many ambitious women in Vodacce do, Domenica joined Sophia's Daughters young. Ennio helped her by teaching her to read in secret. She immersed herself in Rilasciare philosophy while her brother practiced dueling and bribed her with books to help him cheat at lessons.

Under the codename *cielo giallo*, "Yellow Sky," Domenica found herself running the Vodacce side of a Daughters' operation to smuggle *Streghe* to the Sarmatian Commonwealth. Her opposite number, a Sarmatian Rilasciare agent codenamed "Tripe Soup," began writing her to discuss logistics. Their correspondence soon expanded to cover philosophy and personal anecdotes, details blurred on the latter, of course.

For three years, Vespucci remained ignorant of her correspondent's identity, until around the time the Sarmatian Prince Aleksy began courting. At this point, her correspondent began implying he was a servant in the Palace with intimate knowledge of Prince Aleksy's courtships—a trusted confidant of the prince, in fact. He sought advice on suitors and began sending Domenica detailed descriptions of courtships, at which point Vespucci took a guess at his identity and wrote back, *You should marry me*.

Domenica's father was a second-tier shipping magnate; accordingly, she was no fit consort for a man who might become a king. But Vespucci knew her correspondent, knew his contrarian, impulsive tendencies, knew she was a little bit in love with him—and could intuit he felt much the same. The gamble paid off; Aleksy acquiesced to an engagement, and she sailed with her brother to the Commonwealth.

Their first face-to-face meeting, mere days before her writings helped inspire Aleksy to Golden Liberty, was marred by a coup attempt masterminded by the Książę Kazimierz, Marcen Sabat. In the aftermath of that, Domenica saved the prince and the king, earning herself a warm welcome into Théah's most radical Royal Family.

## Portraying Domenica Vespucci

Veiled but no beauty, Domenica Vespucci is easy to ignore. In Vodacce, it serves as a survival strategy, but here, that is just how she likes it. She stands back and lets Aleksy work a room, but swoops in and saves conversations when needed.

Years in a clandestine organization have taught her to enjoy people underestimating her. Publicly, she plays the dim foreigner, still struggling with the language, but privately, she speaks with no accent and makes Aleksy shout with her sharp observations.

Domenica is a cunning woman who cares more for her new adopted Nation than the one she grew up in. She uses her power over fate to help her husband, but rarely uses it beyond that. She pushes herself to be the epitome of what Uppman claims everyone should be, and only uses her power when absolutely necessary.

## Story Hooks

+ Domenica's father has approached her and Aleksy, seeking a position in the Sarmatian Court. Vespucci is convinced her father actually came here to spy for a Merchant Prince, but can the Heroes prove it?
+ A small-time printshop has somehow acquired Domenica's commentary on Uppman. The printer sells copies of the commentary cheap, and their appearance with Domenica's name has caused a scandal. Vespucci hires one of the Heroes to reveal himself as the "real" author and the rest to do damage control.

# Landon Cross

Landon Cross grew up in the small town of Baelig in the middle of the Síocháin Forest in Avalon. The rumor of the town is that his mothers, both animal trappers, made a deal with the Sidhe to grant them a child in return for protecting the Sidhe animals. They refuse to verify the rumors, but Cross does have an almost Sidhe-like appearance.

The truth, of course, is less strange than the fiction. Cross's mothers adopted him from an orphanage in Carleon, where he was left as an infant. The small gold pendant he wears around his neck is one of the only hints to his heritage, along with his pale skin and stark white hair, which shines silver in the sun.

Cross learned his mothers' trade of trapping and hunting, and seemed to have a knack for dealing with the wildest of the woodland creatures, even those touched by Glamour. Despite a near idyllic childhood and upbringing, the question of his heritage always bothered Cross.

When Daníele and the other Sidhe came from Bryn Bresail, Cross felt compelled to speak with them. He traveled to Carleon and through a bit of fast-talking and quick wit, gained an audience with the Sidhe emissary. They did not know his parentage, but agreed that he probably had Sidhe blood somewhere in his ancestory. Not satisfied with such a vague answer, Cross pressed them further.

He did not get the answers he wanted, but instead got a job. Daníele liked his perseverance and mettle, and wanted to help him find his parentage, but this would be a big endeavor for them. In exchange, he would have to perform a task for them, outside of Avalon.

Within a week, Cross had a ship, a crew and a letter of writ from Queen Elaine. He first went to Montaigne, where he brought what appeared to be a blank sheet of paper to an old hermit in a forest. He signed the paper and gave it back to Cross, thanking him profusely for his efforts.

Next, Daníele sent him to Ussura, where he had to track down and gain the favor of the Leshy Vir'ava. In the course of doing so, his privateer crew made friends with some local Ushkuiniks when Cross was able to soothe a particularly violent vodyanoi. Enough so that the greater Brotherhood of the Coast members offered to aid Avalonian ships traversing the Maw.

Now Cross and his crew are in the Sarmatian Commonwealth, charged with finding a dievas in the Sanderas Forest. He doesn't know what greater good his trip will end up serving for Avalon, but he suspects there is a secondary reason. That, or Daníele just enjoys sending him to dangerous parts of Théah.

## Portraying Landon Cross

Landon Cross is slight of frame and shorter than the average Avalon man. He keeps his nearly translucent skin covered in multiple layers of light clothing to reflect the sunlight. He wears a wide-brimmed hat to cover his shock of silver hair. When he grins, which he often does, his sharp teeth poke down over his lip.

Cross is a friendly man, though he is full of mischief and unusual ideas. He never approaches a situation the way people expect, and it serves him well to remain unpredictable. He is a trained hunter and trapper and is skilled at all types of ranged weapons, and he isn't so bad with a sword either.

He is helpful if asked, though his number one priority is Avalon and his deal with the Sidhe to find out who his real parents are. He refuses to do anything that might jeopardize that arrangement.

### Story Hook

- Cross has heard stories of *Katabasis*, a way for a losejas to kill his dievas, and is looking to possibly head out with a losejas in search of the dievas he is looking for. The problem is, no losejas is willing to take him on such a personal quest, and the people within Voruta refuse to act as guides. Will the Heroes go with the Avalonian, or possibly find a losejas who is willing to take him along?

## Rugilė Savickė

Before the king was the King, Rugilė Savickė took care of him.

The first time was in a field hospital set up by members of Grandmother's Shawl used primarily to house refugees blinded by quicklime. Stanisław Gracjan, brought there after being wounded in battle, had a habit of quoting texts in fever dreams that soon grabbed Rugilė's attention. Before the war, she had been a book peddler on a donkey's back, a round-spectacled Yachidi Curonian autodidact who read every text she sold from a sack. This fellow bibliophile intrigued her and so late at night she read to him and they became fast friends.

She noted he was going blind and, hearing of her background with books and the quicklime-blinded, he asked her to accompany him back to his castle, to become his reader and book collector, for though born to power, the written word kept him sane. She agreed.

Over time, she fell in love with the king, and she and Małgorzata orbited warily for years. She tutored Aleksy, and taught him to hide from Małgorzata in the kitchen. When she struck the queen, she committed treachery, but it was also a long time coming. In prison, the queen (who knew her ways of coping well) forbade her books. A fellow prisoner slipped her the Rilasciare's writings, Uppman's notebooks, and she read them.

It did not strike her as strange when Uppman called for the death of Kings—for hadn't she just been betrayed by a king herself? Hadn't she just learned that even when the best man she could imagine was a monarch, the world remained twisted and unfair? Maybe death was a harsh punishment, but nobility certainly needed to go away.

When Stanisław fetched her from the prison, she read the journals to the king, daring him to order her to stop, order the journals seized and burned. He never silenced her; he let her read, and when she asked, *"May I show these to your son?"* He said, "I trust you."

She showed them to Aleksy, and she and Stanisław spoke of them no more. When Aleksy dreamed up Golden Liberty, and Stanisław signed it into law, she stopped herself from asking if the notebooks had inspired them.

## Portraying Rugilė Savickė

Rugilė Savickė's wide eyes and round face make her look much younger than her age, an impression not belied by her quick, birdlike movements. Her hair remains dark, with only a few streaks of grey peppering her temples.

Almost inevitably she stands by the king's side, holding a book in her hand. At diplomatic functions, she is deferent, if a bit too protective of Stanisław. In private, she is an energetic teacher, always eager to share her newest knowledge.

### Story Hooks

+ Savickė is Stanisław's shadow, his reader, his writer, his constant companion. She still loves him, but a decade of Małgorzata running the palace and a stint in prison have not left her unwounded. Domenica and Aleksy want to engineer a reconciliation between the two, but that will be a delicate maneuver—Rugilė's a new noble *and* a Yachidi, and Stanisław remains married. They ask the Heroes to help engineer a clandestine meeting without revealing Aleksy or Domenica's involvement.

+ Rugilė Savickė has joined the Rilasciare body and soul. Even now, with the Golden Liberty, she has work to do. She knows Małgorzata Domagała still has designs on the throne, and works against her at every step. She is torn between that and her duties to the king, whose health worsens every day. She needs someone to help her poison the Sejm against Domagała when she can't.

# Małgorzata Domagała
# (Queen Consort & Księżna Drajewicz)

Małgorzata Domagała is the oldest daughter of the Drajewicz house, and inherited the title of Księżna when she was barely sixteen. She grew up immersed in the politics of the Sejm, and for the most part has always had what's best for the Commonwealth in her mind. Her marriage to Stanisław was purely convenience, but it also put her in a position to do the most good.

The most galling thing for Małgorzata is that she served as a good queen. The country prospered under her rule. City coffers stayed full, Castillian refugees received passage to the Commonwealth, and she wrangled the Sejm into a semblance of coordination—the country worked. Given that, why should her domestic abuses matter? The country never suffered under her rule. And if Stanisław had not wanted to suffer, well, he should have been her partner, instead of hiding under black moods and letting her run the country alone.

Even before Golden Liberty, Domagała thought the Sejm a mistake; the Commonwealth needed more centralized control, à la Queen Elaine's Avalon. Golden Liberty she considers a disaster in the making. In the Senat, she is fond of saying "if illiterates can vote, mobs rule." Democracy may work in times of peace but it can hardly stand stress, hence Małgorzata's scheme.

The Ussuran General Winter plans to invade the Commonwealth, and Domagała knows this. She made an alliance with him: he promised her the Sarmatian throne in exchange for a warm-water port and unfettered access to the River Sejm.

What General Winter does not know is that she plans to betray him. She refuses to be the Ussuran's puppet queen, nor let the Commonwealth become General Winter's vassal state. Instead, once General Winter's invasion has impressed the citizens of the Commonwealth with the need for strong leadership, she plans to step forward and take the throne on her own merits—and beat the Ussurans back.

## Portraying Małgorzata Domagała

Małgorzata has the brittle pride of someone who has been in the wrong for many years but would break before admitting it. Her posture is impeccable, her beauty dramatic, perhaps even more so with her face lined than when young.

Her manner is haughty but otherwise impassive; her cold blue eyes are by default dismissive. Her skin and hair are so pale as to be near-transparent, and her long, precise fingers tremble almost imperceptibly.

Domagała, a tremendously competent administrator, demands the same competence from her underlings and allies. Should a Hero oppose her and prove himself competent, she tries to talk him over onto her side: she genuinely fears mob rule and will even swallow her pride. She shows her tremendous temper only in private, and those she abuses, verbally and otherwise, are always under her power.

## Story Hooks

+ Małgorzata served as the Commonwealth's *de facto* ruler when the Inquisition's purges started in Castille. She could not stand the idea of a Nation killing its own intelligentsia, so she set up a shipping lane dedicated to smuggling Inquisition targets out of Castille. Now, those who oppose her threaten to tell the Inquisition where to find the refugees. Can the Heroes stop the Czerwony from bringing the Inquisition to their door?

+ Domagała has a plan to get rid of Golden Liberty. She proposed a law within the Sejm with arcane language, expressly to confound the uninitiated and make it appear beneficial. If the law passes, she can reinstate the distinction between noble and commoner, removing their rights to vote. Will the Heroes convince the Izba Poselska to vote against the new law?

# Ugnė Urbonė
# (Księżna Janusz)

Ugnė Urbonė (pronounced: OOG-nea OOR-BON-nea) is a Curonian through and through. She is one of the few sitting in the Senat, and it makes her bold and mostly exasperated with the petty concerns they hold. She is sarcastic and full of wit, challenging the others to think before they speak. She peppers her speech with provincial idioms the way other posłowie (Senators) do not. When she votes, she votes determinedly pragmatic: "Who will pay for this ship? Who will unload this cargo?" When Senat members start arguing semantics, she yawns.

She is a Curonian national Hero, in part because of her manner: Curonians, never not tired of Rzeplitan pretensions, admire her irreverence. Besides, she is the Senat's foremost defender of Curonian interests, to the point where she argues quite seriously that the capital should be moved into Curonia. On top of that, she is an active and dedicated member of the Ratas, known for assisting in the captures of more rogue losejai than any other living being.

No Biały, she sneers at Szablewo snobbery and seems mostly unbothered by Golden Liberty. No Czerwony, she fiercely protects Sanderis (fond of saying it is less dangerous than democracy—both test power and responsibility) and argues that the military should arm itself to fight Ussura (she especially worries for Złotogóra, which provides Voruta with most of its food).

Ugnė's name has in fact become synonymous with being skeptical of both factions, and (to her own chagrin) she has been taken up by those who feel the same—especially Curonians—as an icon. The Curonians will do whatever she says, trusting her to always have their best interests in mind.

Of course, that means if the monarch elections come down to Małgorzata or Aleksy, she could serve as the Kingmaker. Or Queenmaker. Ironically.

Or she could throw her own hat in the ring once Stanisław I dies and try to wrest the monarchy away from the current dynasty. Though Ugnė is not as popular as Małgorzata or Aleksy (Curonia is half the size of Rzeczpospolita, after all), monarchy voting is a current hotbed of political action. The Senat are the only ones who can legally vote, as of right now, and who they may vote for is anyone's guess. Many of the new nobles are pushing for Izba Poselska voting rights, which could tip the vote for monarch closer in her direction than anyone would suspect, as plenty of Biały and Czerwony would rather have her in power than the other candidates.

For her own part, Ugnė is more concerned about dealing with an inevitable war with Ussura, or stopping some kind of ridiculous Biały versus Czerwony civil war, than she is about voting rights in the Sejm. Though if she were somehow voted in as Queen, she would do a damned fine job of it.

## Portraying Ugnė Urbonė

Ugnė Urbonė is bigger than her body. When she walks, she takes long strides and swings her arms wide. In the Senat, she is a menace. She burps and yawns and swears like a peasant, and acts conspicuously Curonian in idioms and accent—let no one forget that the Commonwealth is not all Rzeczpospolita!

If you see her with the Ratas or administering her Księstwo (mostly Voruta; the Sanderas resists administration), she clearly possesses substance behind that style. Late nights after doing business, her eyes bruise with care, and danger to either prompts a white-lipped intensity impossible to mistake.

In her home, she is welcoming and accommodating. She believes in Curonian hospitality and shows it to any who come calling. She might even make you her famous cepelinai if you stay the night. She only cares about business that affects her, feigning boredom or anger if someone asks her to get involved in anything outside her own sphere of influence.

### Story Hooks

+ Ugnė is widowed, has no children and plans to go on *Katabasis* soon—a tradition that sends her deep into the Sanderas Forest to attempt to destroy her dievas. She wants to choose an heir before she goes, at least provisionally, and hires the Heroes to round up suitable candidates.

+ Urbonė's husband took his own life three years ago, and she bound herself to the dievas who convinced him to do it. Determined to destroy her husband's demon, her own trips into the Sanderas have netted her nothing—other dievai fear her dievas and refuse to sell him out while he rides her senses. Can the Heroes enter the forest and discover enough about Ugnė's dievas to destroy him?

# Azucena Esquivel

Azucena Esquivel fled the Castillian Inquisition on a ship chartered by Małgorzata Domagała. She made her way to the capital, intending to offer her services to the Queen, and discovered that that the King had banished her. Hoping to discover why, she took a job as a Palace guard.

She asked questions. Her quiet curiosity brought her to the attention of the little prince, who interrogated her in his twelve-year-old way, and then asked her to teach him swordfighting.

As she watched Aleksy grow, Esquivel became convinced that he would make a great king. He took his responsibilities seriously and clearly *wanted* to make his Nation better. The Sejm, she despised—the nobles only obstruct, and treat the king with insufficient respect—but Golden Liberty made her uneasy. How could rule by all not devolve to mob rule? The king and prince, both fine rulers, had made themselves more powerless by allowing it. They may have tremendous faith in human nature, but Azucena does not. After all, she grew up with the Inquisition.

As a sworn member of Los Vagabundos, she protected Aleksy during Marcen Sabat's coup attempt. After that, she supported the Senat's insistence on reforming the *slachta*, the royal guard, and was named their leader.

Even as leader of the slachta, Azucena remains conflicted enough to think of leaving to serve Małgorzata. For all that she is a monster in her private life, Queen Małgorzata was a superb proxy leader. When Golden Liberty goes topsy-turvy, Aleksy and Stanisław will not retake power. So who but the queen can seize the reins and impose regnal order when the mob starts making Inquisitions?

## Portraying Azucena Esquivel

Azucena Esquivel is quiet, reserved and still. She prefers to be overlooked, blending in as just another piece of furniture in the room. The position of bodyguard suits her; people often ignore soldiers flanking Royalty.

Force her to speak about something that makes her uneasy and suddenly she turns into a fiery, gesticulating, stereotypical Castillian. Such passion, she says, does not suit her; she would rather stay silent and keep her own counsel than risk conflict by sharing her opinions.

# Jan Noreyko and Gintarė Žilinskė

When only sixteen people ran the Sejm, knowing the law was a sucker's game. The law shifted to what the Sejm said it was. If any ancient decree seemed inconvenient, they overlooked or overturned it. Jan Noreyko, an energetic law wonk, nephew of the scion of House Tokarz, was a man whose obsession with legislation made him a pariah. No one cared all that much that he could cite city codes or obscure laws, especially when his peers were all connected to the Sejm nobles in some way.

With Golden Liberty, that all changed. Suddenly the law became everyone's business, and knowing what it actually *said*—all the ancient decrees and obscure loopholes—granted one power during meetings.

Noreyko became plenty popular after Golden Liberty, as every old noble who wanted something over the rank-risen peasants consulted him on obscure points of law. By Golden Liberty's six-month anniversary, Noreyko's services were so popular that Tokarz bought him a townhouse two blocks from the Sejm so members of the Senat could consult him on all occasions. He became the first official Sarmatian lawyer.

When the now-noble peasants heard about this, they decided they too needed a lawyer, in order to stay abreast of the old nobles. It seemed the most politically prudent thing to do, even if they didn't really know what good a lawyer could do for them. Their search brought them to Gintarė Žilinskė (pronounced: gin-TAR-ea JIL-ensk-ea), one of the only people in the city who could match Noreyko's knowledge and fervor for the law.

She also happened to be Noreyko's former archivist, assistant and lover. Her townhouse sat on the opposite side of the Sejm from Noreyko's, and her library matched his, book for book. And while Noreyko fought for the status quo, Žilinskė fought for the new nobility.

Cue a rivalry that destroyed their friendship, partnership and love affair all in one day.

When the peasantry recruited Žilinskė, Noreyko offered to help pay for her townhouse across from the Sejm. Žilinskė refused, telling him that she could afford her own arrangements. He then started refusing to discuss cases with her. She did not want to be rivals. But it seemed he was intent on setting her up as such.

Instead, she wanted him to come work with her and help create a new, better Commonwealth by assisting the Izba Poselska. Noreyko refused. The Senat had helped him start up, and their money was what had brought them both into prominence. He would be betraying his family if he started assisting peasants, and she was betraying him by doing the same. And anyway, was she really convinced this Golden Liberty thing was a good idea?

Žilinskė threw a mug of sipping chocolate at him in response to that question. Noreyko went home and pulled up precedents for a few particularly repressive curfew laws his uncle could cite in the Sejm the next day. He was convinced Žilinskė was working on a lost cause, and was determined to show her as such by beating her in the Sejm.

Žilinskė went home and felt bad about throwing sipping chocolate at her lover. The next day, she heard Noreyko's uncle citing those curfew laws when arguing for a suite of regressive anti-peasant policies. And she viewed it as a declaration of war. Then— well, they both dug in after that, rationalizing their positions with shows of self-righteousness. Now, eighteen months past Golden Liberty, neither speaks to the other because why would they? Their former friend—former lover—represents everything wrong with this country.

They snipe at each other's clients, send subordinates to spy on the other and generally put their noses up at anything the other says or does. For two people who claim to want to have nothing to do with each other, they certainly spend a great deal of time invested in what the other is doing.

Either way, the Sejm has never been more active with confirming past precedents and setting new ones. The new nobles show a fervor for pushing through new legislation, and the old nobles have a penchant for stymieing anything the Izba Poselska puts forward.

## Portraying Gintarė Žilinskė

In public, Gintarė Žilinskė has fierce, scrappy dignity. She is mousy and ever agitated, but has the hard-bitten look of someone who pulled herself up by her bootstraps.

In her office, when she thinks she is alone, she talks to a Jan who is not there. She spends a lot of time asking, "what would Jan do?" and predicting arguments his clients might make. She practices her scowl in front of the mirror in case someone asks about losejai, but confront her on it unexpectedly and she just as likely becomes flustered.

### Story Hook

- Gintarė recently began consulting with losejai who want to construct airtight deals with dievai. She keeps the connection secret, because her more superstitious clients may leave if they find out. But it seems that Jan's apprentice has found out somehow, and threatens to reveal it to her other clients. Can the Heroes help her deal with her blackmailer?

## Portraying Jan Noreyko

Jan Noreyko is the archetypal absent-minded bureaucrat, the sort who gets ink on his hands and in his hair, the sort who cannot find books in the library now that he no longer has an archivist in his employ.

If asked about Gintarė, he starts arguing with her as if she is there, then shakes his head distractedly when asked about this. If asked about working with losejai, he has a rebuttal planned, a nice spiel about harm reduction and the danger of poorly planned contracts, but it comes out stiff: he is not a very good actor.

### Story Hook

- Jan Noreyko began consulting with losejai who want to construct airtight deals with dievai. He keeps it a secret hoping Gintarė won't find out and take his business. The problem is, his last bit of advice backfired on his client, and now she looks to take it out on him. Can the Heroes help him ward off this angry Sorcerer?

# Jędrzej Jerzy Maciejowski

Jędrzej Jerzy Maciejowski was born to an old noble family who had for the past century lost more and more favor with the rest of the Sejm. First, they became Objectionists, when most of Rzeczpospolita was Vaticine. They then decried violence and the War, and eventually his father became a small voice against so many dissenters. To avoid too much political blowback, the family moved to Curonia when Jędrzej was young.

His father's ideals stuck with him as he grew older, and Jędrzej also despises violence, viewing those who use it as weak and bullies. It's no wonder that he joined the Močiutės Skara early in life. He travels all over Théah with the organization, doing all he can to help people touched by violence and war.

The Shawl is where he met Lina, a fellow agent, and a losejas. Maciejowski had always been enamored by the women he met, but Lina captured his fancy like no other. She liked him, but he idealized her, which made her uncomfortable. He saw beauty in her, and refused to see any of her flaws. She tried to enchant him to see the bad parts of people as well as the good. The tricky dievas turned it into a curse to always find fault with someone he might love.

After that, he found living alone to be the best way to avoid heartache. While working with the Shawl, he has grown to hate politics, as he has seen how power corrupts, leading to violence, bloodshed and worse. He now goes by the name Andrzej Kisiel, to dissassociate himself from the politics of the Senat, where he ostensibly has a seat since his father passed.

Kisiel is torn by this prospect. He wants nothing to do with the corrupting power the Senat poses, but he also knows that having a member of the Senat on their side could help the new nobility a great deal.

## Portraying Jędrzej Jerzy Maciejowski

Jędrzej Jerzy Maciejowski, or Andrzej Kisiel as most know him, is a typical Sarmatian with dark hair and crystal blue eyes. He is easygoing and often friendly, though when being serious, he takes on an icy demeanor.

Kisiel is a passionate man, mostly in the form of laughter and helping those who need it, but when angered, he goes into a blind rage. Quick to lend a hand, and slow to anger, Kisiel is one of the Shawl's most trusted agents.

# Estera Sabat
## (Księżna Kazimierz)

Marcen Sabat, Rzeplitan scion of House Kazimierz, ruled a Curonian Księstwo but never identified much with other Curonians. He grew enamored of big city life during his time in the Senat, and he never could convince himself that the Curonians were really civilized.

Thus, when his daughter Estera was born, she had barely learned to walk before he sent her off to Budorigum—the height of Rzeplitan civilization—to be fostered with a passel of younger Drajewicz. Growing up in Budorigum, Estera insisted on dressing only in black, stole from the other noble children and took to climbing the drainpipes and turrets; from this, she gained the nickname *czarna kotka*, "the Black Cat."

It had always been the elder Sabat's ambition to marry Estera to the prince, and even before the prince officially began seeking suitors, Estera pursued him. The pursuit led to no marriage, but a friendship bloomed between the two; Estera admired how Aleksy could engender trust, and he admired her verve and daring.

Circumstances sorely tested that friendship when Marcen Sabat decided to counter the Golden Liberty (and Aleksy's decision to marry a Vodacce woman) by attempting a coup against the Royal Family. Estera betrayed her father in order to protect Aleksy; the coup ultimately failed and the Sejm stripped the Książę of his titles, passing his properties to Estera.

Estera Sabat, Księżna Kazimierz, now rules the wealthy Curonian city of Sperus and its surrounding lands; however, her life remains far from simple. A powerful movement, centered in Sperus, seeks to vote her out of power.

To them, she is a Rzeplitan raised in Budorigum with a reputation for slippery business, a daughter of a traitor and a black-clad thief, who rumor has it, has been spotted climbing onto people's roofs at night. And they aren't far off the mark. The only thing keeping her in power, in fact, is Prince Aleksy's wholehearted endorsement of her, a situation she resents to no end.

## Portraying Estera Sabat

Estera Sabat dresses in all black, and sits and lounges like a cat. She has sandy blonde hair, always tied back and kept out of her way, and tawny eyes. She is lithe and muscular, though shorter than most Curonian women.

She always looks relaxed, as if she does not care if you stay or go. It is a lie—she is desperate—but if you confront her on it, she snaps at you that desperation does not do a thing.

She has kept her cool all these years by faking a confidence she does not have, and perhaps if she is lucky, someday the mask will become her; but right now, once the facade drops, she reveals sharp motion and bitter pride, close to tears.

## Story Hooks

+ Under her father's influence, Sabat has lived a life of Villainy, by thieving and taking whatever she wanted. Her sudden change of heart against him in his coup has left her conflicted. She intends to kill the leader of a treacherous band of hunters to stop unrest in her city. Can the Heroes convince her to find a less Villainous way to deal with the city's issues and set her on the path to Heroism?

+ Estera's detractors in Sperus are actively working to remove her from her position. They have no replacement; that kind of planning is too far beyond their current scope of blind hatred. Instead, they have a simple plan to assassinate her one night. Will the Heroes try to save the Villainous Księżna? And if they do, what becomes of Sperus?

## The Brotherhood of the Coast

The Ushkuiniks are river pirates, a branch of the Brotherhood of the Coast that primarily operates in Ussura. In Ussura, they famously get along with hostile water creatures. In the Commonwealth, they apparently share this relationship, since only their ships can reliably sail through the Sanderas Forest to deliver food and people to Voruta. The prices they charge are ruinous in Voruta, but the people pay up anyway; after all, what is the alternative?

The rest of the Brotherhood of the Coast operates openly in Stróż Bay but the King pays privateers to keep them off Sarmatian ships. The Sejm does not adore this—why pay pirates to fight pirates?—but thus far no posłowie has proposed an alternative not obviously worse than the current situation.

Many of the privateers who earn coin from the King are members of the Brotherhood themselves, using the writ they gain from the Sarmatian Commonwealth as a hammer against Vodacce and Crescent ships.

Many of the Brotherhood ships simply ignore the privateers though, offering them additional coin to leave the pirates alone when they have found a Sarmatian ship laden with goods traveling out of the bay.

## Die Kreuzritter

In all the Sarmatian Commonwealth, only one living being claims to be a member of die Kreuzritter. An itinerant who lives in the swamps of Saulės Mūšis, she comes from nowhere and fights with a dracheneisen spear. She calls herself Jadvyga Jasaitytė.

She is probably insane, but where she goes, the residents of Saulės Mūšis fear a little less. She started teaching spear fighting classes to all those in the swamp who want to learn, and after classes she is often trailed by a passel of "ducklings"—orphaned children, disabled people, disrespected elders—the castoffs of society together at sunrise, learning to fight.

## Los Vagabundos

In the Commonwealth, Los Vagabundos and the Slachta have a lot of overlap. Both are controlled by Azucena Esquivel, who tries valiantly to use them for very different purposes. Members of the Slachta, after all, are very public figures; they act as goodwill ambassadors and bodyguards to the prince and king. Los Vagabundos, meanwhile, like to operate from the shadows; they sneak and spy and uphold the good, but *silently*. Unfortunately, for all Azucena's attempts to divide their responsibilities, both wholly concern themselves with the safety of the king and his son, so much so that instead of acting as a separate organization, Los Vagabundos most often acts as the Slachta's shadow half, doing the dirty deeds that the members of the public-facing Slachta cannot be caught doing.

# The Explorer's Society

A branch of the Explorer's Society in Rzeczpospolita operates out of Szablewo and spends most of its time exploring the city's underground caves. Every Septimus, the *Collegium Maius* lends it a room, which members then transform into a mini-museum display focusing on one of the cave system's wonders.

Though the University bans students from exploring the caves on pain of expulsion, a student who explores nonetheless frequently finds herself recruited if she graduates. A Society member in Szablewo is a sought-after guest lecturer and frequently donates copies of his finds to the University Library; in exchange, the Library allows him to copy and request texts as if he were a full-time member of the University staff. Currently trying to equip a Sarmatian expedition to the New World, the Society has begun writing to other branches, asking for tips.

There is another branch of the Explorer's Society in Curonia operated entirely by vagrants. Its members live in Saulės Mūšis (pronounced: SOWL-yes MOO-shes) and seek to map the territory, to record accounts of unnatural happenings, to sketch and dissect the fruits on the trees. They have basically no money—Odiseo sends them brushes, ink and paper—and produce stunning results labeled in untutored hand. Members have written other branches of the Society asking for supplies, but thus far the results have been slow in coming.

Neither Sarmatian branch of the Society has any idea that the other exists.

## Favor in the Sarmatian Commonwealth

Heroes who are members of the Explorer's Society in the Sarmatian Commonwealth may earn Favor in the following ways:

- Creating a map of the crystal caverns under Szablewo is worth 3 Favor. If the map is particularly accurate or uncovers a new chamber, it is worth 4 Favor.
- Bringing necessary supplies to members in Saulės Mūšis is worth 4 Favor.

# The Invisible College

When the Inquisition began cracking down on Castillian intellectuals, the queen set up a shipping lane dedicated to smuggling targets out of Castille. The queen (now *de facto* merely a powerful Księżna) no longer controls the Commonwealth, but the shipping lane remains, smuggling intelligentsia from all over Castille into Szablewo.

The Invisible College, therefore, considers itself in debt to the Księżna—debt doubled by the fact that Małgorzata Domagała has used her own funds to create positions in Szablewo universities for intellectuals who have impressed her (as well as many whom she has impressed in turn—as a Drajewicz she hardly lacks education).

Scholars who owe her their lifes and positions include Alvara Arciniega, the inventor of the reflecting telescope (though currently on loan to Ussura), Iratze Eneko, the first to discover the *placebo* effect, and Annunciacion Valla, a philologist working to disprove the provenance of several writings attributed to the Third Prophet.

## Favor in the Sarmatian Commonwealth

Heroes who are members of the Invisible College in the Sarmatian Commonwealth may earn Favor in the following way:

- Helping the Invisible College move a persecuted academic from Castile to the Commonwealth earns 5 Favor.

Heroes who are members of the Invisible College in the Sarmatian Commonwealth may spend Favor in the following way:

- Gaining an audience with Queen Małgorzata costs 4 Favor.

## Močiutės Skara

During the War of the Cross, even the warlords loved the Grandmother's Shawl. Cute little ladies cleaning up the battlefield, baking cookies and darning socks—you could rest easier knowing *someone* tended to your wounded. Everyone adored and infantilized the "Grandmothers," which perfectly suited their purposes; when the war stopped, the world did not know why but the Grandmothers laughed behind their hands.

Officially, Močiutės Skara remains headquartered on the Sarmatian-Ussuran border. Unofficially, while they still have offices there, the actual important work is all done in Memel, but since revealing their connection to the radical pacifist creed *Anashid* (a Memel-based sect of heretical Dīnists) would damage their oh-so-harmless reputation, they do not do that. Currently, they chase the rumor that General Winter plans to invade the Commonwealth—they suspect at least one member of the Old Nobility quietly supports him, but who?

## Knights of the Rose & Cross

The Knights of the Rose & Cross had a long tradition of gifted knights and a select few noble benefactors within the Commonwealth. When Golden Liberty raised everyone to noble status, people clamored to join them, as many a new-made noble sought to prove his elevation more than just political convenience.

At first, the Order spent a great deal of time attempting to vet the new recruits, pairing them with seasoned members and testing their skills. But the applicants outnumbered the Knights, and they began turning away anyone without the best training or coin to back them. This means many of the new nobility, though skilled and willing to help, are turned away at the doors.

Now, the Rose & Cross has more Knights than they know what to do with, but few benefactors to really help fund the Society's actions. The current number one goal for the Knights of the Rose & Cross in Sarmatia is to find benefactors amongst the old nobility.

## FAVOR WITH OTHER SOCIETIES

The Most Noble and Ancient Order of the Post have garnered a great deal of respect in the Sarmatian Commonwealth, and some of the other Secret Societies in the Nation have started using their services to their own ends. As such, agents of the various Secret Societies can work with the Order of the Post. Here are a few examples of earning or spending Favor with the various other Secret Societies.

Heroes who are members of the Rose & Cross in the Sarmatian Commonwealth may earn Favor in the following ways:

- Delivering a parcel (or a package of letters) for the Post earns 4 Favor.

- Assisting a postal carrier in making a delivery earns 1 to 3 Favor, depending on the significance of the assistance.

Heroes who are members of the Invisible College in the Sarmatian Commonwealth may spend Favor in the following ways:

- Having a postal carrier deliver somewhere not on her usual route takes anywhere from 1 to 3 Favor, depending on the danger or distance to the location of delivery.

- Getting access to the Post's maps costs 4 Favor.

## The Rilasciare/ Sophia's Daughters

Domenica Vespucci wrote extensive commentary on Uppman's journals. Aleksy crafted Golden Liberty inspired partially by her commentary. That alone would be a scandal, were it known publicly; Biały, especially, would be delighted to draw the line between Domenica, Aleksy and the Rilasciare. Given their work with Sophia's Daughters, it is no surprise the Rilasciare protect the Prince and the Princess Consort: both are Uppman's Friend and during Marcen Sabat's coup, the Rilasciare were instrumental in helping bring down the traitor Książę.

# The Most Noble and Ancient Order of the Post

The Knights of the Rose & Cross received an influx of new recruits after the Golden Liberty, but few of the new nobles had money to offer by way of benefactors. They did, however, have horses.

Horses in the Sarmatian Commonwealth are a funny thing. The most popular breeds have long legs and undergo training to take riders through difficult terrain; for their facility navigating marshes in particular, they are nicknamed "swimmers." All these would-be knights had swimmers, and when a passel of them met in Budorigum they considered delivering long-distance messages. After all, carrying messages under the right circumstances seemed quite Heroic, with all the frozen marshland and narrow mountain passes, but as it was, only the rich could afford riders to carry letters and well, that wasn't fair, was it?

And thus the Most Noble and Ancient Order of the Post began.

The name started out as a joke; none of those in the original Post had been nobles for more than a month. But the service they offered was not a joke, not when people began to count on them to carry medicines to isolated outposts, seed corn into snowed-out towns, family heirlooms to far flung relations and deeds and wills that people were willing to kill for.

Out of necessity, the Post became cartographers: many of their current routes started out unmapped. They now possess the world's most detailed maps of the Commonwealth, in itself technology many kill for: they have sent copies to the king and a few others. They used to make woodcuts of the maps, print them by the hundred and sell them on the cheap, but after a copy of the maps let a bandit gang effectively terrorize the Sarmatyzn River for a month, they started keeping their newer maps secret.

They have also started helping coordinate and organize other Knightly Orders, facilitating town-to-town communication to help networks of villages catch brigands, repair bridges, build roads and the like. It helps that nearly every village has a Knightly Order of its own: in Rzeczpospolita, the Sarmatism craze swept the rural areas hardest, and those in Curonia refuse to call them Knightly Orders, but many towns have militias that serve the same purpose.

## Favor with the Most Noble and Ancient Order of the Post

The Most Noble and Ancient Order of the Post is concerned with reviving chivalry in the Sarmatian Commonwealth. Some do this by performing their duty of letter carrier with the utmost respect for privacy and discretion. Others do this by making a general call to the people to perform knightly service in the Nation. Either way, the ultimate goal is to prove that honor and gentility is alive and strong in the Commonwealth.

Heroes who belong to the Order of the Post may earn Favor in the following ways:

+ Delivering an important message in a timely fashion is worth 3 Favor, especially if no one was the wiser of your delivery, other than the sender and recipient.
+ Helping a new Knightly Order is worth 4 Favor. This could be to help them organize, solidify their code, secure a place to meet or any other activity that furthers the goal of organization.

Heroes who belong to the Order of the Post may spend Favor in the following ways:

+ Requesting aid from a Knight costs 3 Favor. A Knight is typically Strength 5 and possesses the Dueling Academy Advantage in any school of your choosing. If you spend an additional 2 Favor, the Knight you recruit can have an additional Dueling School of your choice.
+ Access to a letter or otherwise private missive costs 2 Favor. While normally the honor of the postal carrier involved is of utmost importance, sometimes the information contained in a letter takes precedence. Gaining access to such information may require the Hero to offer to take the letter to its final destination in order to preserve the honor of the original postal carrier.

*Places*

# Rzeczpospolita

Neither Rzeczpospolita nor Curonia has yet violently contested the Commonwealth's unity, since their unification in the mid-1500s. This is remarkable, particularly given that even now, Rzeplitans and Curonians grow up speaking separate languages—though a century ago a wise enough Sejm mandated that nobles, at least, needed to learn both, though few bother to use Curonian. How this will play out now that the Commonwealth's entire population has been ennobled remains unclear. That said, Commonwealth conventional wisdom has it that Curonians are much more likely to call for the Commonwealth's dissolution than Rzeplitans are. This is for a few very valid reasons.

First, historically, Dominykas Dega, the Curonian king who put together the Commonwealth, famously favored Rzeczpospolita over Curonia. Not only that, but he was inordinately tactless with his favoritism: for instance, not only did he reorganize Curonia into Księstwa along Rzeplitan lines but he also gave

those Curonian Księstwa Rzeplitan names (this is why various Curonian Księstwa have names like "Gancarz"). He also mandated that Rzeplitan be the official language of government, the language of education and the only language spoken in the Sejm.

Dega knew Curonia lacked wealth compared to Rzeczpospolita and believed the Curonians could be pacified with money. Though in a sense true, the ever-pragmatic Curonian nobles, rather than wasting time taking offense, simply took their places in the Sejm and passed a slew of bills appropriating Rzeplitan money and recruiting experts to build infrastructure in Curonia—hospitals, highways, universities, all the things Curonia could not afford as a destitute sovereign nation. Dominykas Dega ended his reign with an empty treasury, its money poured into building up Curonia.

A powerful patriotism has grown up, though, in the wake of Golden Liberty, and perhaps that keeps this tension from turning truly ugly. Though

Budorigum has remained stubborn, many Rzeplitans from outside the capital have spoken up in favor of moving or perhaps rotating the Sejm. Followers of Sarmatism, especially, have thrown themselves behind it. What started, some say, as a silly trend has led to some very serious talk about national unity. Several members of the Izba Poselska have even spoken up in favor of all votes being done by mail, with the Post or other Rose & Cross members hired to carry written communications.

Rzeczpospolita boasts the Nation's capital city, trade borders with Ussura and Vodacce, the Nation's largest universities and hospitals and the largest stretches of fertile land. Rzeczpospolita also feels the first impacts of war with other Nations, and the Księstwa have larger debts due to this.

## Szablewo (Księstwo Drajewicz)

Some call Szablewo "The First City"—they say it was built in Numanari times and continued through the Empire's fall and as the Commonwealth rose up around it. The Numanari ruins, buildings and tombs amidst the city seem to support this. Others call it the "Endless City" or the "Crystal City" for the subterranean crystal caves found below—white limestone and crystal corridors run underneath the streets, geodes, hollows and drops for explorers hungry for glory and eager to die.

But most call Szablewo "University City," the name synonymous with education. Forty-three colleges are located there, with all Senat an alumnus of one of these institutions. The colleges admit members of the sixteen and their families, and, after that, the children of the wealthy. Occasionally colleges offer scholarships, but mostly they do not court the brilliant: as the Domagała are fond of saying, they *make* the brilliant.

Małgorzata Domagała, Queen Consort and Księżna Drajewicz, controls Szablewo. The vast majority of citizens are her loyalists, and no wonder she made their great city even greater. As Stanisław's proxy in the Sejm, she pushed through the "University Tithe"—currently, ten percent of all Crown revenue is earmarked for higher education. Before the Sejm enacted the Tithe, the University struggled with debt; now, all the colleges operate in the black. Conveniently, the Księżna's work with the Invisible College has prompted Castille's outlaw intelligentsia to immigrate *en masse* to the city.

## The University of Szablewo

The Colleges have names, but are referred to as "The University" or "Szablewo University" as a whole. Built of the city's bright white limestone, in a mix of Numanari and Gothic styles, the Colleges are a sight to behold—especially when you step inside. Six observatories, a to-scale orrery, depicting the six known planets and their positions around the sun, and the largest library in eastern Théah grace the halls.

Because of their dependence on the University Tithe, the Colleges have the most to lose from Golden Liberty; already, the Sejm talks of reallocating the Tithe—to the Church, classically, or to the Most Noble and Ancient Order of the Post. Many who dislike Małgorzata resent the Tithe for its associations; they say (and not without some truth) that she forced the bill through the Sejm with no regard for the democracy of even the pre-Golden Liberty posłowie.

Moreover, many deputies, loudmouths in the lower house, have made it clear they view the University as a privileged palisade and wish to tear it to pieces as punishment accordingly—as a result, many Szablewo citizens stand with the queen against those who want to cut the Tithe. A popular opinion in Szablewo has it that the University should at least be restricted to non-criminals who can read, in an effort to keep those loudmouths out of the system.

The citizens of Szablewo most upset about the Sejm's burgeoning hostility towards the College system are the new immigrant Castillians, who have seen this sort of thing before. Esteban Verdugo and his allies excel at presenting what they do as populism, good at creating mobs when convenient, and masterful at turning popular sentiment against the privileged elite when it suits their purposes.

All the situation needs now is the charge that intellectualism is somehow ungodly, that the elite are anti-Vaticine. Plenty of fuel for that fire starts with Szablewo's rivalry with Budorigum's Three Sisters University and ends with rumors that the queen is a losejas. Szablewo has never been a fortress town, but sooner or later, they may have to start defending themselves.

## The Crystal Caves

No one has mapped the Szablewo caves, not entirely. They change too fast, chambers cracking and collapsing from underground earthquakes that never quite reach the surface, leaving behind their only evidence: ruins for returning spelunkers and new crystal corridors to explore.

The caves are white limestone, smooth to the touch and highly reflective—light from entrance shafts bounces throughout the corridors, giving an illusion of ethereal illumination. The larger caverns contain soda lakes, water bitter to the taste and totally lifeless, save for strange silver fish that live nowhere else.

The underground hides secret churches, dating from the days of Numanari persecution, pre-Vaticine shrines and altars of mystery cults and odd skin-eating sarcophagi with jewel-clad skeletons trapped inside.

Amethysts grow like thistles in the caves, climbing the limestone walls and then descending as purple crystal chandeliers. The caves are deadly and every college forbids students from exploring. Students inevitably spelunk anyway, hoping to see what no one has ever seen before: a river new-revealed by an earthquake or a cavern about to be sealed.

They have even begun trying to leave evidence of their own presence, hoping another spelunker will find it, checking back later to see if it's missing. In the most stable parts of the caverns, small graffiti markings declare a student's name or a symbol she has chosen to use to denote herself. Every now and then, a newly unearthed room might hold the mark of someone who came before, the chamber lost and resurfaced through the ever-tumultuous earth's passing.

Ever pragmatic, the Explorer's Society provides a rough map of known sites (frequently updated and deliberately unfinished), and the group advises spelunkers not to steal semi-precious stones or jewels from skeletons. New sites are to be reported to the Explorer's Society immediately; an individual who finds one gets discoverer's credit and amnesty from the University.

## The Cloth Hall & Guild Houses

Once upon a time, the University was not the only industry in Szablewo.

The Cloth Hall held tailors, spinners, weavers, wool-combers, scutchers, retters—the list goes on (everything but dyers—Szablewo has always bleached its cloth with lime). In the hall, they sold what they made, the finest pieces for the highest prices. In the Guild Houses, a block to the west, workers trained and packed cloth and goods stamped for export. Cloth exported from Szablewo always received a stamp with bright white wax embossed with the Drajewicz twelve-pointed star signifying its excellence—or it did, until a series of disasters happened.

First, the linen manufacturers began experimenting with fungus-assisted retting. This seemed like a good idea at the time—it meant the retters no longer had to stink up the river—but created linen which, after some wear, was revealed to be of relatively poor quality.

Unwisely, the manufacturers decided to export the fungus-retted linen anyway, perhaps believing Szablewo's reputation could absorb the hit—and maybe, in another year, it could have.

But that year, clever counterfeiters decided to forge the Szablewo stamp and add it to their low-quality cloth, which they then used to flood the market—the end result, of course, destroyed the reputation of Szablewo's textiles.

The industry still has not recovered and the Guild Houses are sad shadows of what they used to be—it is a rare apprentice who comes in wanting Szablewo certification anymore. Most of the clothiers who used to live in the area have moved to other cities, and people talk of selling the Cloth Hall itself, ghostly and half-abandoned now, to one of the colleges.

Unsurprisingly, the entire disaster has led to an upswing in town versus gown rivalry, as the remaining clothiers resent the University sitting pretty on the Tithe while the less-prestigious workers of the city suffer. The Colleges' tendency to respond to this complaint with "you brought this on yourselves" or some variant does nothing to help.

## Budorigum

Before it became the capital, Budorigum was famous for beds of red clay suited for brick making, which lay not far from the riverbanks. The first brickmakers were Crescent migrants, imported en masse by Książę Cieslewicz in 1333 AV; these migrant workers gave Budorigum's culture a notably Crescent bent, and today the city's architecture appears mostly Crescent in design.

Crescent, that is, except for the bricks: in a brick-making town, every building sports brickwork, even the enormous triple-domed mosque in the center of the city. Along with brickwork, the city became known for its brilliant glassworks when a cadre of converts discovered the sand that lined the Sejm could be mixed with small amounts of clay to produce a multitude of stained glass hues. Even to this day, most windows in the city contain stained glass of some sort—a point of pride for Budorigum's residents.

In 1442 AV, Budorigum became the capital; the Sejm was built in six weeks. Townhouses for traveling nobles were built on the blocks around the Sejm, and the demand for clean water quickly led to aqueducts and drainage canals. The migrants had collected water in great brick cisterns and dumped their waste directly into the Sejm. Noble families flaunted their wealth by building parks, public squares and elaborate brickwork fountains; a cadre of aristocrats fond of horse-racing even went so far as to build a racetrack next to the Sejm which could seat 100,000 people. This was rather over-ambitious; to this day, the stadium has never been filled.

A second migration into the city began directly post-Golden Liberty, with scads of "New Nobles" eager to live near the Sejm. Predictably, this has driven Budorigum's real estate prices through the roof and the Sejm currently debates what, if anything, should be done about that.

### The Sejm

The original Sejm was ugly; a great brick building slopped together as a sort of irregular rectangle. Various improvements have done nothing for the overall aesthetic, with the possible exception of one: in 1593 AV, seven parallel corridors were built to attach the Sejm to the stadium.

Originally, this allowed the ruling sixteen to make public announcements efficiently. However, when Golden Liberty began, the corridors gained new purpose: namely, the stadium (which by this point had failed as a business) was declared the meeting place of the Izba Poselska, the "house of deputies" or "the lower house," where the New Nobility vote.

The Senat still maintains the power to decide the timing of votes, though the Izba Poselska has put some limitations on this. First, the Senat and the Izba Poselska must vote simultaneously, which is meant to prevent the Senat from scheduling the Izba Poselska's vote at times when people could not—or would not—make it, such as public holidays. Second, a member of the Senat must announce, on the stadium floor, when they schedule a vote to happen, with at least four hours' notice.

This, in theory, allows at least the Budorigum-based members of the Izba Poselska ample time to arrive at the Sejm. After the Senat announced two votes at midnight to an empty stadium, the Izba Poselska began posting a 24-hour watch in the stands, volunteers charged with raising a cry should the upper house announce more votes that are inconvenient.

Given that the Commonwealth has more than 100,000 citizens, it is possible that one day the stadium might fill beyond capacity. In that case, the Izba Poselska has set up a protocol for the creation of polling stations and has passed a bill disallowing the Senat to end voting until 12 hours after calling the vote. The stadium has never overfilled yet, but the Izba Poselska likes being prepared.

### Duelist's Square

Duelist's Square is exactly what it sounds like: a public square surrounded by swordfighting schools. Ennio Vespucci, the Princess Consort's brother, initiated the setup of the square, representing all well-known styles of sword fighting (though Ennio gave Ambrogia, his favored style, the best of the bordering buildings). The circular mosaic at the center of the square displays two duelists clashing; the circle itself is the perfect size for exhibition matches, and every Sunday afternoon at least one school puts on a show.

The swordmasters are imported, promised prestige and subsidized by Ennio. In the capital, the phrase "getting Ennio's attention" has become synonymous with "being a brilliant duelist." As such, a swordmaster not so lucky as to have a school in Duelist's Square competes to set up classes nearby; she hopes that she or her students may catch Ennio's eye.

Also holding court in Duelist's Square is an office belonging to the Duelist's Guild; membership in the Duelist's Guild, after all, separates real sword fighters from brigands. The rise of dueling culture in the Commonwealth, however, has its obvious downsides.

Largely sedate about matters of "honor" pre-Golden Liberty, Commonwealth citizens now recast honor as a point of personal pride worth spilling blood over, especially among the youth. Where duels used to be over serious matters, long-held disputes or even personal insults, people duel each other over the most trivial matters. The Duelist's Guild attempts to put an end to this trend, but so far, none of its well-meaning pamphlets written to discourage frivolous duels had much in the way of an impact.

## Pocket Parks

The nobles who came to Budorigum when it became the capital carved out public squares and parkland. Even before the city had a substantial upper class, people made attempts to beautify it. In particular, the Crescent migrants planted rooftop gardens, lush facades and mini-jungles with tall grass, small trees, ornamental shrubberies and beautiful vines that cascaded either onto the next roof or down the home's brick siding.

The brick town of Budorigum has a surprising element of wildness. Vines shade cool streets and unexpected trees grow in unused alleys. The nobles who moved into the city took the aesthetic and expanded on it. Old clay beds, sheer-edged and hollows were flooded to make deep impromptu lakes and swimming holes surrounded by trees and ferns, knit together by old quarry tunnels and bordered by the houses of those who wished to live nearby. They called these lush water and vegetation spots within the otherwise bricked city, "pocket parks."

Now new arrivals challenge Budorigum's pocket park aesthetic by not knowing how to treat the parks with respect. City-organized cleanup crews can mostly deal with litter, but vandals pulling up plants to spell out political messages is another mess entirely, never mind the hordes of Izba Poselska, so determined to vote that they camp in the parks and willingly sleep homeless.

Within the city, a heated debate rages as to whether the parks should be fenced off or guarded. On the one hand, that might curb the damage, but on the other hand, perhaps a fence misses the point of a park. As for waking up unwelcome sleepers—well, what good Budorigum citizen has not napped in a park from time to time?

Making matters even more complicated, a cadre of real estate developers have begun pressuring the Sejm to let them pay the government for parkland. Pocket parks are nice and all, but with so many new arrivals desperate for housing, letting developers build over the parkland might ease some of the strain on the market, even as it also enriches developers.

## The Three Sisters

The city of Szablewo has 43 colleges; classically, the upper class is educated there, in sedate winter gardens and amongst dreaming spires. But for those who lack the wealth or pedigree to be allowed into "the White City," they rely on the Three Sisters— Budorigum's universities.

Szablewo has long had reason to consider the Three Sisters second-rate. A Szablewo education is relatively secular; the University, packed with Vaticine, Yachidi, Dinists and followers of old faiths, tries to encourage a cool neutrality amongst the faithful. In 1446 AV, a Vaticine priest and would-be professor, Alicja Lis, took exception to this, pulled up her roots, moved to Budorigum and founded the Three Sisters—a trio of colleges (nicknamed *Jadwiga*, *Bona* and *Wanda*) built specifically as Vaticine educational institutions. The sophisticates in Szablewo derided this as backwards, but the colleges succeeded—two centuries later, they still graduate students.

Stereotypically, a Three Sisters student falls into one of two categories—either she is devout and wants a cloistered education or her family is neither well-bred nor wealthy. Post-Golden Liberty, partisan politics have added a third archetype to the mix: the red-clad Czerwony not sufficiently subtle about his politics, either expelled from a Szablewo school or bullied until he transferred.

In fact, the fight between Biały and Czerwony is, for the Sisters, the gift that keeps on giving. A prestigious professor, upon finding himself unwelcome in Szablewo's halls, often seeks a position in Budorigum, and the Sisters are always happy to hire. If this partisan infighting keeps on going, and the Szablewo Colleges keep pushing people out, the Three Sisters will soon rival Szablewo's finest.

### Lottan Mosque & Stanisław's Cathedral

The triple-domed Lottan Mosque is a glazed, intricate brickwork, a multi-colored masterpiece where each brick is varnished a different hue and light leaks in through stained-glass squares, stacked like bricks, that serve as windows. It is a tour de force of Crescent and Commonwealth architecture made only more impressive by the fact that it was built mostly by impoverished migrants who spent their daylight hours making bricks.

Sometimes called "the Night Mosque," the stories say the migrants built it all at night. The Mosque's current Imam, Rabia Saliah, is the country's most prestigious Dīnist leader and when she first met Stanisław, she gave him the deed for the ground adjacent and told him to build a Cathedral.

Budorigum has plenty of churches, of course. On side streets, they are nearly as common as mosques. Budorigum even has two basilicas; Three Sisters' graduates made sure of that. But Budorigum's last Cathedral saw its steeple blow off in a storm. The tower collapsed a mere month before Stanisław stopped using his wife as his proxy. Since then there has been no Cathedral. Budorigum's Cardinal lives in a Church.

Adjacent to the Lottan Mosque, Stanisław's Cathedral stands half-built. The Archbishop, Andrzej Radziwiłł, gives sermons there on sunny days and sometimes on rainy ones, saying that Theus' house is ever under construction, so who is he to scorn unfinished ceilings? He and the Imam have struck up a friendship, to the amusement of the capital.

Finishing the Cathedral has been on the list of budgetary votes for the Sejm for the past few months, but it has been exceedingly difficult to get the Senate to approve the budget, since the Izba Poselska did so in record time.

# Curonia

More than a century after unification, Curonia remains the poorer part of the Commonwealth. Rzeczpospolita has dozens of universities, multiple lucrative industries and enormous cities; Curonia still consists of almost all marsh farms and tiny villages haunted by dievai. Rzeczpospolita's population also numbers twice that of Curonia's, but until eighteen months ago this hardly mattered: in the Sejm, where the Commonwealth passed laws, a Curonian noble strategically wielding the *liberum veto* possessed just as much power as a Rzeplitan one. Now that is no longer true. In the Izba Poselska at least, the majority always rules, and almost always, the majority is Rzeplitan.

This is enough to make many Curonians upset.

Ugnė Urbonė, a Curonian Senat member, has proposed moving the capital to Curonia. This would solve at least a portion of the problem: a Curonian deputy would no longer have to make the long voyage to Budorigum every time she wished to vote, while for a Rzeplitan, voting would come with a higher cost. Unsurprisingly, the voters of Budorigum refuse to support this plan, and since they include the Sejm's most active voters—by virtue of where they live, at least in part—that has become a bit of a sticking point.

While Curonia may be poorer than Rzeczpospolita and marginalized in the government, the people there have a stronger sense of unity than those of their sister nation-state. Most of this stems from the struggle to maintain cultural identity following the unification with Rzeczpospolita. The Curonian language fell into disuse, their religion overrun by the Vaticine faith and cultural norms discarded in favor of the more popular Rzeplitan ones. While these changes affected Curonians, the people also resisted such changes. In Curonia, a Curonian speaks her native language, burns offerings to her gods and follows her ancient traditions, and all her neighbors do the same, supporting her decision to not let Rzeplitan popularity crush the old ways.

Moreover, though stylistic Sarmatism has not much penetrated Curonia itself, many Curonians nonetheless strongly feel the need for a National unity, even one that comes at the cost of haggling with privileged, ridiculous Rzeplitans. There are a couple reasons for this. First and most pragmatically, with General

Winter at the border, many Curonians worry that the country faces invasion. Quibbling, even over things like capitals, seems rather pointless in that context.

Second, the Biały and Czerwony quarrel currently dominates the public consciousness. Though Curonian Biały and Czerwony exist, the vast majority of Curonians are not enamored of either side: Aleksy is an idealistic pacifist, oblivious to the threat of invasion and too suspicious of Sanderis, while Małgorzata is a domineering snobby intellectual who wants to limit the franchise and cares only for Szablewo. Standing outside the political frenzy and exasperated by both Biały and Czerwony, many Curonians have decided (somewhat influenced by stereotypes), as the responsible, sober down-to-earth people, to calm the passionate Rzeplitans before the Biały and Czerwony conflict actually gets dangerous. Hence the rise of the *Jasny* (or "clear"), a faction of mostly Curonians who make it their unofficial duty to help Biały and Czerwony hammer out compromises and de-escalate whatever quarrels they find.

It is also an open secret that many Curonians hope the split between Rzeplitan Biały and Czerwony allows for the election of a Curonian monarch, most likely Ugnė Urbonė. Even many Rzeplitans hope that if Ugnė wins the election, the Biały and Czerwony struggle will fizzle. That said, many Commonwealth citizens, Curonian and Rzeplitan both, also fear that if the loudly pro-Curonian Ugnė is elected queen, Curonian and Rzeplitan tensions might then come to the fore.

## Saulės Mūšis (Księstwo Czyż)

This ancient city is the oldest in Curonia and stands as a testament to the power of the dievai and the folly of those who try to work against them.

### The Fall

Saulės Mūšis was the Curonian capital until 1262 AV. It fell under the reign of Petras V. Petras made a series of Deals with a dievas (pronounced: DEE-ah-VAS, plural dievai: DEE-ah-VI) he adored (now called Saulė since people telling the story retroactively name her after the city). Saulė, of course, was very powerful, and so Petras's rule went unquestioned.

Though Petras started out wise, as he stayed with her and grew more deluded, until one summer equinox, at the height of his arrogance, he declared he wished to make the Seventh Deal with her, bring her into the world and make her his wife. When noon came that day, Saulė was nowhere to be found. Instead, at the moment when the sun reached its zenith, the city burned to the ground.

No one knows what really happened, but neither Petras nor his dievas were seen again.

The days after the fall of Saulės Mūšis were known as the days of the Fallen Inquisition. After the city fell to the flames, the Curonian Vaticine Church vowed to put a stop to all Sanderis Sorcery—a disaster of that scale could not be allowed to happen again.

In response, many of the country's losejai came together to form the Ratas—a network of alliances and partnerships with a twofold purpose: to keep the losejai safe from all the organizations who would end them and to keep the rest of the world safe from the losejai.

## Saulės Mūšis Today

Saulės Mūšis burned, but the stone survived. Now it is a skeleton city, all archways, doorways, altars and streets, overgrown with trees that split the sidewalks and grow strange fruits out of season.

The fruit in Saulės Mūšis is what scares people.

The trees, bushes, shoots, vines and plants bloom and bear all year, even when frost covers the ground. In Saulės Mūšis, if you eat what grows in the ruins, you will always be sated, but what unnatural fruit ripens even in Decimus? Ambrose Davidson, the traveling Avalonian scholar, nicknamed the stuff "færie fruit," and the name stuck.

People say it is planted by dievai. It is the best fruit you have ever eaten, too: ripe unpecked cherries, melons, raspberries. But once you consume it, you always want more—the people who come to Saulės Mūšis to stave off starvation almost always stay in the ruined city the rest of their days.

Given that the fruits' effects are public knowledge, most cautious and privileged people avoid Saulės Mūšis. But the place has become a magnet for vagrants, the starving, the destitute and those willing to eat strange fruit for the guarantee of life free from hunger. Others may shudder or sneer, but to that a citizen says, "Would you have fed us?" In the city, she may be a plaything of dievai, but at least she is not desperate or starving.

And indeed, a sort of patriotism grows around Saulės Mūšis these days. A citizen calls himself an apple-eater; some write pamphlets advertising the old city's wonders, not entirely satirically. Others have formed a branch of the Explorer's Society dedicated to mapping the ruined city. They have begun sending sketches to Odiseo and have been recognized officially.

An apple-eater takes pride in the fact that his city is a place of sanctuary. Criminals who make it to Saulės Mūšis and eat the fruits of the city do not get taken in by law enforcement because, really, why would they?

The Książę Czyż, who technically controls the city's Księstwo, does not want to touch it, and law enforcement rarely sends an agent in lest she decide to stay. Plus, conventional wisdom goes, what dangers does a criminal pose to all but the people of Saulės Mūšis once he has eaten færie fruit? He almost certainly stays in the city and the people of Saulės Mūšis can take care of their own.

Still, strange things happen in the city—more now than before. Sometimes residents simply vanish—there one day and gone the next. Sometimes a new person appears, or an old one reappears, changed. She has no memory of her alteration, though she has claws now or cannot feel the cold. And when fog covers Saulės Mūšis, citizens sometimes hear screams—always too distant for cause to be visible but not distant enough, just the same.

## Pallet Houses & the Great Stone Cathedral

Housing in Saulės Mūšis is a problem; all the old wood burned and nobody wants to cut down the fruit trees. Sperus has started shipping old pallets, broken or rot-patched, to Saulės Mūšis for the price of whatever nonliving treasures the denizens of the city can stand to send down the river. The dead timber has been a godsend and Saulės Mūšis citizens use it to construct houses.

Before building with pallets, much of Saulės Mūšis spent the winter sleeping in the Great Stone Cathedral, the city's only large building made wholly of stone. Even with the pallets, a large Saulės Mūšis contingent—called, unimaginatively, Traditionalists—still sleep in the Cathedral come winter.

According to them, it lets citizens catch up with each other and build community. Sleeping between pews, the lack of privacy may become wearing, but that is what summer is for. A person who prefers pallet houses values privacy and chooses his company more highly. He also admits he finds the Cathedral scary, given its history.

Originally built by Vaticines, during his reign, Petras V converted it into a place of worship for Saulė, Petras' dievas. Considering she burned down the city, this makes people understandably wary—and besides that, the bloodstained altars are creepy.

A person staying in the Cathedral may have the right of it though; she is far less likely to disappear during the winter than those in the pallet-houses. Those who value privacy (and in a homeless city, there are many) live dangerously—all who vanish do so alone or in pairs.

## The Sanderas Forest

Old tales of the Sanderas almost always involve adventurers wandering the forest, searching for dievai to strike bargains with. The dievai notoriously like to play hard to get. They hide in bone houses and set would-be losejai impossible tasks, like pulling a spill of poppy seeds out of the soil before sunrise. Old tales of the Sanderas do not lie: even today, wandering the woods is the surest way to find a dievas willing to bargain.

There is only one settlement near the Sanderas, Voruta, a city built on the lightning-struck plain in the forest's heart. The Księżna of Voruta is and always has been a dedicated Ratas member: the Ratas controls Voruta and therefore controls easy entrance to the Sanderas. Those who seek to use the woods to make deals with dievai must first pass through the Ratas, and the Ratas knows that not everyone who wishes to deal with demons deserves to.

But the Sanderas does not just exist for people to meet dievai. Non-losejai and those who have already bargained with dievai also wander into the woods. The only thing dievai like doing better than tormenting humans is tormenting other dievai, and those in the woods eagerly sabotage those who have already latched onto a human. More than one losejas has learned a new Deal, or a piece of a Name, by pleasing a Sanderas dievas.

The Ratas calls venturing into the Sanderas *Katabasis*. A dedicated Ratas member tries to venture into the Sanderas at least once every seven years, to glean more information about her dievas.

## The Fires of Gabija

Two roads go into the Sanderas, one from Złotogóra, one from Sperus. Those roads, built by the Ratas in the thirteenth century, used magical rituals now lost, and except for those two roads, the Sanderas is unmapped. Paths appear and peter out, bone houses change places and any losejas unwise enough to put his trust in a compass needle swiftly ends up circling back on his own footprints. The only beacons worth seeking are the Fires of Gabija, ever-burning pyres that appear frequently but irregularly in the forest.

The dievai say Gabija the Red, a powerful dievas who killed her losejas after making the Seventh Deal,

created the fires. General Ratas policy is to kill on sight any dievas who manifests bodily, so they say Gabija is no dievas at all—the dievai who insist so must be lying.

Someone who distrusts the Ratas distrusts this statement in particular: he says the Ratas left Gabija alive purely for pragmatism's sake. Her pyres make the Sanderas traversable and she never appears outside the forest. She walks the woods as a woman in a red dress, and she is scrupulously fair—even generous— with her pyres, so long as those who use them play by her rules.

Anyone who ventures into the Sanderas with the blessing of the Ratas memorizes the protocols for the pyres before she goes. Fires should be banked only with their own ashes and extinguished with clean stream water—gory stories circulate about losejai who tried to stamp the flames. Salt thrown into the fire pleases Gabija and nothing tempts her wrath like bloodshed in the firelight. Those who fight near the flames more often than not suffer immolation. The flames' protection is for everyone. Enemy losejai may— and often must—share the same fire when night falls in the Sanderas. Wild animals stay away from the flames and so too other dievai.

It is not uncommon for groups of losejai to accumulate around the pyres come nightfall, with Sanderis practitioners from all over Curonia exchanging stories and sleeping by the flames.

## Voruta (Księstwo Janusz)

The middle of the Sanderas forest is a place where no trees grow, a lightning-struck plain and a surface vein of bituminous marble with sprays of scarlet and snow-white coral.

This is where Voruta stands.

The Ratas built Voruta to assist with Katabasis. In the middle of the forest, it provides a safe house, a haven. Much too large for its current purpose, from 1266 AV until the Commonwealth's formation, it served as Curonia's capital as well, declared so by a Grand Książę who wanted to encourage the nobles to destroy dievai.

Today, large portions of the city stand empty, basilicas and ballrooms, baroque and splendid, waiting for nobles who will not return 'til the Commonwealth falls. But the city still stands. It is an eerie city.

Somehow, so close to the sun-dappled forest, the daylight in Voruta never looks right. Always bluish-white on the black-red-white marble, the light never looks warm. The only warmth comes from lamps kindled at night. And how does it always look that way, so overcast, with the forest always sunny?

The city stands for the sake of Katabasis, and at any one time about a seventh of the people staying in the city are losejai or potential losejai trying to gin up the nerve to enter the Sanderas. Much of the rest of the city exists as industry to serve these losejai, to boost their morale. So despite the unnerving sunlight, the city is beautiful and businesses and monuments exist to encourage serenity, some in stranger ways than others.

Famously, losejai visit the black marble dome, set with lanterns to look like stars, where sound is muffled and those who enter lie on mats. Music plays, and those that lie can watch the false stars move their paths, slowly, an eternal, predictable, warm, calm night.

## Poetry Houses

Less respectably, though no less strange, poetry brothels peddle intimacy on curtained beds in rose-lit chambers, less often sex than services more serene. A person pays for someone to give him warm milk and tuck him into bed, or to have someone read his favorite poetry out loud or simply spends silver on massages and mulled wine. He pays for anything to calm his nerves, as it never does well to enter the Sanderas agitated.

Others prefer the museum that stores the heads of those dievai killed when they appeared bodily; vicariously recalling triumphs always comforts. And then lastly, a scholar can head over to the Scholomance, hoping for a bit of Sanderis research to give her an edge.

## The Scholomance

The Scholomance is Théah's foremost school of Sanderis—not that there is much competition. Head down to its basement (and down, and down—built into what was once the black marble quarry) and you hit a labyrinth, a seeming-infinite library of hand-bound codices and a card catalog containing various descriptors.

This is where a person looks up his demon.

# KATABASIS STORIES

The promise of a better understanding of life and self-discovery is often enough to draw someone into the forest. Those who go likely get something out of the experience, even if it only leads to a better understanding of her own lot in life. Such a venture is a lonely one, as the trek often involves danger.

A Hero with Sanderis may inevitably want to embark on Katabasis as a Story. Just like any other Story, the player should determine the goal of her Hero's Katabasis. This could be as difficult as "Learn a way to destroy my dievas" or as simple as "Gain a better understanding of my powers." In general, the reward for this kind of Story should be purchasing a new level of the Sorcery Advantage.

You can run these Stories as solo mini-sessions for the losejas Hero if the others are not interested in participating.

## Katabasis

Some losejai believe that deep in the Sanderas Forest lies a secret, a way to destroy her dievas without killing herself or making a Seventh Deal to do it. The Ratas does not condone the idea, promoting scholarship and understanding over superstition. That does not stop a regular pilgrimage into the Sanderas, called Katabasis.

The story goes that once every seven years, a dievas who is bound to a person becomes weakened. Something about the bond to the mortal world makes them vulnerable. If the losejas can find the dievas' origin in the Sanderas Forest, she can kill it.

Few know where the origins for the legend come from. No one knows anyone who has actually destroyed a dievas this way, but the stories persist. A steady stream of losejai wanders through Voruta hoping to go on Katabasis, or speaking of it. The few who gather enough nerve to go out into the forest come back changed in some way.

Many view the act itself as a form of self-discovery and life affirmation. Those who embark on one Katabasis take up the pilgrimage once every seven years, believing without fail that destroying her dievas this way is absolutely possible.

## The Weeping Walls

No one knows why those who return from Katabasis always come back at sunrise, but look at the top of Voruta's northern facing walls and you would think the city suffers a siege every dawn. After all, many a time, it is not just the losejai who go to Voruta—family and friends wait while the losejas wanders the woods.

Their friends, family and even other losejai mount the walls before the sun rises, and hold a silent vigil until well past noon. They wait on the wall for seven days, and in those seven days, nine-tenths of the losejai return. That other tenth are usually just gone, but cruelly, not so often that their relatives and friends can abandon hope.

Stories tell of a losejas returning from the woods three, five, even seven years later, and sometimes even sane when she does. Sometimes when a losejas leaves for more than seven days, family, friends or lovers enter the woods to fetch her. This occasionally works, but not so often that the Ratas encourages it.

A losejas in the Scholomance looks for a sketch of her dievas or a matching description in files that losejai through the ages have added to with accounts of their Katabasis and descriptions of Deals. Ratas members, cross-collating descriptions, have managed to name, manifest and destroy nearly a hundred dievai, though how many more remain uncounted is unknown.

The Scholomance, of course, is not only a library—it is also a school. Though few in Szablewo deign to consider a Curonian College their equal, it probably is. While Szablewo's courses tend towards the theoretical, though, the Scholomance's classes teach the intensely practical. Rhetoric, for instance, is taught as a series of debates, definitely allowing dirty fighting through bad discourse. The College assumes a Scholomance student intends to be a losejas, and there is no use coddling him or letting him keep his hands clean. When a pious type denounces the Scholomance as a school of dark magic, this might be what she means.

## The Remainders

The permanent citizens of Voruta call themselves the Remainders. In some ways, it is self-deprecating. Their city runs on a service economy, and most of them make their money serving losejai. Therefore, they are the remainders; those left when all the questers and Heroes leave.

Those who see only the wry self-deprecation miss the other meaning—namely, what it means to *remain*. A Remainder knows he lives in the middle of the Commonwealth's most dangerous location, and when the questing losejai leave, he *stays*. Many are not wealthy.

Indeed, Voruta, with all its galleries and palaces sitting empty, is a popular spot for destitute urbanites looking to avoid paying proprietors. The current Księżna Janusz, Ugnė Urbonė, has begun experimenting with giving longtime squatters deeds to these properties on the condition that they repair and beautify them.

The Remainders live inside a city surrounded by a forest full of dievai, and when asked what could kill Voruta the answer is always the same: a famine. Nothing grows on the lightning-struck plain, so Voruta completely depends on food shipped in from the outside: pickled beets from Złotogóra, cranberries from Sperus, smoked fish and beer brought in on the Wyrzk by the Ushkuiniks. When an ice storm briefly stopped Złotogóra from sending food up, prices rose so fast the city went into a panic.

The city's current *voivode's* "governor" primary priority is making sure that never happens again. She has been spending money out of the city's coffers, buying food that does not spoil: white rice, dried peas, salt, liquor, vinegar.

The Remainders have been following suit and many add their own twists. They make Budorigum-style rooftop gardens, cultivating fish in flooded quarries, raising chickens on kitchen scraps, growing mushrooms in cellars, even keeping bees overlooking the forest—thus far Sanderas pollen has shown no ill effects.

## Złotogóra (Księstwo Szczupak)

The Sarmatian Commonwealth borders Ussura, so of course there are Ussuran immigrants. Most embrace Sarmatian culture, though not all wish to assimilate completely. Hence the creation of Złotogóra, often called "Little Ussura," a city of bathhouses, with onion domes and matryoshka dolls that mostly lives up to its name. Like most cities built on nostalgia, it is a bit of a parody. The *chay* (tea) is spicier and the architecture more elaborate than it ever really was in the old country. But that only makes it more delightful. Residents, tourists, even scholars looking to study well-preserved traditions of Ussuran craftwork and cooking come to embrace the experience.

Of course, that does not mean some things do not come off differently than the immigrants intended.

### Hot Springs

Złotogóra hosts a glorious set of hot springs and as such, bathhouses are abundant. In Ussura, bathhouse culture lacks modesty but is rarely sexual. The same is not the case in the Commonwealth. Here, nakedness brings to mind associations recent immigrants do not always expect. This created a subgenre of erotic bathhouses, steamy, dimly lit and appropriate for sex. Jennys make a fine living, as do discreet herbalists.

Non-erotic Ussuran bathhouses also exist in the city, of course. Less of a tourist draw, they tend to be painted turquoise while erotic bathhouses are painted red—outdoor hot springs are considered turquoise by default. Locals who like to sneer at tourists make lots of japes about erotic bathhouses, but it is not uncommon for those same locals to try out the red-painted places every once in a while.

### The Mirrored Plaza

The plaza at the center of town is paved in mirrored mosaic tiles, courtesy of an eccentric Księżna who loved the look of her face, even in miniature. Torches dot the square at night, reflecting light for a perpetual twilight; in the dark, the mosaic looks like water, and flâneurs float on the surface.

Moving to the Sarmatian Commonwealth, many immigrants miss the easy hospitality of Ussura. Houses dark and closed at night and food only had for coin—that is not the Ussuran way, so it is not done in Złotogóra either. Hence, in the Mirrored

Plaza, Złotogórans set up the trencher table, a table of fruits, meats and cheeses that anyone can eat at any time. Złotogóra residents are expected to donate to the trencher table, and every year they choose a "chef" to make sure the trencher table's contents stay fresh.

The Mirrored Plaza also hosts Bartok, Złotogóra's unofficial mascot, a tame bear. Brought by an immigrant a century ago, Bartok never seems to age or die. He eats from the trencher table, sleeps in the square and occasionally takes a liking or disliking to tourists, who then receive appropriate amounts of respect or derision. Residents suspect he is a Leshy and take it as lucky he bound himself to the city.

In past winters, the plaza and the roads that lead off it have frozen over; rather than fight it, the citizens each Decimus don skates and navigate their mirror-bright highways with practiced grace.

In this season, the divide between locals and tourists is especially broad. The devastating ice storm two winters ago prompted debate as to whether citizens should begin preemptively sanding the roads. Last year, tradition prevailed until Primus, when vigilantes with buckets began sanding roads at midnight, sending skaters spinning the next morning.

## The Ice Storm & Leadership Crisis

Twenty months ago a terrible ice storm tore through Złotogóra. Many died, including the Księżna Szczupak and her only daughter. The Księżna's nearest heir now is her distant niece, but nobody knows where she is. Instead, since the storm, an informal council of rich city dwellers have taken up administration.

Citizen consensus holds that this arrangement should not last forever, but currently no one can agree on what constellation should replace them. Should they try to find the Księżna's niece, last seen in Eisen? Should they choose another noble to govern the Księstwo? Or should they do away with nobles altogether and try administering via some kind of elected body?

Complicating that dispute, the feared Ussuran General Winter currently has cast his eye toward the Sarmatian border. His forces have been there for nearly two years now and Ussurans say he can control winter weather. Złotogóran conspiracy theorists now hold he caused the ice storm.

## Memel (Księstwo Gancarz)

In 803 AV, the self-proclaimed Prophet Irshad bint Jamila began preaching her creed—a creed she called *Anashid*, "songs" in the Crescent language—in Iskandar. In 813 AV, she died, many say killed by the Crescent Empire. At that time, the Empire violently expelled her followers and most fled across the Curonian border. There, amidst the marshlands, they built Memel, a city made in mourning—in Curonian, Memel means "mute."

But what was it about Anashid that made it so hated by the Empire?

First, Anashid holds that the individual is morally responsible for preventing as much death in the world as possible. In particular, Anashid favors active responsibility over innocence. Refusing to serve in an army may be righteous, but serving in an army and sabotaging it is more righteous still.

This makes followers of Anashid gadflies, unwilling to simply appease their consciences passively. An Anashid who sees beggars starving in terrible poverty might, for example, donate all her money, then, driven by her own sense of active responsibility, steal from other wealthy people—or worse, worm herself into power and then legally force the rich to donate.

Anashid, then, is anathema to any status quo. The rulers of the Crescent Empire were displeased by it, and more so when they realized Irshad claimed not to be merely an Imam but a Prophet—someone with a direct link to the divine. That meant she had to be deified or falsified; she could not be dismissed.

She could, however, be destroyed—and the Empire's leaders were quite happy when she died.

When Curonia took the Anashid in, they did it on two conditions. First, that the Anashid serve as Curonia's first line of defense against the Crescent Empire, and second, that the Anashid (including native Curonians who converted to the faith) be lawfully required take on distinctive surnames so as to identify them.

The first promise, the Anashid keep and take very seriously. Many Anashid still nurse a grudge against the Crescent Empire and their schemes have thus far stopped three would-be invasions. The second—well, a lot of Anashid still use the surname "al-Memeli," but many more do not. The surname bears stigma, as many non-Anashid dislike the thought of appointing

those who believe in "active responsibility" to politically sensitive positions.

The Anashid dogma, and their Prophet's own willingness to engage in subterfuge in service of this dogma, makes Anashid a natural fit for many secret societies. Anashid claim to have co-founded the Močiutės Skara and Anashid faithful may additionally be found in the Rilasciare, the Rose & Cross, the Invisible College and Los Vagabundos.

## The Honeypot

Memel is a Crescent city in miniature, down to the narrow streets shaded from the sun and the marketplaces selling silk and spices only open at sunset and dawn. That is no accident: the city makes a tidy sum from tourism as travelers come to experience Crescent culture (or an approximation, anyway) without risking their lives or learning another language.

Many Crescent customs are butchered for the sake of Sarmatian sensibilities. Foods are not as authentic as you might find in Crescent cities, and the buildings have distinctly Curonian influence. But, to the casual tourist, this is the next best thing to visiting the Crescent Empire, and it is certainly a less dangerous trip.

But as well as a honeypot for tourists, the city also functions as a honeypot for invaders.

The Anashid take their promise to protect Curonia from Crescent invasion very seriously. In that vein, Memel's Anashid pay off unscrupulous archivists in the Crescent Empire to forge records saying that in previous invasions, the city of Memel has always been easy to take. It helps that the Ansheed keep in close contact with their families in the Crescent Empire, giving them an easy in.

Thus far, it has worked: since the ninth century, every time the Crescent Empire tried to invade the Commonwealth by land, it started by taking Memel, and every time the Empire has tried to invade the Commonwealth by sea, it started by taking Memel's port. Every time a Crescent army tries to take Memel, the citizens of Memel put up a token resistance and open the gates. Inevitably, the real nightmare for the Crescent army lies inside.

Memel is a walled city. Invaders enter through the front gates into a maze of mud-brick and mosaic tiles, dazzling camouflage designed to distract the eye. Residents know of numerous secret passages that tunnel under the walls, but to an outsider, he sees only one exit, same as the entrance. It can be blocked, and the city remade into a trap.

The Prophet Irshad urged her followers to find alternatives to murder. The Anashid listened, and today Memel houses the largest community of Castillian-trained Boticarios living outside Castille. When turning back invasions, Anashid are locally known for their use of nonlethal but nonetheless dangerous elixirs. Crescent armies sent to the Commonwealth have returned deaf and dumb or plagued with hallucinations.

## Sperus (Księstwo Kazimierz)

Sperus is all dikes now, sandbanks covered in cranberries separated by shallow waterways. In the fall it floods, the berries wet-harvested and floodwater kept through the winter where it freezes to protect the vines. Come spring, the ice melts, the water drains and the cranberries grow again.

It was not always this way.

Sperus used to be a little swamp town, the haunt of houseboat-dwelling hunters and trappers. But Marcen Sabat, the Książę who owned the land, was an ambitious man determined to monetize the swamps. He had his soldiers plant cranberries in Sperus, then set about creating Commonwealth demand. They took the New World import and marketed it as an exotic delicacy. Sabat then showed it off at salons in sauces and preserves. Nearly overnight, Sperus became a boomtown, drawing in farmers from all across the Księstwo.

Funny thing, boomtowns: everyone may be rich, but they are rarely happy.

The hunters resent the tree-cutting farmers, and the farmers resent hunters who trample the crops. Brawls are common, especially in the bars and brothels that line the outskirts of the city. At night, sneaky farmers sink houseboats and hunters set farmhouses aflame.

The city cannot survive like this: if a peace is not reached soon, Sperus will fall. And while the ruling Księżna tries to keep order, her presence only fans the flames.

### The Sabat Family

When Marcen Sabat ruled as Książę, he used martial law to keep the peace. Curfew came at sunset and soldiers patrolled in boats throughout the evening. His daughter, Estera, killed the curfew and ended the dreaded soldier patrols. Now she wonders if her father's measures were the only thing keeping the city from chaos.

Estera rules the city, nominally, but no one trusts her. Her father tried to kidnap the prince and Estera gave him away. Some cannot forgive Marcen for the kidnapping and some cannot forgive Estera's betrayal. Furthermore, Estera's reputation for theft has started to haunt her. To her father's friends, it proves her dishonor, while to her father's enemies, it proves she is just like her father.

### The Boat Drivers

The Boat Drivers started out as Vodacce-style gondoliers, punting passengers between houseboats and islands. Now, with bodies falling in the water, they have become Sperus' makeshift police.

Say you are a hunter. You want to burn some farmers' houses. You take a gondola to the farmers' island because that looks less suspicious than driving in your houseboat, and as you leave the gondola, you light a burning brand. You walk two steps only to find that gondoliers surround you now (or if you were subtle and lit up only once you neared a farmer's house, maybe a gondolier followed you). Thus far, the gondoliers have stopped only obvious crimes, but they are developing good instincts, getting better at knowing when to leave a boat to follow someone onto shore—and training themselves in sword use so they can bring saboteurs down.

### The Sunken City

In some parts of Sperus, houseboats sit tied to spires that jut just above the waterline. Sperus was once the site of a city built in folly from heavy stone on soggy ground. The city sank—that much is clear—and now only cupolas and minarets remain above the water, serving boaters as impromptu anchors. No one knows who built the city or when—the water has wiped out all signs of age—but the architecture styles suggest something Crescent, despite the fact that the Crescent Empire never successfully occupied Curonia for more than four years' time.

The curious agelessness of the city, combined with the fact that even the oldest Curonian records do not mention it, has led Scholomance scholars to speculate it might have been built by the ancestors of those who later founded the Crescent Empire as early as the Old Kingdom.

Nowadays, hunters and trappers rope their houseboats to the spires and tell the farmers the waterlogged ruins are haunted. A would-be explorer who dives deep, hoping to catch glimpses of the larger ruins, finds herself stymied by the muddy water. A few trappers have tried to map the city by swimming through it blindly, though the disorientation engendered thereby leads largely to injury—and useless maps.

# Sanderis

Much about Sanderis is unknown. The Ratas, the organization that governs all losejai, purposefully obscures information about their art from the wider world. Despite this, the people of Curonia are intimately familiar with the dievas, and the stories that go with them.

Mothers tell stories about dievai to scare unruly children, but the truth is darker than anyone thinks. The dievai are very real, and very powerful creatures. Rumors and legends do not do them justice, and only those who have seen their magic firsthand know how truly destructive they can be.

The biggest problem is that the dievai, though honest, always try to twist the words of losejas, making her simple request into something it wasn't before. This has led to various disasters and catastrophies all across the Sarmatian Commonwealth. The stories of these events, like the legend of Saulės Mūšis, get twisted and confused in their own right, probably due to the influence of the dievai themselves.

Many people believe these beings are simply wild, needing only a firm hand to get ultimate power. This leads people to do dangerous and often Villainous things in the name of taming them.

Unlike a sorcerer in another Nation, who must either earn her powers or be born with them, anyone in the Sarmatian Commonwealth has the ability to become a losejas. Anyone can be approached by a dievas, and simply accepting the Deal he offers gives one incredible powers. Someone who does make a Deal finds herself quickly under watchful eyes, ready to stike her down if she makes one mistake.

## The First Deal

Among the losejai there is but one unifying theme: each one of them has made a Deal with a dievas. While the individuals vary and the terms of the Deals are each unique, there is no way to learn the art of Sanderis without entering into such a contract.

These contracts come about in one of two ways: either a dievas attempts to convince someone to accept her Deal, or the potential losejas seeks out a dievas to attempt to gain her power. No matter how the Deal forms, it always represents what the Sarmatian desires most in the world. However, the cost is always high, commonly the death of a loved one or one under the protection of the Sarmatian. But it is not always something so dire. The dievai play the long game, and sometimes the cost of the first Deal seems almost comically small. "In two years time, a man named Piotr will come to you and ask you a question. You must answer him with "yes," is a Deal which may seem innocent enough at first look. However, two years later a man named Piotr could come to the losejas and demand to take his daughter with him as a bride. Only then would the true nature of the Deal come to light.

Most losejai are enticed into their contract by a dievas. Who is chosen and why is a mystery known only to the dievai. Sarmatians who would never consider making a Deal are targeted, while those who hunger and yearn for the power find themselves stymied and may never encounter a dievas. Most often, a targeted person does not even realize she is being enticed into forging a Deal until it is already too late. A dievas hides his true nature while growing close to his target. A dievas can appear in a human form if he so desires, and while he cannot physically interact with anything in our world, he can speak to his intended target.

A perceptive Sarmatian may realize that her new friend has never touched her arm, picked up a cup, conversed with anyone else in a busy room or suddenly vanished when she turned her back, but these signs are lost on many. Especially because some dievai are powerful enough to create the illusion of touch, even going so far as convincing a losejas that the two are lovers.

This pursuit can take place over a period of time, often days but sometimes weeks or even months. During this time the masked dievas gains the trust of his intended and learns of her deepest desires. To the Sarmatian, this new individual seems to be a new friend, a potential lover or a sudden ally. To the dievas, it is all just a game, a means of increasing the likelihood that his Deal will be accepted.

Once the dievas feels that he has his target enthralled, the dievas reveals his true form and offers his target a Deal. At this point many feel close to the dievas and so strongly want what he offers that only those with the strongest will refuse the offer.

While it is much less common for a Sarmatian to seek out a dievas than to have the Deal brought to her, it is possible to initiate a Deal yourself. Sarmatians tell many folk tales about the means one can use to summon a dievas. And while many are just that, some of the stories contain a bit of truth.

A legend from the hills of Curonia claims if one gathers specific items and buries them at a crossroads, a dievas appears willing to make a Deal. There is no guarantee that this will be successful. A Sarmatian could bury the needed items at a crossroads and have no dievas appear, and the next day another could bury the same items at the same crossroads and be approached. Only the dievai truly understand the choices they make. Once the dievas makes contact, the Sarmatian makes the request for what she wants and the dievas offers her a Deal.

Scholars in the Ratas wonder why so many more losejai have their Deals initiated by the dievai. The best theory that has been brought forward is that to the dievas, the act of enticing an unknowing target to accept a contract is more worthwhile. Being sought out by a potential losejas removes that aspect of the contract and is, in some twisted way, less fun for the dievas.

A single group in particular, the *žynys* (pronounced: JEE-NEES), or priests in Curonia, are much more likely to have contact with the dievai. These people act as spiritual guides for the people of Curonia, and make a point of understanding the pomp and ritual surrounding the dievai. This devotion seems to attract the dievai, though the reason is unknown. Some believe the dievai mistake the scholarship as worship and enjoy the attention.

## The Ratas

While a sorcerer from another Nation may be aligned to a number of different factions, or even act completely on her own, a Sanderis user belongs to a larger organization, even if he does not know it. The Ratas governs each and every losejas beginning the moment he makes his first Deal. A new losejas finds himself approached by members of the Ratas within days of making his contract and gets informed of his new allegiance to the organization. Ratas members make it exceptionally clear to the new losejas that he has only two options. He can either join the Circle or be eliminated. He gets no time to contemplate his answer. If he does not immediately agree, then the Ratas agents attack without remorse and do everything within their power to obliterate the losejas.

Upon joining the Ratas, each member selects a new name to be referred to by other losejai. This is a holdover from the earliest days of the Ratas. Even then losejai knew that they empowered their Deals by knowing the true Name of their dievai. Those first members believed that all names had power and did not trust their peers with their own names. Over the decades this has proven to be false. However, the tradition still stands amongst the Ratas today, though the organization has no formal rules for this chosen name. Often the losejas takes the name of an animal, such as Sokół, the Falcon, or a title from before she accepted the Deal, such as Kowal, the Blacksmith. While a losejas is free to use her own name in any other aspect of her life, amongst all interactions with other losejai, from formal meetings to encountering another member at a tavern, she uses her chosen name exclusively in communication. To use the birth name of another losejas is an extreme taboo.

# RATAS FACTIONS

To those outside the Ratas, it appears that the losejai form a unified front. However, this is far from the truth. Within the Circle, a number of factions, while loyal to the overall organization, have no love lost between each other. A member of the Listeners, who gather secrets from around Théah, has no reason to support a member of the Circle of Storms, a militant faction wanting to see the overall power of the Ratas grow. Infighting is common, and this stops any one faction from becoming too strong within the Circle.

It is unlikely that any within the Ratas know of every faction, but other major powers include the Red Eyes, who want to reduce Ratas oversight on the use of Sanderis Deals, the Order of the Question, who seek a way to remove dievai from Terra completely and the Puppet Masters, who seek to gain control of the dievai and use them to their own ends.

Heroes with Sanderis may choose to become a member of any—or none—of these factions in game. Treat these factions like additional Secret Societies the Hero can be a member of, though keep in mind that the goals of the Ratas may come into conflict with the goals of the Secret Society, and she must manage them both. A player should work with her Game Master to define the Ratas faction she wishes to be a part of.

Membership in the Ratas is not limited by age or experience. Upon joining the Circle, a losejas is a full member, a *Członek*, with all the rights given by the organization. There is no shame in remaining at this level and the majority of all Ratas members do not change their rank over their entire lives. Some do chose to dedicate more of their lives towards the Ratas. With time and dedication, one can advance to the *Rada*, the Inner Council. Those who join the Council make the decisions of the Ratas. Additionally, it is possible to join the Valytuvas who enforce the judgment of the Circle.

Beyond that, the Mistrz is the leader of the Ratas. The current Mistrz, a woman called Wiedźma, the Witch, has been the master of the Circle for as long as anyone can remember. The eldest members of the Ratas recall Wiedźma being firmly entrenched in her role when they first joined. Additionally, she still appears as young and beautiful as she was decades ago. Many believe this to be due to her Deal, although no one knows the specifics.

## The Valytuvas

In one of its most important roles, the Ratas monitors the actions of the losejai. Each member of the organization, even the newest members with only a single Deal, are capable of incredible destruction. Because of this, the Circle must police its own to ensure that no ill will comes toward its members. However, the Ratas follows unusual ethics. Evil acts, even the most monstrous of murders, are beyond the purview of the Circle if done through conventional means. As long as the losejas does not use Sanderis, a member can kill indiscriminately and see no punishment from the Ratas.

The Ratas generally overlooks small uses of power. The repercussions of these acts are small enough that little concern is paid to them. However, they fully investigate large acts. If the Ratas finds a losejas has invoked her Deal for more than a minor act, it dispatches the Valytuvas to determine what caused the losejas to act. Depending on the severity of the use of power, the Valytuvas may take a statement or, in the case of more drastic actions, require that the losejas return to the Ratas to stand before the Mistrz. In the most extreme cases, such as using Sanderis to kill without cause, the penalty is death. They may levy other punishments for lesser crimes, but the Mistrz issues the final verdict. No member of the Ratas would act against her judgment.

How the Ratas determines when a losejas uses her powers improperly remains a mystery to the rest of the losejai. While at times it may be obvious, as there are only so many ways that an entire city can be plunged into complete darkness at a whim, other uses of Sanderis are more subtle. That the Ratas still finds out about these subtle misuses has led many members to believe that they make Deals to unearth this information.

When a losejas has been found to have fully given in to the evil nature of his dievas, the Valytuvas dispatch in a different role altogether. In this role, they truly embody their title, Purifier, and seek out the rogue losejas to stop him before he can cause too much harm.

Once the Valytuvas find their target, they give him a single opportunity to repent. If rejected, then they use their full might to kill the losejas. Because a losejas with no conscience can, and will, use the full might of his Deal, the Ratas gives the Valytuvas a special permission: they may use Sanderis as they wish with no fear of investigation. This does open the concern that a member of the Valytuvas may abuse her power and use her sorcery outside of her mission. The Ratas claims to have safeguards in place to keep this from happening; but when members ask for specifics, the Ratas gives no answer.

## Joining the Valytuvas

Joining the Valytuvas is more complex than advancing in rank to join the Narada. The first step in joining the Valytuvas is to seek out a mentor already a member of the Purifiers. In order to convince the veteran to take you on as an apprentice, you must demonstrate your worth.

Each mentor sends the new recruit out to complete a specific task. A formality in some ways, the mentor is the sole determiner of what quest he requires to prove yourself. A losejas who already has a good relationship with the Valytuvas may be sent down to the library to retrieve a book while another Valytuvas may send a less trusted recruit on a mission to retrieve a Syrneth artifact.

Once the losejas completes the task to the Purifier's satisfaction, the recruit becomes a full apprentice. As an apprentice, the losejas shadows the Valytuvas. During this time, the apprentice receives training in combat, stealth, tracking, research and investigation as well as the role Sanderis can play in each of these areas.

While a Purifier needs these skills to complete her duties, this also allows the mentor to determine if an apprentice should have the freedom to use Sanderis at will without repercussion. If a Valytuvas member abused that power, it would blow back on the mentor just as much as the rogue Purifier.

Once a mentor determines that an apprentice should join the ranks of the Valytuvas, she is sent to one final test with the Mistrz. This test takes place in the Wymagnine, a specific hall in the Ratas headquarters only accessible to the Mistrz, for the sole purpose of testing new Purifiers. The apprentice enters the room, empty except for the Mistrz and an archway that the recruit must walk through.

The consensus amongst the Purifiers is that when walking through the archway, you face your greatest fear in your mind. Those able to face it walk through the archway successfully and join the ranks of the Valytuvas. A recruit who cannot face her fears backs out of the archway and the mentor dismisses her from her duties as an apprentice. There is no action taken against those who fail the final test, and a losejas who fails may go back to her previous duties as though nothing changed, but she may never again attempt to join the Purifiers.

No one knows if the archway really conjures a threat into the mind of those who walk through it, but the thought of facing your fears is enough to cause many potential students to back away without ever going through. Those who do refuse to speak of what happened to them.

## The Seventh Deal

Every member of the Ratas has a theory about what occurs when a losejas makes the Seventh Deal with his dievas. Some are fantastic, others benign, but there is only one truth. The truth is in many ways darker than many of the theories and involves more sacrifice on behalf of the losejas than any of his previous Deals.

Once a losejas makes the Seventh Deal, the dievas is able to leave its world and fully enter ours. It enters the physical world fully embodied and with none of the rules that it was forced to follow when interacting with the losejas.

Before this point, it could only act indirectly. The dievas could ask for a losejas to act according to its goals as a cost of a Deal, but it could not physically interact with anything in our world. This is not the case once the Seventh Deal is made.

Once the losejas accepts the final contract, after the dievas gives whatever boon the losejas requested, the dievas with its full and complete power physically and

# SEVENTH DEAL STORIES

Because of the sacrifices a Hero accepts when taking the Seventh Deal, this type of story is not for everyone. Taking the Seventh Deal not only removes a significant amount of character advancement by removing all Sorcery Advantages taken, but the narrative cost is high as well. Most players elect to have their Heroes reach six Deals and stay there without taking the Sorcery Advantage again.

A Seventh Deal Story can be a good choice to end a campaign. Once an overarching story has come to a place with the end in sight, it may be worth a Hero taking Sorcery for the seventh time to make her final Deal. Players should be fully aware of and accepting of the repercussions of their Heroes making the Seventh Deal.

## The Reaping

While the sacrifice made by the losejas is significant, and often times debilitating, making the Seventh Deal does grant her some benefits. She gains the following abilities:

+ She may spend a Hero Point to learn the current location of her dievas by knowing how far away it is, and in what direction.
+ She may spend a Hero Point to negate a single Monstrous Quality her dievas posesses for the remainder of the Round. This may be done once per Round.
+ When directly interacting with her dievas, she gains Bonus Dice to all rolls equal to her Ranks in Resolve.
+ She does not have to spend a Hero Point to take Actions against her dievas when she is Helpless. The dievas may still attempt to murder her, but she has enough strength to keep fighting until the very last.

permanently manifests. At this time, the previous Deals are forfeit. The losejas is no longer empowered with Sanderis.

This is not the only cost to the losejas. The terms of the Seventh Deal always include a sacrifice, but not a physical sacrifice. A dievas would not simply ask that the losejas cut off her own hand. The sacrifice is always something more. Something deeper.

To make the Seventh Deal, the losejas must sacrifice a part of her soul. What and how varies and each dievas may ask for something different. One may ask that the losejas give up her joy, while another may ask for him to sacrifice his dreams.

These sacrifices are not metaphorical. If the losejas gives up her joy, she literally gives up her ability to feel joy. That aspect of her vanishes—permanently. The dievas uses that sacrifice to become corporeal and enter the world.

While a dievas is undeniably empowered upon entering the physical world, he receives one significant weakness. Here, a dievas can be killed. This death is permanent and only possible when it is corporeal. Any action taken against a dievas in its own world is laughably ineffective; however, in the physical realm, a dievas bleeds when cut with a blade.

When a dievas dies in our world, it completely and irrevocably dies. The dievas cannot cheat its way out of this death. As long as someone deals the final Dramatic Wound to a dievas with the conscious decision to kill it, the dievas dies.

Regardless of the circumstances surrounding this encounter, a Hero receives no Corruption for killing a dievas. This is not to say that the circumstances themselves could not give Corruption. Simply, the act of killing the dievas never gives a Hero Corruption.

Once a dievas dies, the aspect that the losejas sacrificed to provide form to the being dies as well. In the case of the losejas who sacrificed her joy to make the Seventh Deal, she literally kills her own joy when the dievas dies. The Hero must live with this sacrifice for the remainder of her days. Knowing that the sacrifice helped kill something truly and completely evil makes this easier to accept, but it is still one of the most difficult choices anyone in Théah can make.

# Dueling in the Sarmatian Commonwealth

The declaration of Golden Liberty granted all subjects of the Sarmatian Commonwealth nobility. Farmers, brewers, freeholders, carpenters, all those who toiled the land now obtained a direct voice in the future of the Commonwealth. Nobility also granted the power to create knighthoods and Chivalric Orders. Sarmatianism spread like wildfire throughout the Commonwealth.

Men and women have always gathered to discuss local politics. Prior to Golden Liberty, their voices often went unheard. *Voivodes* previously handled threats to the community. Now the new noblemen and women have an investment in the betterment of their communities. Every village has a community center, whether it resides in the basement of the local Church or at the long tables of the Beerhall. Locals discussed matters and hashed out ideas and concepts before presenting them to the Senat.

Disagreements obviously arose since communities competed for limited resources. Sarmatians are a proud and passionate people. This passion leads to challenges settled by the clash of steel. In order to maintain civility, they looked to the writings of Lech Kościuszko. A twelfth century Rzeczpospolitan philosopher, Kościuszko's writings centered on Chivalry and Civil Discourse. The popularity of these concepts spread across the Commonwealth. Book printers ran easily accessible pamphlet-sized booklets. Soon, the newly appointed nobility referenced the various works and quoted the pamphlets from memory. This gave direction to the new nobles. They could abide by the codes written and be the Heroes and defenders they wished to be. With the feudal reign over, and the abuses of noble lords in the past, the commoner could espouse Chivalry and ensure the new nobility remain noble.

Chivalric Orders began to appear. These groups of like-minded idealists served as examples of virtue to their comrades. Orders could be founded on the basic tenets of Chivalry, religious ideals or vows to local defense and prosperity. Banding together also allowed a member to hone his swordcraft without reprisal from nobility looking down on the armed peasants.

The following tenets, set forth by Kościuszko in the book *Unanimity in Throes of Discord*, are generally accepted as the Core foundations of Chivalry:

+ Thou shalt respect all weaknesses, and shalt constitute thyself the defender of them.
+ Thou shalt love the country in which thou wast born.
+ Thou shalt not recoil before thine enemy.
+ Thou shalt make war against the wicked without cessation and without mercy.
+ Thou shalt perform scrupulously thy duties, if they be not contrary to the laws of Theus.
+ Thou shalt never lie, and shalt remain faithful to thy pledged word.
+ Thou shalt be generous, and give largesse to everyone.
+ Thou shalt be the champion of the Right and the Good against Injustice and Evil.

Through the tenets of Chivalry, Sarmatians have welcomed dueling as a civilized manner of settling disputes, seeing duels as tests of skill and will. A Chivalrous Sarmatian offers mercy and also accepts the mercy of a better opponent. Duels are rarely to the death since each Sarmatian needs to stand next to each other against the rest of the world. In this way, Sarmatism promotes a sense of solidarity amongst the populace.

Sarmatian Duelists tend to formality when proposing a duel as well as accepting. Chivalry demands respect. Someone that shows disrespect learns the error of his ways—often painfully.

An aspiring Duelist ventures to Budorigum to test her mettle. The capital is rife with conflict, and participants in the Senat almost always need champions. Young new nobles, sword upon hip, are eager to achieve fame and notoriety. Chivalric Orders rise and fall like waves in a storm. Powerful citizens bestow badges of honor and knighthoods and trade titles as currency in a market not yet realized.

## Rightful Order of the Cherry Blossom

One such Chivalric Order is the Rightful Order of the Cherry Blossom. A small farming community named Kwiat Wiśni rests along one of the northern branches of the Zūpan River. Three local men founded the Rightful Order of the Cherry Blossom in honor of the local Cherry Blossom blooming festival. Tomas Petrikonis, Jan Kamionka and Luigi Paglianite joined forces and vowed to protect their community.

Luigi Paglianite, ethnically Vodacce, was born and raised in the Sarmatian Commonwealth. His family breeds a toy dog breed named Pom-pons. These dogs have become popular with the social elite in both the Commonwealth as well as Montaigne. Jan Kamionka is a charismatic barkeep. Small in stature but immense in bravery with a sharp tongue, Jan can unnerve the most stalwart of stoic. Tomasz Petrikonis is a proud Curonian with a knack for leadership. He maintains an even temperament, though Jan often-times lights a fire in Tomasz's demeanor.

Luigi's prosperity with his kennels has allowed the construction of a meeting hall for the Order available to all members to train and study. The Rightful Order of the Cherry Blossom see to the defense of the Kwiat Wiśni both locally as well as in the Senat. All members of the Rightful Order of the Cherry Blossom are skilled Duelists. Tomasz and Luigi practice the Sabat style, while Jan learned Valroux as a youth when studying wine in Montaigne.

## Szybowanie

From high upon horseback, a fabled winged hussar is a fearsome foe. He bears his lance upon his enemies during terrifying charges. His armor can strike fear in any opponent, and he cares for his horse as a fellow warrior. The bond between a hussar and his steed is unbreakable.

A particularly insightful hussar named Kyra Mikita realized that not all situations allowed for equine superiority. She developed the Szybowanie fighting style. The weapon in hand does not matter but instead the style focuses on establishing advantage in the battlefield. The style, based on fighting from any height advantage, not only horseback, delivers when possible a mighty blow named the Eagle's Dive. Szybowanie practitioners constantly maneuver around the battlefield for the most advantageous position.

### Style Bonus: Eagle's Dive

When you fight from any advantageous height (not only horseback), you gain a special Maneuver called Eagle's Dive. You leap down upon your opponent delivering a very powerful blow. Eagle's Dive deals a number of Wounds equal to your Ranks in Weaponry + your Ranks in Ride. A Duelist must spend 1 Hero Point and may only perform Eagle's Dive once per Round.

# Legendy of the Sarmatian Commonwealth

Often, immigrants from Ussura or Eisen remark with relief that (besides the dievai) there are not many monsters in the Commonwealth. And indeed, most of the country's apex predators are not unnatural—but as the cynical Curonians say, wolves and bears still kill when hungry, and humans kill for no reason at all.

In Voruta, the Scholomance works to identify dievai. Thus far they have classified 812 of who-knows-how-many dievai—classified by name-known-under, by basic (though often changing) appearance, by motif, by known Deals and by modus operandi.

Of the 812 thus classified, the listed three deemed by the Scholomance most dangerous have never been contacted and dealt with without eventually turning their losejai into a Villain. At this point, the Ratas officially recommends killing any who bargain with these three on sight.

## Saulė, the Burning Sun

No one has seen Saulė since the days of the last King Petras, but she still gets the top spot on the list of most dangerous dievai. The Villains she creates are those whose passions blaze without restraint; her losejai start intemperate and become ever more impulsive under her influence. In her long lifetime, she has started wars, sparked love affairs that ended kingdoms, burned cities (including Saulės Mūšis)—in sheer straightforward destructive power, Scholomance scholars say she is unrivaled. For all that, though, she disappeared once Saulės Mūšis burned; no one has made a Deal with her in centuries. Of course, she could still be making Deals, but under a different guise—though Scholomance study indicates it would be difficult for her to completely change her motifs.

Theories abound as to where she is now. The most popular theory, albeit the one most vehemently denied by the Ratas, states that she made the Seventh Deal with Petras before burning Saulės Mūšis and now walks the world in a physical body, unfettered. Many who believe this also believe that Saulė and the Sanderas pyre-maker Gabija the Red are one in the same; this despite the Ratas' insistence that Gabija is not a dievas at all. The dievai, when asked, sometimes say this is the case: they furthermore say that Saulė (or Gabija) constructs the pyres in order to atone for her sins. Most losejai, even those who distrust the Ratas, consider that last part unlikely—after all, who has ever heard of a remorseful dievas?

Another theory has it that after the Saulės Mūšis' fall, Saulė (acting bodily or otherwise) stayed in the city. The theory has been gaining ground ever since a Scholomance scholar posited that the strange fruit in the city's remains were her doing, since Growth was one of her known Deals. If so, she has been acting as both the city's benefactor and terror—for who but she could be responsible for the citizens' screaming disappearances?

## What's Known

Saulė most often appears as a beautiful woman surrounded by a blazing, sun-like corona.

Saulė tends to stalk an impulsive would-be losejas, making Deals with her, then wearing down her temperance. The Villains she creates are destructive and self-indulgent; she is known for taking her losejai as lovers and is the only dievas Scholomance scholars strongly suspect has survived making the Seventh Deal.

## Laima, the Child-Catcher

Growing older is a terrible thing, for once you grow older, you must never climb trees. Once you grow older, you must do more chores; you have less time to play, and sooner or later your parents start speaking of marriage. Some very clever children have seen this and decided they wish to never grow up; these clever children make Deals with Laima the Child-Catcher.

Laima's children never grow a day older or a mote wiser: they remain always foolish and amoral, rambunctious and careless as children are, tiny predators with tiny white milk teeth that never fall out no matter how many sweets they eat. They say she lives in the Sanderas Forest, in a cottage built of gingerbread and icing: she helps any losejas who comes across her, so long as he tells her something about a child. Many refuse to.

Laima's children are a constant source of controversy amongst the Ratas. Those who take her Deals are legitimately dangerous: a child's moral naïveté and utter lack of self-restraint combines poorly with Laima's unpredictable sorcery. A child is ill-equipped to undergo Katabasis, which means once she makes a deal, she likely grows ever more insane and dangerous.

But the obvious alternative is likewise fraught: many Ratas are unwilling to simply kill those children. The last little girl who lived with Laima died in the Sanderas Forest four years ago: since then, fear has gripped the hearts of Curonian parents as they wonder if Laima will choose their child next.

## What's Known

Laima most often appears as a very old lady with mossy teeth and mossy hair.

Scholomance Scholars call Laima's only known Deal the "Deal of Time," though they have yet to find another dievas who offers anything comparable. Laima's children may manipulate time: most notably, they do not age.

Laima appears to a child who insists he won't grow up—though how she finds him, no one really knows. Under her influence, her charge loses whatever grasp he had on maturity, quickly becoming an amoral creature, self-indulgent and vicious. Though he stops aging under her care, Lamia's losejas often die quickly; a powerful child is almost always poorly equipped for self-preservation.

## Perkunas, the Righteous Storm

They say the first losejas who summoned Perkunas mourned the fall of Saulės Mūšis; horrified by the fruits of Sanderis, he summoned Perkunas to rid the country of all losejai, starting with the nascent Ratas and ending with himself. For ten years, they say, he led the Fallen Inquisition, and brought the losejai near extinction before he died by his sister, an experienced Sanderis practitioner who, once she had killed him, summoned Perkunas herself.

As he had been determined to rid the land of losejai, so she was determined to rid Curonia of all Vaticine oppression—and so she started her own twenty-year reign of terror, taking down entire towns she accused of "collaborating" with the Vaticine, until, two decades

in, no Church stood in Curonia. Only when she turned on her subordinates (at this point lacking other enemies), accusing them of pro-Vaticine sympathies, did she finally see defeat.

Those who summon Perkunas always wish to purge the world of evil—and Perkunas seems to want that as well, with all the times he has left the Sanderas looking for losejai. Often, whatever evil Perkunas and the losejai see, they succeed in completely eliminating. Most famously, the ethnic Khodynts, who used to live in Northern Curonia, suffered extinction by one of Perkunas' losejas.

Less famous, but perhaps more insidious, are all the *ideas* that have been eliminated by Perkunas. One losejas claimed that Perkunas had eliminated the concept of his family, completely eliminating them from his life because they were a distraction. The Scholomance scholars who recorded it found an entire book on Perkunas, but swore they had never seen the book before. No one seems to know where that book is now.

## What's Known

Perkunas most often appears as bearded man with his face in shadow, dressed in black and white and riding a fiery steed. Unlike most dievai, who wander weaponless, he always wears the traditional Sarmatian cavalry saber.

Perkunas does not approach people with Deals; he must be summoned from the Sanderas forest. You would think that meant fewer people summoning him, but there is always some chump who thinks the current evil he fights is worse than all the other evils that have ever existed in history, and therefore justifies his extreme tactics (like summoning Perkunas).

Perkunas, clever devil that he is, never asks his sorcerers to do anything that might break *their* moral code; the terrible things he asks his losejai to do as favors always directly devastate only those who somehow, in some way, embody the evil the losejai want to destroy. (If it is not obvious how they embody that evil, Perkunas is always happy to tell). In doing so, he further radicalizes his sorcerers; after all (as the Numanari philosopher Publius once said) it is human nature to hate those whom you have hurt.

## The Silver Knights

Sometimes, when all seems hopeless, when fires burn and Villains triumph in the Commonwealth, suddenly a Knight appears.

The Knights always wear old-fashioned armor, like something out of the twelfth century, and their conduct, even in dark forests and dank slums, is impeccably chivalrous. They save children and fight Villains and appear always in full plate; they never speak or raise their helms to show their faces. Many believe the Knights act as the *genius loci* of the Commonwealth itself. They wander all parts of the Nation now, and always act alone, but the žynys say that if the Commonwealth is ever truly threatened, the Silver Knights will gather and fight the threat as one force, and on that day, they will speak again.

### What's True

When the organization that eventually became known as die Kreuzritter marched from Eisen determined to find demons in the east, they joined a detachment of mixed Rzeplitan and Curonian Knights who sought the birthplace of the dievai, called the Silver Knights. During the trek through the Crescent Empire, the leader of the Silver Knights, a woman called Anna, had a series of dreams that led her to believe the birthplace of the dievai was "in a garden, in a mountain" to the west of their current location. She and her Knights split from the bulk of the Eisen forces, marched into Ashur and plundered the First Garden. In doing so, they became immortal, but also lost their voices.

Only then did they discover the Garden had a Guardian.

The other Knights, upon seeing the Guardian, drew their swords, but Anna had always been wise, so she knelt at his feet instead. Writing in the dust, she begged the Guardian for his mercy, explaining that they were foreigners who had come hoping to find the birthplace of demons but now had transgressed by plundering the Garden.

The Guardian acknowledged that they had transgressed terribly, but agreed to let them go, so long as they went home and never left the soils of their home countries again. When they reached the border where the Crescent Empire, Rzeczpospolita and Curonia all touched, they silently swore to become eternal protectors of their homelands.

## Toasting with Water

Legend says that a losejas can only raise toasts with alcohol. Water toasts are strictly forbidden. If she does raise a glass of water, her dievas gains a foothold and learns all her dark secrets, allowing him to corrupt her. This does not cause too many problems, since most Sarmatians prefer hard liquors and wines over water.

In rural areas, where liquor is hard to come by, a losejas may find herself in a bit of a bind. The rumors say that if you force a toast with water, you can spot losejai in the crowd by who refuses to drink, or even raise their glass. Those who do not wish to anger the powerful people always have some kind of alcohol on hand to offer instead of water when toasting may be in order.

### What's True

A losejas can raise a toast with water, and the origin of the legend is rather sad. In rural Curonian villages, people suspected of being losejai are frequently ostracized, especially when their Deals are not approved by the local žynys. Such was the case of Motina, who made a fortune in her tiny village trading in herbal medicines. A jealous žynys accused her of being a dangerous losejas.

Not an actual losejas, Motina was also not above lying, so to win back her community's trust, she spread the rumor about the water—then raised a toast with a water glass on the žynys' birthday. The žynys, a losejas himself, did not think the local water safe, so he filled his cup with wine before drinking, thus inadvertently confirming the rumor.

It has been a couple of centuries since then, and the tale obtained a life of its own. Nowadays many losejai believe they tempt fate by toasting with water, a supposition dievai find highly amusing and do not bother correcting. Some losejai even travel through unfriendly lands with drops of mead hidden in hollow rings or secreted inside their sleeves. When found (as they often are), the rumor gains more currency.

To make matters worse, in many rural towns, the water *isn't* safe to drink. A traveler from those towns calls down suspicion on himself by refusing to drink water elsewhere. Finally, Rzeczpospolita has protocols governing when it is and is not meet to raise a glass to *any* toast. A Rzeplitan trying for honor often encounters suspicion when, for example, she fails to raise to a stance she disagrees with.

## The Hanging Tree

Once upon a time, so the story goes, a young man saw all his comrades killed in war. When he came home, he couldn't stand the burden of surviving when everyone he knew was dead. In a moment of pure despair, he decided to kill himself.

He wrapped his belt around the nearest oak tree and made to hang himself. As he dangled in the air, choking for breath, dying, his life came into full clarity. His comrades were dead and gone, yes, but he still had his life ahead of him.

In the span of a few seconds, but what felt to him like long minutes, each of the fallen soldiers came to him on the tree, and told him a final wish, what they needed him to do for them before he could die. As they did so, they put a little cut in the belt. Once the last one was finished, and when he realized that he had no real desire to die, the belt suddenly broke under his weight, and he fell to the ground. He broke both his legs, but he lived.

When the man lay dying many decades later, he asked his family to bury him beneath the same tree. Afterwards people said that if someone wished to end her life, she should first wrap her belt around one of the trees' branches and leave it there for a week and by the week's end, legend said she would no longer feel the urge to die. So that oak came to be the Hanging Tree, and every year hundreds of women and men wrap their belts around the branches and beg the ghost of that long-ago man to free them from the urge to end their lives.

## What's True

Several "Hanging Trees" exist in the Commonwealth, each claiming to be the original. All are strung with belts and hose, and all have partisans (including many formerly suicidal) swearing to their effectiveness.

Explanations proffered include that the soldier haunts them all, that each was the site of a suicide (unsuccessful or otherwise) or (the theory newly offered by Castillian researcher Iratze Eneko) that the trees, along with the stories, act as a *placebo* to the suicidal. Since the placebo effect is not much understood yet, this last theory remains controversial, with many sending Eneko hate mail regarding her attempts to "ruin" the sacred trees.

Regardless of which is the original or just a copy, the trees are all afforded a great deal of respect, and anyone seen tying a belt or visiting the tree is likely to gain a lot of sympathetic attention.

Some tend to the trees, bringing fresh water and fertilizer to those places where a tree looks to be in need. These people also keep an eye out for would-be suicides, offering them comfort and solace. Many say that just having others around to listen to and try to comfort them is enough to stop any thoughts of death.

## Rusałka Week

They say in the last days of Numanari rule, a sinister mystery cult controlled Szablewo. Every year, seven weeks after the spring solstice, they ritually drowned seven boys and seven maidens over seven days to call a thunderstorm to cleanse the city on the eighth. They terrorized the town, taking the children of political adversaries and any who would question their rule.

Seven years into their rule, the mystery cult made a mistake: they drowned a sorcerer's sister. The sorcerer was a powerful necromancer, and she tried to revive her sister, but the cultists stopped her before she could finish, leaving her poor sister as an undead wretch, a rusałka.

In an act of vengeance against the cultists, the sorcerer, so the story goes, cast a spell that raised all the spirits of the sacrifice victims as rusałka. Seven weeks after the spring solstice, for the seven days of sacrifice, these invisible spirits came into Szablewo and stole the breath of all who lived in and around city.

Many people died to the rusałka, until the people revolted and overthrew the mystery cult. When the rusałka were to come again, the people put on white masks, to show their mourning for the dead. The rusałka were appeased by the gesture, and angry at any who did not display it. Those who did not put on the masks died by loss of breath.

Thus the citizens of Szablewo learned to don masks for the seven days of sacrifice seven weeks after the spring solstice, and even today, no one may enter Szablewo or the surrounding area for those seven days without a nose-and-mouth-covering mask.

While an entire festival has grown up around what is called "Rusałka Week" the locals warn that the danger of not wearing a proper mask is very real. The rusałka are insidious and will find any who try to get by without one. Even in the home, and while sleeping, people must wear their masks, or risk drowning to a rusałka attack.

## What's True

In Szablewo, for seven days, seven weeks after the spring solstice, everyone wears nose-and-mouth-covering masks. Laws in the city and surrounding areas prohibit appearing in public unmasked, and for good reason: seeing breath stolen is terrifying. The rusałka victim gasps and then begins to drown with no water near. Sometimes bringing the victim indoors or giving him a mask dislodges the rusałka, but in most cases, nothing can be done. However, rusalki are native to Ussura and do not travel. One can rarely find them further south than the Boyars River. So it is not water spirits that plague the townspeople.

Plowman's Lace is a small flowering plant that grows only in and around Szablewo. For seven days, seven weeks after the spring solstice, it releases very poisonous pollen. Breathing in enough of the pollen causes the bronchial tubes to clench shut, leaving the breather drowning, surrounded by air.

A sinister Numanari mystery cult once ruled Szablewo, but their sacrifices have nothing to do with the flowering plant. The story came about after an explorer came up from the Crystal Caves, claiming she found great mosaics explaining the story of the sorcerer. What had been a complete mystery now seemed to have some kind of explanation, and the people accepted it.

And it seems likely Szablewo's citizens would not be entirely well-served by learning of the rusałka's true origins. Over the centuries, Rusałka Week has become a cultural institution, a festival of masks in the Vodacce style, filled with the sort of sins usually frowned upon in the University City. During Rusałka Week, masked citizens gamble, have anonymous sex and drink to excess.

People compete throughout the rest of the year to make the most beautiful, elaborate masks for Rusałka Week, where they show them and trade them (in many parts of the city it is considered déclassé not to have a new mask each day). The weekly carnival provides a chance for the usually uptight citizens of Szablewo to let loose, and perhaps it would be a little cruel to deprive them of the excuse.

Chapter 3

Ussura

# USSURA

*"Where you see a frozen river, I see a bridge. Where
you see a blizzard, I see cover from bombardment.
Where you see a forest of monsters, I see scouts and
allies. The same things which lead you to disdain
us make us strong enough to overcome you."*
—General Winter

Once upon a time, in a faraway ice-and-snow-covered
land called Ussura, there lived a mighty Czar who had
a husband and two sons borne by his best friend. His
husband and elder son died, he disowned his younger
son, and he married a clever young woman in hopes
of getting a proper heir.

But before that could happen, he died mysteriously;
both his younger son and his new bride claimed the
throne. The son wanted to reign from the old capital
and keep to the old ways; the bride erected a new
capital, gleaming and modern, and sought to make
everything in Ussura as contemporary and new as
what she had built.

No one in Ussura knows for sure what will happen.
Not the boyar in his castle, nor the priest in her
church, nor the rider on the steppes, nor the merchant
from the east or south, nor the nomad who wanders
the country, nor the muzhik in her shack nor the
spirit in the forest or the river.

But the contestants for the Czar's throne will have
to bring together all those people to rule unopposed—
and that is what they have set out to do: to see the
people of Ussura set up before them like dolls in a
house…or chess pieces on a board, as it were. Ussura
is a house divided, old versus new, but otherwise poised
to go to a capable set of hands, if only one could take it.

# A Nation Built on Class

You can usually tell an Ussuran's social class from her appearance, especially her hair color. Boyars have light-colored hair and beards, usually blond; whereas muzhiks have dark hair, as well as darker skin from the sun or from Cathayan ancestry. Different regions and families may have different attitudes towards boyars fraternizing with commoners. Rare as it may be, no one will string you up for being a boyar with dark skin and hair, a commoner with light skin and hair, a dark-haired person marrying a light-haired person, etc.

That said, many Ussurans make assumptions about someone else's class, wealth and education based on her coloring. Moreover, the fact that the upper classes have more western Théan ancestry and the lower classes have more indigenous and Cathayan ancestry is not lost on anyone, especially in the current political climate dividing the country on class and visual lines.

The boyars' favorite, Ketheryna Fischler Dimitritova, ethnically Eisen, looks the part, with strawberry blonde hair and light blue eyes; whereas the lower classes' favorite, Ilya Sladivgorod Nikolovich, has his Crescent surrogate mother's dark eyes and hair. Many muzhiks suspect Ketheryna's push to modernize the country and advance its technology only further divides the classes.

A typical Ussuran has a somewhat mixed heritage regardless of what he may tell you about how his pureblood family comes from west Théans, Khazari nomads or Crescents. This is less true with a boyar, who selects with more discrimination her family's marriages and lineages, but even the noble families tend to have at least one Khazari or Crescent leader somewhere in their family tree.

## Ethnic Groups in Ussura

People living in Ussura range from Théan descent, Crescent descent, and those native to the land, born in the steppes.

Though centuries of intermarrying has made Ussura less divided along physical boundary lines, the cultures of these various people continue to influence Ussura to this day. Architecture, education, food and even customs and stories can all point back to these major ethnic groups within Ussura.

## Khazari

The nomadic horse riders and herders who occupy Molhynia's eastern and northeastern steppes migrated west across the Szabla River to escape Cathayan imperial expansion. They settled among eastern Ussura's indigenous peoples. Their steppe horsemanship tradition has influenced all Ussura and is one reason an Ussuran does not worry that her Nation has few modern roads. The old horse trails remain as reliable as ever, especially in winter when crossing frozen rivers is easy. If foreigners can't figure that out, that is an invasion Ussura need not worry about.

A Khazar happily identifies as Ussuran, but his tribal identity is also extremely important. He has a long tradition of raiding neighboring tribes and killing to steal livestock, but no Khazar takes it personally—it is just something you do. He has had less success convincing other ethnicities to accept his "no hard feelings" attitude towards robbery and violence. He also loves travel, working with other Khazari as mercenaries, bodyguard or musician elsewhere in Théah, the Crescent Empire or Cathay during young adulthood before returning to the steppes with money, scars and stories. Outside Ussura, these mounted mercenaries are commonly called "Cossacks," an old corruption of the word "Khazar."

Khazari are also notorious for their habit of collecting religions. The oldest Khazar religion, Turăism, worships the ancient sky god Tură. Nowadays many Khazari are Orthodox, Madhyamika, Yachidi, Vaticine, Dīnist or various combinations of the foregoing. Missionaries find converting Khazari easy, but convincing them to drop previously held beliefs impossible. Khazari abhor the concept of killing another human over a religious dispute (as opposed to because you covet her horse or her grazing land, both perfectly reasonable).

## Crescents

Crescents in Ussura, though a minority, dominate the markets. For as long as there has been trade, they have come to Ussura to exchange Crescent goods, medicine and resources for Ussura's riches: furs, metal ores and agricultural products such as wheat, livestock and dairy.

Ussura responded to early missionary work in the Second Prophet's wake with a widespread "thanks, but we're fine with what we have." Yachidis and Dīnists have nevertheless spread through southern Ussura thanks to wide-ranging Crescent traders. Dīnist congregations often worship in the same building as Orthodox assemblies without conflict. After all, Ussura has no Orthodox or Dīnist Inquisition. Crescent influence appears in Ussuran architecture, particularly government and religious buildings; no one knows where Ussuran churches' famous onion domes originated, but some historians point to Dīnist minarets as a possible antecedent.

Crescents in Ussura represent a powerful financial force, attracting both Ilya's and Ketheryna's attentions. Ilya is technically and ethnically half Crescent: he wasn't raised in Crescent culture, but he has spent a good deal of time in Crescent enclaves throughout southern Ussura and maintains good relationships with prominent Crescent merchants, entrepreneurs and investors. Ketheryna, who built about half her entire new capital full of expensive machines and structures on credit, desperately pursues Crescent support as well. She promises boosted trade with the Empire, exclusive access to rare Ussuran resources such as demantoid gemstones and even boyardoms for particularly generous contributors. Yet Lady Arzu of Gallenia, Ussura's most influential Crescent, doubts Ketheryna's promises. After all, she has said the same to many Théan diplomats. Can she really make good on so many promises in so many different directions?

## Tamatama Nomads

Caravans of the Tamatama, an ethnic group originating far to the southeast in Agnivarsa, travel throughout Ussura, mostly along waterways between major cities but occasionally via ancient horse trails non-Ussurans don't know. Nowadays, you are most likely to find them in Veche Province.

Ussuran Tamatama are mostly Dīnist. They occupy a peculiar but comfortable social position as entertainers: musicians, dancers, actors and suchlike. Their traveling lifestyle means the Tamatama rarely intermarry with other groups, though this is a matter of convenience rather than prejudice. A Khazar on her way to adventure through the rest of the world often links up with Tamatama caravans for part or all of the way, swapping songs and updating one another's maps.

Some wider-ranging Tamatama bands are responsible for the cross-pollination of dance styles throughout different parts of Théah. Thanks to the Tamatama, ballet, a physically and technically demanding performative dance form originating in Montaigne, has become all the rage at many boyars' courts, especially in modern Bashanta. Ketheryna's Imperial Theater in Bashanta, which features the latest mechanical contraptions and special effects systems for stage performances, has hosted many Tamatama performances.

## Ilya Sladivgorod Nikolovich

Czar Gaius Iriney's first marriage was a love match with another boyar, Nikolai. With a surrogate mother, Nikolai had two sons, David and then Ilya, whom the Czar formally adopted. The Czar loved his adopted sons, and named David heir to his throne. But Nikolai's family had a history of falling-sickness, a disease characterized by violent seizures.

Falling-sickness is rarely fatal, but first Nikolai and then later David died of heart failure during particularly bad episodes. Even though Ilya's seizures were not nearly as severe, a combination of heartbreak and anxiety over his heir's viability led the grieving Czar to disown Ilya. He planned to remarry in hopes of producing a "stronger" heir.

Ilya, barely fourteen, confronted the Czar before his entire court. He had lost one father and his brother. Now his other father pushed him away? After an angry, undignified confrontation, the Czar banished Ilya to the far east of Ussura. Ilya replied that he was leaving anyway.

Ilya left Pavtlow in anger and planned to never return, his father's decision hurting more than he would admit. He vowed to prove his own worth by being a Hero to the people of Ussura, even if he couldn't be their czar.

For four years, he rode throughout Ussura as a *bogatyr*, using Leshiye gifts to help right wrongs and deal with threats. He stole horses with Khazari in Molhynia, drank and danced in Siev's taverns in Veche, defended Cathayan caravans from bandits in Gallenia and prayed in mountain monasteries in Somojez.

When he learned of his father's death, he returned as fast as he could to Pavtlow. Once there, he discovered his onetime friend Ketheryna had claimed the throne herself in Bashanta.

While Ilya's travels garnered him widespread popular support, the nobility backs Ketheryna's drive to modernize the country. Having spent time out in the country with people unlikely ever to see any of her fancy inventions, Ilya is not so sure.

## Portraying Ilya

Down-to-earth, adventurous, and a traditionalist. Ilya is the people's champion, a daring, cosmopolitan young man. He has dark hair and shining brown eyes, and his youthful dark beard is shot through with reddish streaks.

In his gazes into the middle distance, you can see his grief and regret about his youth and relations; yet Ussura's land and people are his surrogate family. He struggles, however, to find a coherent vision for Ussura's future. Everyone knows Ketheryna's plan. The people know Ilya's qualifications, but what does he want to do?

When Ilya speaks to convince, he is calm and commanding. No one denies his experience. He refuses to let you forget the good his adventures have done for Ussura. He speaks of Ketheryna with respect, regret and frustration. Ilya's populism, personality and compelling narrative makes him a convincing candidate for Czar, but he does not get specific with his ambitions: their absence is his greatest weakness.

## Story Hooks

- Shortly after Ilya returned to the capital, myriad individuals declared themselves the true banished prince, seeking power for themselves. The Knias Douma, overwhelmed by the claims of the Ilyas, prepare to ignore them all in favor of supporting Ketheryna, unless the true Ilya can show some proof of his identity. Can the Heroes help Ilya prove he is the real deal?
- Ilya's mother, Vera, has reappeared in the capital, saying she misses her son and requesting a place in Ilya's new government. Ilya could use an ally, but he barely remembers this woman. She seems to have an agenda and refuses to take no for an answer. Can the Heroes help Ilya discover Vera's secret?

## THEN FALL, CZAR

Who stabbed the Czar with an icicle?

**Dimitri Babineaux** is a lover, not a fighter—but has big muscles and the most personal grievance against the Czar. Did fear for his beloved's well-being and freedom drive him to murder?

**Metropolitan Lyuba** sees potential in Ketheryna's modernization. She grew up in Eisen, lacking Ussurans' native respect for the spirits Lyuba wants purged from her religion. Assassins aren't usually her style, but violence is. Perhaps she seized the opportunity to promote her religious movement.

**Ilya** is a Hero. He wouldn't stoop to murder his own father, would he? Could he kill his foster father, who disowned him for his illness after he lost his biological father and brother? But even if he wouldn't, perhaps one of the false Ilyas who conspires to take his place would.

**General Winter** is Ussura's most notorious purveyor of ice-flavored death. Destabilizing Ussura's government divides any possible organized opposition to his ascent.

In **Matushka's** eyes, did the Czar's disowning Ilya and marrying Ketheryna without asking her first delegitimize him? An icicle through the heart is her style, after all.

**Ketheryna** is a practical woman and had more to lose with the Czar's death than most others. Is she really too calculating to have killed him out of love for Dimitri?

# Ketheryna Fischler Dimitritova

Ketheyna Fischler Dimitritova was born in Eisen to a newly appointed Eisenfurst and his Ussuran wife. When she was still very young, her mother died to a Horror attack, and her father spent a great deal of time obsessing over how to keep her from suffering a similar fate. She grew up sheltered, but not secluded. Her father ensured she had the best education he could find and ensured she was trained to defend herself versus Horrors.

When Czar Gaius Iriney's progressivist recruiters swept through Eisen seeking promising scientists, a young half-Ussuran noblewoman's inventions left them speechless. To amuse herself, Ketheryna had scavenged parts from the Fischler city streets to construct a lantern which projected a map of Eisen onto a wall as a pattern of light and shadow; a graduated glass tube with a bulb on top and water in a reservoir underneath, responding to temperature changes; a set of conjoined rulers which slid back and forth to produce her math exercises' answers; and a tiny clockwork songbird that could fly across the room and explode (an unintended consequence still under investigation).

The Czar's recruiters offered her father, Falk Fischler, a small fortune to whisk her away to court in Pavtlow, and he jumped at a chance to send her to a safer home. She settled in happily, and eventually fell in love with the half-Montaigne ballet dancer Dimitri Babineaux and then found out the Czar wanted her hand in marriage. Her father had accepted on her behalf without asking her first.

On her wedding night, Ketheryna found the Czar's corpse in her nuptial bed, an icicle driven through his heart. His household thereafter claimed he died in his sleep after consummating the marriage. But when Ketheryna claimed the throne and married Dimitri without mourning, rumor spread that Ketheryna and Dimitri themselves assassinated the Czar.

Ketheryna moved the Czar's court to Bashanta. On her orders, Prince Bogdan of Veche expanded this tiny village into a new "city of the future," full of modern art and architecture and the latest technological advances. Many Ussurans doubt Ketheryna's motives and intentions. Is an Ussura with roads and technology really Ussura? Is this all a plan to sell Ussura out to her western neighbors?

## Portraying Ketheryna

Ingenious, visionary and eager, Ketheryna talks fast and thinks faster, always testing some new invention. Her blond hair and bright blue eyes help her fit in with Ussuran boyars, even if her skin is darker than most.

She is helpful if asked, but she assigns some crazy mission in return, like "steal an experimental telescope back from the Inquisition," or "help me secure funding for a new university in Bashanta." She respects Ilya's pull with the Ussuran people, but thinks he aims too low. They used to be friends once, and she is still sympathetic to his cause, but she would rather have him working for her, rather than watch him keep Ussura firmly in the past.

She wants Ussura now to be what Castille was a hundred years ago, even if burying tradition is the price. Ketheryna is brilliant and engaging, but also a technocrat, with little idea what rural Veche's muzhiks or northeastern Molhynia's Khazari raiders care about.

## Story Hooks

+ A chambermaid in the Pavtlow court comes to the Heroes with evidence identifying the Czar's murderer—but she thinks someone knows and is trying to kill her before she goes public.
+ A sudden and unexpected diplomatic mission in Eisen has forced Ketheryna to leave Bashanta abruptly. Everyone expects Dimitri to reign in her place, but Dimitri is a ballet dancer, not a politician—and some of the most canny political actors in town plan to take advantage of Ketheryna's absence.

# Altai Khatun

Centuries ago, the Iron Khan's hordes thundered across Théah and Cathay. But upon his death, logistical breakdowns and individual ambitions split history's largest empire into squabbling khanates. Altai Khatun (the feminine of Khan) is one such khanate's last scion. Her clan fled to Ussura after their foes banded together to drive them from the throne.

Ussura's most celebrated Knight of the Rose & Cross, Altai Khatun, dreams of empire, but mistrusts political power. What good is an empire that time and entropy inevitably sunder? But culture and ideas can ride eternal. She wants a khanate of the mind, a set of ideals spread throughout first Ussura, and then the world: bravery, camaraderie, strength and—most problematic—freedom of religion.

"My religion is the only correct one" is still a widespread, deadly idea, especially after the War of the Cross and Cardinal Esteban Verdugo's ascent. Altai thinks Théah needs some old-fashioned Khazari interfaith sentiment. Why follow just one religion when you could have half a dozen, just in case one turns out to be wrong?

Anywhere humans oppress one another over how to worship, Altai Khatun's band of kheshigs (honor guards, a Khazari leader's elite guard) rights wrongs and defends the innocent in the name of whichever religion is under threat. But personable as she is, Altai still makes enemies who worry that her "khanate of the mind" masquerades as a dry run before a more traditional khanate of the bow.

When Altai rides through western Ussuran cities, progressivist Westerners and Orthodox purists often give her a chilly reception. Metropolitan Lyuba's Schismatist movement, which advocates purifying the Ussuran Orthodox Church of folkloric influences, decries Altai's ecumenism as a war on the truly devout. Schismatist mobs have interrupted Altai's riders at everything from public prayers to dinner parties, sometimes violently—then blamed the "bloodthirsty Cossack raiders" for the ensuing melee.

For her own part, her own political leanings are less clear. She only wants what is best for the nation, and believes both Ilya and Ketheryna have a chance of doing good. The last thing she wants is a civil war, despite those who suggest otherwise.

## Portraying Altai Khatun

Altai Khatun is a quintessential bogatyr: bold, brave, good-looking, flush with patrons and admirers, always on her way to her next adventure. She has dark skin and long, silky, dark hair that she keeps braided down her back. Her eyes are tawny brown and always full of life and laughter.

She automatically trusts anyone she judges honorable and heroic: make a good impression and she immediately invites you along to help her drive off bandits or rescue heretics from the Inquisition.

But while she recognizes her influence over the Khazari, she hesitates to get involved in politics, conspicuously changing the subject at any mention of Ilya or Ketheryna. She is unlikely to openly support either unless war is imminent.

### Story Hooks

+ Altai Khatun's faithful stallion Borya has been horsenapped! This legendary war horse is as valiant and clever as Altai herself (or so she reports—no one else can understand him). Who could the culprit be? Is a political enemy drawing her into a trap? Maybe the Heroes can help her spring it without getting caught.

+ A prominent Inquisitor has challenged Altai Khatun to a public debate about religion. Altai is not that kind of public speaker, and besides, she recognizes an obvious trap. She needs a champion, and only the best orator among the Heroes will do. The rest are on bodyguard duty.

# Archduke Aleksi Pavtlow Markov v'Novgorov

Alyosha (the diminutive name for Aleksi) of Novgorov was not always a prince. Once a goblin merchant who lived in the Borovoi Forest in nearby Somojez Province, he bought and sold at the local goblin market under the auspices of Borovoi the Forest Walker. One night he came across Masha, a scared young lady in an abandoned hut in the forest. Transforming himself into a young human, he sat with her through the dark night, giving her gifts from his day's trading and telling her legends of the forest, transforming noises and growls in the night into stories.

Masha was the daughter of the Archduke of Novgorov, who had run away because she did not get along with her stepmother. When she returned to her home in Rurik, she insisted the goblin come along—although, of course, she didn't know Alyosha was a goblin. She introduced him to her relieved parents as the man who helped her in her time of need, and they rewarded him with gifts and adopted him into their family as Masha's brother.

When the old Archduke died, Alyosha was as surprised as anyone to find he had been named heir. Masha declined the title, preferring to take holy orders as an Orthodox priest; so it fell to their adopted son. The trouble was, Alyosha never entirely got the hang of acting human and is capricious and temperamental—normal for a forest goblin! It has been difficult to learn an entire new species' etiquette (and consciously change his appearance to mimic human aging), but Alyosha thinks he does a good job.

Now it is all Alyosha can do to keep up with the vicissitudes of political activity in Ussura. Traditionally, Archduke Novogorov leads the Knias Douma, but he has no desire to do so. He does have political opinions. As a happy adoptee, Alyosha supports Ilya, sympathizing with the fact that some people do not believe he deserves to ascend the throne because he is not biologically related to the former Czar.

He also worries about Metropolitan Lyuba's initiative to reform the Orthodox Church, because it would eject entities like himself from the old faith. Alyosha has little confidence in himself as a political actor. He may have to step up, even if he risks revealing his identity. After all, no one has made a "no goblins on the Douma" rule, yet.

## Portraying Archduke Alyosha

Alyosha may be a goblin from the Borovoi Forest, but he has a genuine interest in helping others and a good head for numbers. He masks his obvious discomfort with human ways via mood swings and misdirection. He misses his life as a goblin, but he cannot resist the challenge and fascination of living as a human. He has a good friend in Masha, who still lives in Pavtlow as a member of the Orthodox Church.

## Story Hook

+ Masha suspects that her confessor at her religious order, the only person in the world besides herself who knows Alyosha's secret, is about to go public with it. But to whom? Can the Heroes help guard his secret?

# Prince Bogdan Siev Benediktov v'Vladimirovich

Prince Bogdan, age thirty-eight, thinks himself unlucky. He dresses well, but he is middling in stature, neither fat nor thin, with green eyes, thin blond hair and a blond beard that is, well, not that impressive in a land of impressive beards. He is one of Ussura's most powerful boyars—but he rules Veche, sparsely populated, yielding less tax revenue than his fellows on the Knias Douma. He isn't particularly smart and not nearly as well-spoken as others on the Douma. Prince Bogdan still remains one of the richest and most powerful people in Ussura. He just doesn't feel like he is.

The man takes dangerous risks that rarely pan out. When Ketheryna decided to move her capital to Bashanta in his province, he promised her he could build the city of her dreams in a ridiculously short time period. He pulled in muzhiks from all over Veche and overworked them—in some cases to death—to produce the glittering jewel that is Bashanta in scant over a year. He did finish the city on time, but in return, the fields throughout Veche lay fallow as the muzhiks who normally worked them toiled in the capital, or died. Now Prince Bogdan doesn't know if his people can survive the coming winter and hopes he can purchase enough food from surrounding provinces.

Two years ago, when General Winter's army swept into Veche, Prince Bogdan knew he had found a winner. Hearing rumors of border raiders and aggressive boyars frozen to death, he thought, "This is a man I could trust." Then a soldier with frozen eyes appeared at Prince Bogdan's castle door demanding Bogdan quarter and feed the terrifying silent army who brought winter wherever they went. Bogdan agreed right away.

The trouble is, Bogdan had already sold out. The Inquisition has paid him well for the privilege of sneaking Inquisition spies through Five Sails into Ussura. Few Vaticines live in Ussura, and many of them are Khazari; but Cardinal Esteban Verdugo still has designs on Ussura's population.

Bogdan's own court even hides an Inquisitor, though he doesn't know whom. He dares not use his family's power of turning into a bear, lest the Inquisitor report him to Verdugo. Moreover, the Inquisition wants to stop General Winter, a clearly dangerous sorcerer who threatens the Vaticine world. Can Prince Bogdan continue to serve two masters?

## Portraying Prince Bogdan

Prince Bogdan is privileged, insecure and just average. He has fair hair and skin and grey blue eyes. He hunches his shoulders and looks down at the table. He meets the Heroes' eyes only with trepidation and mumbles his sentences' ends.

He apologizes frequently, but seems wounded that he has to. Prince Bogdan, utterly convinced of his own inferiority, counteracts it by glomming onto others who seem exceptional. He prays one of his two bosses grows so powerful the other can't touch him—but will that boss then come down on him?

### Story Hooks

- Prince Bogdan accidentally double-booked a visit from General Winter with a visit from Cardinal Fátima Campos, a prominent Inquisitor on El Concilio de la Razón. Bogdan begs the Heroes to help him divert one or the other as he frantically rearranges his castle to keep them from meeting.
- As Prince Bogdan becomes less sure of his own personal safety, he realizes it is time to draw on his family's most ancient and reliable ability: transforming into giant bears to devour the opposition. He is rusty at this, but he trusts his interpersonal skills with bears better than his interpersonal skills with humans. Is it safe to let this bumbling man use such a dangerous weapon?

# Lady Arzu Sousdal bint Erdoğan v'Riasanova

At eighteen years of age, Lady Arzu is the youngest, most contentious Knias Douma member. Gallenia's Riasanova family descends from Ussuran nobility who intermarried with Crescent merchants. A devout Dīnist, she attends Knias Douma meetings in traditional dress: a fur-lined jacket, robes, veil and turban from Iskandar.

Her faith sets her at odds with the devoutly Orthodox Metropolitan Lyuba. Her outspoken desire to open her eastern border to Cathayan traders, and to reduce the number of Cossack patrols on the border, worries the Khazari and Koshchei in the neighboring province of Molhynia. Lady Arzu knows Ilya worries about foreign influences from any direction, while Ketheryna thinks that Ussura should open westward, not eastward. Lady Arzu's informants in the Secret Societies have also indicated to her that Prince Bogdan might support General Winter, whom she fears and hates. She has tried to warn the others about General Winter without betraying the fact that she knows more about him than usual, but so far no one else recognizes the threat. She is friendly with Archduke Alyosha, but he is the only one.

Lady Arzu's unpopularity has made her a frequent target for peasant revolts, political assassinations and other violent antagonism. She has been able to stay alive and afloat due to her connections to multiple secret societies in Ussura. El Vagabundo has a long-standing relationship with her family, having saved her parents from various assassination attempts. She also contracts the Ushkuiniks regularly to move goods along the riverways to buyers elsewhere in Ussura. She maintains friendly relations with Altai Khatun, who respects the Riasanova family's commitment to free religion even as she suspects Lady Arzu's friendship with Khazari enemies on the east side of the Szabla River.

Only Lady Arzu's closest confidants know she seriously considers an offer of leaving Ussura and joining the Crescent Empress. It is not just a cultural decision. Most Gallenians have at least partial Crescent ancestry, including family in the Empire. Trade with the Empire pays for their food and clothing.

Lady Arzu would have less power under the Crescent Empress' regime, but she considers it a small price to pay for a government that has offered her people more support than Ilya or Ketheryna has.

## Portraying Lady Arzu

Fiery, self-assured, inexperienced. Lady Arzu is quick to speak, quick to interrupt and likes to state her opinion bluntly and forcefully, without any diplomatic leavening. The Knias Douma's reaction combines grudging respect for her strength of character and annoyance that they keep losing arguments to someone who doesn't really even argue with them.

Lady Arzu's connections to various Secret Societies give her acute insight into other people's secrets. She knows more about secret societies than any other Ussuran, so if you drop any hints that you belong to one, she finds a subtle way of letting you know she knows. If you need someone to help you coordinate between societies, she is the best at making that happen.

## Story Hooks

+ Rumor has it that the "Crescent merchant" Lady Arzu plans to meet in Sousdal is actually a diplomat representing either the Crescent or Cathay. Her people wish to block her actions, afraid she is going to sell Gallenia to an eastern power. Lady Arzu asks the Heroes to go to the meeting in her stead to ease suspicions.
+ To protest Lady Arzu's open-borders plan, Gallenia's most powerful boyar has blocked a major trade road from Curonia into Ussura, which goes directly through his castle. He has announced his intent to defend it against all comers from either side until Lady Arzu renounces her plan.

## Koshchei "the Deathless" Breslau Aglayev v'Pietrov

Koshchei has a reputation as a bad man. You can tell just looking at him: he looks like a skeleton with waxy skin stretched over it. It feels uncomfortable looking into his hollow eyes. At Knias Douma meetings, he almost never speaks and almost never blinks. When he does offer an opinion, it is terse. His voice, a death-rattle, makes everyone on the council shudder. He got that way by hiding his soul and his death in an egg inside a duck inside a hare inside a treasure chest buried under a tree on a faraway island off the Vodacce coast. Until someone cracks open that egg, he will never die.

Koshchei rides throughout Ussura, an unkindness of ravens presaging his arrival. His visits are always the same. Sometimes he does the talking, but more often a gigantic raven perched on his shoulder speaks for him. He professes his interest in a child, and then offers her family a truly staggering bounty in exchange for her. Gold. Jewels. Livestock. Even land. The family rarely refuses. Sometimes, when they refuse, she disappears anyway.

When Koshchei's new captive rides through the doors of his castle, it really gets weird. Inside his castle's forbidding walls, black stone frozen over with ice, exists a tiny city, its towers reaching high into the sky, but also burrowing deep into the mountain underneath. Everyone in town, mostly women and children, bustles about happily as though without a care in the world.

For hundreds of years, Koshchei has maintained a guise as a villainous black widower to hide what he really does. He uses a network of common ravens to spy on Ussurans throughout the country, watching for mistreated children. He then uses his money, power and scary looks to dissuade their abusers from looking for them.

### Portraying Koshchei the Deathless

Fearsome, terse, misunderstood. In public, Koshchei speaks as little as possible and moves with deliberate, fearful slowness. Ravens often attend him; the largest raven perched on his shoulder speaks for him. Inside the walls of his castle, though, he relaxes. He is polite, solicitous, always asking his wards whether they

## THE KNIAS DOUMA

With the Czar still undetermined, the boyars of the Knias Douma have fractured and fallen to bickering. While the five great families never truly agreed on anything, they were united in their dedication to Ussura. Now, the boyar families' loyalties are split between Ketheryna and Ilya, causing a standstill in the government.

If the families supported one monarch over the other, they might be able to come to some consensus on the matter and get things moving again. Instead, many of the Douma, much like the rest of Ussura, are unsure which of the two to support. The Pscov family, with a strong leaning towards Ketheryna, has attempted to call the Douma to vote upon a unanimous support, but everyone else is completely hung on the issue.

It seems the families seek outside confirmation, possibly from Matushka, and refuse to act in the case they pick the wrong monarch. It also means that the government has ground to a halt, with only Ilya's and Ketheryna's individual actions moving Ussura forward.

need anything from the outside world. He even lets a trusted few return to the world outside once safe from their former families, keeping in touch with them via raven and recalling them if they come into trouble.

### Story Hooks

+ A number of boyars have hired bogatyrs and deployed a small army to ride on Koshchei's castle to get "their children" back. Koshchei is worried. The adults in the castle can fight, but they number few—and even if they do fight, Koshchei's secret will be out. Can the Heroes find another way?

+ Koshchei's precious egg-duck-hare-treasure chest combination lies on an island off the Vodacce coast. He wants to move it to northern Molhynia where he can monitor it more easily. He needs help—either to do it for him or to guard him on the way.

# Metropolitan Lyuba Veche Klimentova v'Pscova

The Pscov family's impressive religious pedigree could have elevated Lyuba higher in the Ussuran Orthodox religious hierarchy than her current rank of Metropolitan bishop. Within the Orthodoxy, the Metropolitan is more than just a spiritual leader, but also a community leader. Higher up the hierarchy, few of the faithful take on political careers.

Her Knias Douma duties occupy much of her time, preventing her from climbing much further. Nevertheless, Lyuba's greater ambitions have already embroiled Somojez Province in a turmoil threatening to engulf all Ussura.

Metropolitan Lyuba thinks the Church's rituals honoring domovoi, the Leshiye and other local spirits are a distraction at best, diabolism at worst. If the Ussuran Orthodox Church is ever to reach beyond Ussura, it needs to abandon what makes it distinctly Ussuran. Especially miscellaneous spirits. She has not only expressed these preferences extensively and eloquently in public, but also reformed major churches in every city and large town in Somojez. These reforms change rituals' symbolic details, centralize power in the hands of high-ranking clergy (whom she personally approves) and strip out any mention of Ussuran spirits.

Her grassroots support is not pretty. Lyuba's Schismatists, an angry, violent mob, intend to purge the Church of impure elements. When a public figure such as a priest speaks out against Lyuba's reforms, Lyuba need not do anything herself: a mob of Schismatists inevitably besieges that public figure's house, breaks windows and starts fires. Rumors abound that Schismatists have even learned to murder their own houses' domovoi.

Many boyars support Metropolitan Lyuba's reforms as well. Since noble families often supply senior priests, they welcome the centralization of power. They also associate the Leshiye and house-spirits with vulgar superstition, thinking themselves above such things. But much of the Ussuran intelligentsia warns that Metropolitan Lyuba's movement resembles the Third Prophet's supporters to an uncomfortable degree.

## Portraying Metropolitan Lyuba

Pious, zealous and ruthless, Metropolitan Lyuba is an impassioned speaker. She has silky, thick black hair, pale skin, and dark eyes. She is not conventionally attractive, but has a way of speaking that draws in even the most discerning listener.

Metropolitan Lyuba sees herself as Orthodoxy's Third Prophet, though her sermons do not have nearly as much explicit fire and brimstone. In fact, as the public face of that movement, Lyuba is the picture of propriety and respectability.

She is the most dangerous kind of demagogue: her language, proper and politic on the surface, subtly incites her followers' lowest common denominator to enforce her will with violence. When speaking, she sounds like a press release or as if she memorized her speech ahead of time, which she has.

Her intentions are not necessarily Villainous in nature, but her results certainly are. Even the best intentions can lead us astray. Can the Heroes help Metropolitan Lyuba correct course?

## Story Hooks

- Lyuba's Schismatist ideology gains traction amongst muzhiks. The streltsy (imperial guard), chafe at the violence, disorder and heresy Schismatists represent. The streltsy guard captain has planted false intelligence to lead the Schismatists into a trap, hopefully causing a riot and giving the streltsy an excuse to suppress them. The Heroes must intercept the information and simultaneously attempt to lead the streltsy onto a less Villainous course.

- Metropolitan Lyuba finds those people who accept gifts from Leshiye deeply concerning, and believes they embody what is most problematic about the Orthodoxy. She contacts the most observant or discreet Hero, hoping to recruit him into a "research division" (read: Inquisition) of her reformed church.

# Gertrude Schmidt

Gertrude "Trudy" Schmidt was born in Ussura, and shortly thereafter abandoned in the Borovoi Forest near the border with Eisen. A wolf found her in the forest and took her in, caring for her as its own. When she was still young, the wolf lead her to a tiny settlement at the edge of the forest in Eisen and left her there. She remembers little from her time with the wolf, though it sometimes comes back to her in dreams.

Trudy grew up on a farm, and like most children in Eisen, learned to defend herself from Horrors. Trudy chafed at farm life; chores bored her, work bothered her and staying in one location was the worst. At seventeen, she ran away from home into the forest. There she survived by following animals and hiding when the Horrors came. Eventually, she crossed the border back into Ussura and immediately the land called to her. For the first time in her life, she felt like she was home.

The land itself seemed to lead her, until eventually she found herself face to face with the wolf of her youth. Now older, she realized this was no ordinary wolf. It taught her how to speak with the animals and eventually, how to change into a wolf herself.

She eventually made her way to Veche, where she tried to use her gifts to help others. She had a string of bad luck, picking friends and lovers who eventually turned out to be Villains of the worst sort. This finally ended when she fell in love with the wife, Ekaterina, of her good friend Timofey—who was a murderer and a madman, though Trudy didn't know this until after she developed feelings for his wife. Trudy brought the full wrath of Matushka down upon Timofey, and freed Ekaterina from his company.

Now they live together, just outside of Veche, close to the Borovoi Forest. Trudy continues to do Matushka's work, using the pathways found in the Forest to travel all over Usssura.

## Portraying Gertrude Schmidt

Compassionate, powerful and a bit too naive, Gertrude Schmidt embodies everything you would expect from someone touched by Matushka. She is tall with dark hair and bright green eyes and has a bit of a feral quality to her. She helps those in need, despite what trouble it may bring her, and rarely asks for anything in return.

# Owen Laslo

Owen Laslo was born in Dunkeen in Inishmore before the War of the Cross ended, but he missed joining the fighting by three years. His father was a merchant and his mother a fisher. He grew up with the love of the sea from his mother, and hoped to join the navy before the war ended. Instead, he ended up on a merchant ship as a sailor, which was a small consolation to his dream.

Laslo's first voyage took him to Vestenmennavenjar by way of the Maw, and made landfall in Vendel. There in a tavern, he met a pirate captain named Dina from Ussura. After drinking and gambling the night away, Laslo had earned not only her respect, but a position on her ship. They set sail two days later.

Dina's crew were members of the Brotherhood of the Coast, and raided up and down the Maw, always in contest against Vesten Raiders. Laslo served with Dina for several years before becoming shipwrecked near Rurik.

The Vesten Raiders had warned the pirates time and again to leave their waters, but Dina refused. Instead, she continued to offer them the chance to join the Brotherhood. This time, instead of the normal exchange of pleasant threats, the Raider ship brought its cannons to bear on hers. The ensuing fight was bloody and messy, and destroyed Dina's ship. Few sailors survived, and the pirate captain herself went down with the ship.

Laslo washed ashore, and found himself stranded in Ussura with no job, no friends and no one to vouch for him. Ever the pragmatist, he went in search of a new ship to serve on. As he searched, he learned that he had earned quite a reputation in Ussura. The fierce red-haired Inish man who served with Dina was easily recognized wherever he went. Stories of his time at sea preceeded him, and everyone knew his name.

In a way, this was a blessing, but in another it was a curse. No honest merchant ship would hire such a character, and few pirate ships made port in Rurik. On the other hand, people got out of his way and generally did what he asked of them—if not out of respect, then out of fear.

Soon, Laslo found that he could put his reputation to good use as a mercenary. People hired him to do all sorts of jobs, from guarding merchant caravans to shaking down debtors for payments due. He was good at it, and quickly had more jobs than he knew what to do with. So, he began hiring other people to help him with his jobs. Within short order, Laslo became the leader of a prominent mercenary company, employing sell-swords, guards, thieves and even a few jennys.

Now, anyone seeking a mercenary in Rurik is likely to use Laslo's crew. The company doesn't run itself, and most of his time is spent dealing with business, but Laslso owns a small riverboat that he sometimes takes out to help the Ushkuiniks.

## Portraying Owen Laslo

Owen Laslo is a gruff man with powerful muscles from years of hard work. He is in his early thirties and still has a youthful vigor. His hair remains a deep red, which he keeps shorn short, though his beard is full.

Laslo might be a mercenary, but he is loyal to a fault. His own personal sense of honor does not allow him to back out of deal once it's made, and he always holds true to his word. He is a shrewd businessman, and will not take a job that he is not confident he can accomplish, and he holds all his employees to his exacting standards.

## Story Hook

+ A Villain the Heroes are attempting to remove from power with has hired Laslo's mercenary company to guard him. Laslo's sense of loyalty means that he will not abandon his charge without extreme circumstances. Can the Heroes find enough evidence to make Laslo turn against his employer, or will they fight against the crew to get to their Villain?

# General Winter

Major Akim Maksimovich Lagunov's tribe answered Lord Koshchei's call to defend Molhynia's border from Vesten raiders. But after their general ordered them—against the major's recommendation—to chase retreating skirmishers, a snow squall separated them from the main body of the army. Night wore on. The storm worsened. The sun did not rise the next morning or the one after that. Exposure or starvation laid his soldiers low, one by one, until but a few remained, pushing into whirling white darkness.

Then, light appeared. Two white reindeer's fur, and the gilt ornamentation on the sledge they pulled, gleamed like candles. Mad with hunger, the soldiers lurched toward it, intending to kill and eat the reindeer. The tall, white-haired driver sighed and turned the soldiers to snow, which usually solved such problems. Yet Lagunov, frozen through, kept staggering forward. "You're different," she said. "There's ice already in your heart. I'll sculpt it into something more interesting."

One week later, he strode into his former general's tent, slit his throat with a knife of ice and assumed his command. Koshchei lost contact with the army.

One by one, provincial boyars' castles went silent, besieged in unseasonable whiteouts. Each dead boyar's private security forces received a choice between conscription and the same fate. "Ussurans," he tells his recruits, "receive a unique blessing: Théah's most devastating winters, killing the weak, sparing only the strongest. I plan to share this gift, remaking all Théah in Ussura's frozen, perfect image."

Lagunov is a tactical and strategic genius. Wherever he walks, blizzards walk with him. He pays soldiers richly with pillage and plunder, blessing his finest with a terrible boon: he plunges his icy hand into them and turns their hearts to ice. Their blood freezes into glaciers that race blue beneath their skin.

They never slip on ice. They can run over the top of new-fallen powder snow, leaving no trace. Once their bodies become impervious to cold, permafrost buries consciences and emotions, leaving only logic and absolute loyalty to their dread master. Their enemies nickname these frozen soldiers "snowmen," their warlord "General Winter." He likes the name.

## Portraying General Winter

Cold, calculating, and imperialist. General Winter is the avatar of Ussuran cold and snow. He cares not that his power disrespects and antagonizes Matushka and Tură: gods who could not keep this power from him are too weak.

He doesn't really converse or negotiate: he kills. He only respects those who subscribe to his philosophy or survive his assaults. Dealing with him is a matter of violence and survival, and even his soldiers refuse to speak much when prompted.

But what is his next target? Eisen, the most serious military threat to Ussura, whose border has never been secure? The Sarmatian Commonwealth, whose territory and warm-water ports Ussura has long coveted? Or the Czarina's throne in Bashanta, just west of his Veche base?

## Story Hooks

- A young woman insists she is General Winter's own daughter from a youthful tryst he had at military academy. She shares her father's cold affinity. She needs your help defeating the General and taking his power for herself.
- A soldier arrives at a hospital, frostbitten, begging for help; he recovers quickly, limbs doctors thought lost regaining warmth and vitality. He says he is a medic from General Winter's army who received the blessing of the ice heart, but pulled away halfway through. He has discovered a way to return snowmen to humanity. General Winter wants him and his cure dead.

# The Explorer's Society

Many monasteries and reliquaries high in northern Somojez's forbidding mountains, built into ancient Syrneth structures, sit in the mountainsides themselves. The Syrneth seem to have built these structures for dense occupation, full of corridors and small oddly sized cells forming labyrinthine patterns underneath the rock. Outside, grand plazas, bridges and amphitheaters connect these different structures.

Monasteries often build new structures directly atop these miraculous edifices, some of which hang in midair, bridging vast gaps between mountaintops, suspended by unknown art or science. Attempts to duplicate them have failed so far. The Society debates whether cutting open one of these structures to see what holds it up is worth it—that is, if the monks even let them.

# The Invisible College

Scientific research is not penalized in Ussura, and the Inquisition has no power. In fact, Ketheryna has invited the greatest scientific minds to join her in Bashanta. She gives them places to study and models her universities after those in Castille.

Members of the Invisible College find not only a friend in Ketheryna, but a safe haven in her court. Information, documentation and knowledge may find a permanent home in Ussura, and Ketheryna wouldn't have it any other way. Members of the Invisible College have the leisure to spend time both safeguarding information and starting up new research projects. Bashanta is a choice destination for those fleeing the Inquisition, if they can make the long journey.

# Los Vagabundos

Ussura's lack of roads means Vagabundos without local connections struggle to move and communicate across the Nation's trackless expanse. Nevertheless, a Vagabundo has monitored the Ussuran Czar for some time, with mixed success. Gaius Iriney's death happened on a Vagabundo's watch—in fact, one who held a mask. This Vagabundo nevertheless chose not to get personally involved in whatever happened—and then disappeared, leaving the mask at a drop point for her confused replacement to find.

That missing Vagabundo knows the secret of Gaius' death. The whole organization is in uproar trying to track her down, figure out why she disappeared and determine whether Gaius' death was murder, self-defense, accident or something stranger. The answers have great bearing on Los Vagabundos' next move and particularly on which candidate for Czar they focus their resources to protect.

# The Brotherhood of the Coast

The Brotherhood of the Coast have a difficult time raiding the freezing waters of Grumfather Bay. Some join with the Vesten Raiders and make their home in Eskjo in Vestenmennavenjar, but some base their home from St. Anderson or even Rurik. Unfortunately, few trade ships other than those belonging to the Vendel League traverse the icy depths, and the Raiders refuse to prey on those ships, for whatever reason. The Brotherhood have turned instead to river piracy as a way to make their living in Ussura.

# The Ushkuiniks

You would think the Brotherhood of the Coast has nothing to do in Ussura. The nation does not have warm-water ports, and trade that does come in is primarily from Vestenmennavenjar via the Grumfather Bay. They compete with the Vesten Raiders who are not part of the Society, which makes their jobs difficult.

But their Ussuran inland subsidiary has a history as old as the construction of ships. The first Ushkuiniks—named after the "ushkui," a light flat-bottomed raiding craft, easily transported overland—came from Ussura and Vestenmennavenjar's border. Coasts and riverside communities feared the Ushkuiniks' serpent-headed boats. They attacked and absconded with valuables to their wilderness hideouts. Those very hideouts, far beyond the reach of normal civilization, gave them their most extraordinary capability.

Ussura's rivers, lakes and marshes abound with dangerous supernatural creatures. The two most common, which also inhabit nearby Eisen and the Commonwealth, are the *vodyanoi* and *rusalki*. The humanoid vodyanoi possess fish- or amphibian-like features while rusalki, female water spirits, resemble beautiful women.

Their hideouts in forgotten marshes forced Ushkuiniks to develop rapport with these odd creatures. They learned the strange etiquette of the swamps, knew how to honor and placate rusalki and vodyanoi lest they lose their tempers and break anything humanmade near the water, or lure people in to drown or enslave them.

For the longest time, Ussuran rivers were the only reliable way to move cargo through this vast and trackless country—but punting a barge down a river without checking on its denizens is a great way to get bankrupted, drowned or enslaved. And this is where the Ushkuiniks come in.

They map the Ussuran rivers, and navigate them faster than anyone else by making deals with the natural denizens or otherwise avoiding those who are the most dangerous.

Ushkuinik escorts can guide your cargo, guard it against bandits, placate any spiteful mermaids hiding in trees or shoo away angry frogmen you come across. If you do not pay them, well, pray bandits get you before mermaids do. And if the bandits do get a boat or two, they share their profits with the Ushkuiniks, because they are just as likely a part of that organization as any other.

The Ushkuiniks occasionally venture out into Grumfather Bay. They don't take kindly to Vesten Raiders muscling in on their turf. During a recent patrol around the Bay, Ushkuiniks ran into a Brotherhood of the Coast ship. After a brief scuffle, the Brotherhood ship's captain suggested maybe the two crews had more in common than not, and offered the Ushkuiniks a look at a Brotherhood charter. It was the beginning of a beautiful friendship.

The Ushkuiniks answer to Lazavik, a little old man with a single glowing eye who lives in a hut in a swamp. He is a Leshy (the singular of Leshiye) of sorts, a nature spirit whose health and well-being reflects that of his home marsh.

Originally one of many spirits the Ushkuiniks placated, he slowly grew into an advisory position and then a leadership position. Now that Ussura divides into the Ketheryna and Ilya parties, the Ushkuiniks—whom the crown considered a criminal nuisance until just recently—have become an important political goal for both prospective leaders.

The Ushkuiniks' connection to the spirits of the land is important for both Ketheryna and Ilya. Muzhiks, from whose ranks many Ushkuiniks come, and to whom Ushkuiniks generally donate a portion of their pirating take, usually have the Ushkuiniks' backs. You would expect them to go for Ilya, but Ketheryna has contacted some Ushkuinik captains with offers of complex new boats.

Of course, much like the rest of the Brotherhood of the Coast, the Ushkuiniks have little interest in political machinations. Sure, they accepted Ketheryna's boats, but she's in for a rude shock when they refuse a call to arms or a request for support, as is the most likely result.

## Favor with the Ushkuiniks

The Ushkuiniks concern themselves with not only goods and wealth, but with the spirits of the river routes. While they hold the same Charters and promises that any Brotherhood of the Coast member would, they additionally seek to keep the vodyanoi and rusalka pacified and in place, making them the only ones capable of successfully nagivating the Ussuran rivers.

A Hero who belongs to the Ushkuiniks can earn Favor as he would normally for the Brotherhood of the Coast and also in the following additional ways:

+ Successfully negotiating passage through a major waterway with a powerful supernatural creature is worth 3 Favor and 1 Wealth.
+ Averting a threat to a spirit-occupied wetland is worth 4 Favor.

A Hero who belongs to the Ushkuiniks can spend Favor as she would normally for the Brotherhood of the Coast and also in the following additional way:

+ Gaining assistance from a vodyanoi or rusalka costs 4 Favor and the request must keep the creature near a river. The creature is a Strength 6 Monster with the Aquatic Monstrous Quality. It follows any instruction that does not endanger itself or its home. It fights for the Hero, but only if it thinks it is likely to win. Otherwise, it can clear a river passage, scare off other creatures or spirits or make deals with unknown spirits in your Hero's stead.

# Die Kreuzritter and the Knights of the Rose & Cross

The Ussuran heroic archetype, called the bogatyr, operates at the intersection of die Kreuzritter's and the Knights of the Rose & Cross' agendas. Bogatyr Heroes originated from Crescent legends, but made their way into Ussuran epics hundreds of years ago, probably via Khazari poetry. Their legends attribute them to honorable customs, defending the weak, destroying monsters and doing good deeds. Accordingly, both the Rose & Cross and die Kreuzritter have found Ussura fertile ground for recruiting active members and rich patrons.

For much of Ussura's recent history, the two societies did not get along. Die Kreuzritter complained the Knights insisted on reasoning with monsters during their prolonged rampages, whereas the Knights groused die Kreuzritter swung first and asked questions later. However, a spate of kidnappings by the Sea King, a Leshy who maintains an undersea kingdom amongst Rurik's coastal islands, forced the two Secret Societies to work together: die Kreuzritter cut a path through his monstrous minions, and the Rose & Cross appealed to his better nature once they got there.

The incident started an unsteady equilibrium between the Societies. A newcomer from either Society working in Ussura often partners with a local veteran from the other, purposefully chosen for her contrasting temperament and methods to the newcomer. Not to say the organizations don't work on their own, but now they work together more often than they used to.

## Favor in Ussura

Members of either the Knights of the Rose & Cross or die Kreuzritter can gain Favor in Ussura in the following way:

+ Performing a mission with the other Society is worth 4 Favor to your Society, specifically when the mission is productive to the goals of both Societies. This Favor gain does not stack. For example, if the Knights of the Rose & Cross ask an agent to undertake a mission, the agent cannot also gain Favor for performing that mission alongside die Kreuzritter agents.

## Močiutės Skara

The Shawl's first-ever operations took place here, on the Ussura-Curonia border, where women risked their lives during the War of the Cross to get supplies to refugees. The Society remains active and aggressive in protecting Ussura from the depredations of war. While large-scale warfare has not appeared for many years, conflicts over territory, resources or pride frequently pit boyars against one another. Outside of Rurik, boyars ignored Gaius Iriney's ban on such petty conflicts, where his streltsy could not march on offenders. These conflicts often ruin the lives of muzhiks guilty of no crime more serious than farming the defender's land.

An agent's favorite approach to these situations is to show up, tell the muzhiks on both sides what is going on and then transport all of them as far away as she can, as quickly as possible. Tensions dry up quickly when both sides realize they cannot feed their troops. But Močiutės Skara needs to know about an attack well in advance to get agents into the area, prepare hiding places and move peasants before soldiers realize their dinner's running away.

To this end, the Shawl researches a different kind of information network: Ussuran natural and tutelary spirits such as domovoi. Nearly every household in Ussura has one. They seem to communicate with one another somehow and to predict upcoming misfortune. Will they aid the Shawl's efforts against violence? Or will they find such a request presumptuous?

### Favor in Ussura

A Hero who belongs to the Močiutės Skara in Ussura can earn Favor in the following ways:

+ Stopping a fight between Schismatists and Orthodox is worth 3 Favor.
+ Getting muzhiks out of the way of oncoming war is worth 3 Favor for a village's worth of people, possibly more depending on the size of the population.
+ Recruiting a domovoi to the Močiutės Skara information network is worth 5 Favor.

## Rilasciare

The wide power gap between boyar and muzhik vexes the Rilasciare. Boyars hold all Ussuran power and spend muzhiks like gold. Prince Bogdan's slave-driving efforts to build up Bashanta on the timetable Ketheryna demanded caused thousands of deaths. However, Ussura's low population density and mobility impede muzhiks' ability to organize.

The Rilasciare has had some small-scale successes, inciting muzhiks to revolt against boyars who lacked military power and replacing their former masters with democratic communes. In places like Breslau, the concept of nobility and leadership is almost completely gone, except for when visitors show up and demand Koshchei v'Pietrov make an appearance.

Unfortunately, that same initiative led them to support General Winter's rise. The General began his career as a common soldier, conscripted from a muzhik village and sent to the Pavtlow Military Academy on scholarship. When the Rilasciare first heard of a commoner who could challenge the boyars on the field of battle, they spread information about him and recruited soldiers for his cause. Now, of course, they realize their error. The Rilasciare helped make General Winter into something they really don't want. What will they do about it?

## Sophia's Daughters

Sophia's Daughters rarely make it as far north and west of their home into Ussura. Those who do find both Ilya and Ketheryna gracious hosts, if a bit distracted by their own problems. Sophia's Daughters have found help in an unlikely benefactor, Koshchei v'Pietrov.

Even the Vodacce Princes fear Koshchei's reputation, and when one of their daughters or noble ladies ends up in his lands, they write her off as dead. Only a few Fate Witches have ended up in the safety of his castle, but they seek ways to bring more into his refuge.

Places

# Rurik Province

Rurik is Ussura's heartland and densest province. Four major cities—Ekatnava, Rurik, Pavtlow and Sladivgorod—lie within Rurik's borders. Rurik's Archduke has long been the most powerful boyar in Ussura after the Czar, due to the financial security density and port towns bring. Rurik trades briskly with the Vendel League. In the old days, northern Eisen brought in a lot of trade as well, but Eisen's economy has flagged lately. Rurik is also the terminus of many important navigable rivers reaching into the continent, a natural meeting place for dignitaries from all over Ussura and therefore the most logical capital site. Originally Ekatnava or Rurik was slated to become the Czar's seat, but other provinces complained—probably because they couldn't attack a coastal capital to protest the Czar doing something they disliked.

Rurik's terrain is mostly broken and hilly, with many river valleys. Farming takes place almost entirely in those river valleys, with easy irrigation and rich soil, but the grazing land is not extensive. Rurik has to draw much nourishment from the sea, and inland settlements rely heavily on hunting to add protein to their diets.

The Ushkuiniks, Ussura's local Brotherhood of the Coast chapter, is most active in Rurik, where an Ushkuinik escort has a lot of waterways to guide you down or dead ends to spring a perfect trap (depending on whether or not you pay her). On the rare occasion someone attacks the Grumfather Bay fishing fleet, the Ushkuiniks also venture into the open waters to defend Ussura. The islands in between Rurik and Ekatnava are the rumored home of the Sea King, an ancient Leshy who rules Grumfather Bay from a sumptuous aquatic palace. Every now and then over the centuries, he kidnaps some interesting humans who either join his court forever or escape (sometimes with die Kreuzritter's or the Knights of the Rose & Cross' help).

## Ekatnava

Ekatnava harbors fishers, whalers and Vendel traders. Its strong economy and greater-than-average disposable income have made it Ussura's sporting capital. The all-weather sports of fencing, boxing and wrestling are particularly active. Every few years at midsummer, athletes from across Ussura as well as eastern Vestenmennavenjar and Eisen compete in the Ekatnava Games' field events, contests of strength, races and the like.

Unbeknownst to the city government, the Pavtlow-based Sokolovskaya crime family has successfully expanded its operations to Ekatnava. Taking advantage of Ekatnava's low crime rate to insinuate themselves into city operations on the sly, the family set up protection rackets on the harbor and muscled in on the Ushkuiniks' turf in smuggling and even piracy. With the Ekatnava Games coming up next summer, Boss Filippa Sokolovskaya plans a grand campaign of illegal betting, match-fixing and even alchemical performance enhancement to ruin everyone's fun but her own.

## Sladivgorod

Sladivgorod lies on a vast rift lake between tectonic plates on the Molhynia-Rurik border. More bountiful than the sea, Lake Vigil abounds in tasty clams, snails, amphipods and—most valuable of all—freshwater seals. Local hunters observe strict limits because overhunting seals incurs the wrath of the Riftguard, an ancient, temperamental water-serpent who maintains the balance of nature. Even during periods of bitter warfare between Rurik and Molhynia, fighting on the lake surface was taboo—no one wanted to be snake food.

Today, Sladivgorod is a snapshot of what Ussura might have looked like one or two hundred years ago, all picturesque snow-covered cottages nestled into the hills or overlooking the lakeside. Still, locals stay in at night, for Lake Vigil attracts many Leshiye who hold council with the Riftguard under the stars. Legend has it no hero has ever vanquished the Riftguard except Sarangerel Bogatyr, who tricked it into leaving her alone as she fought her greatest enemy upon the lake's surface.

## Rurik

Rurik City is the local government seat, where Archduke Alyosha's family lives. Vesten settlers here built Ussura's oldest large-scale architecture, straight crenellated walls connecting crude blocky towers. Rurik still hosts many Vesten expatriates. A gigantic marketplace sells everything from traditional Vesten baked goods to shares in Vendel shipping ventures.

The Vendel League's Ussuran headquarters overlooks the harbor, a towering new structure built to look like part of the ancient fortifications. Before the ancient Somojez boyar Vsevolod's conversion to Orthodoxy and subsequent pacifism, he fought bitterly with Rurik over possession of the coastline and terrain between St. Anderson and Rurik. The rivalry between the two cities persists to this day, with their fishing fleets often clashing over who owns the best sites off the coast.

## Pavtlow

A few years ago, Pavtlow had Ussura's most beautiful buildings, best-kept streets and most vibrant court. Now a husk, empty and hollow, the capital goes through the government's motions while the real action happens in Bashanta.

## Streltsy

Until Ketheryna's departure, the streltsy (singular streléts) stood as the Czar's elite guard, keeping order and putting out fires in the capital. Many streltsy's families have served in the same corps for generations.

Whenever angry boyars marched on Pavtlow to protest something the Czar or the Knias Douma had done, the streltsy waited with swords, poleaxes and muskets at the ready. They are probably Ussura's best infantry, though Ketheryna's new personal guard of Eisen mercenaries and General Winter's terrifying snowmen might have something to say about that.

Despite their elite status, the Douma does not pay them well. Many a craftsperson in the marketplace is an off-duty streléts. Rumor has it they planned to revolt against Ketheryna just before she relocated to Bashanta—and that is why she didn't take them with her. The streltsy have exhibited a wide range of reactions to Ketheryna's indifference to them. Some sections considered it the last straw from an office that never paid them as well as they deserved.

These units left their ancestral barracks to set themselves up among the petty crime lords of the city's market districts. Some simply faded into Pavtlow's population of tradespeople or returned to families in the country. A few—mostly the oldest of the guard—still occupy the barracks and patrol the Old Palace's grounds, answering to the idea of a Czar.

## Rampant Poverty

Precious few in Bashanta come to the city without an invitation, but for as long as anyone can remember, muzhiks have crowded Pavtlow. Most of those who lose their livelihood elsewhere in Ussura come here, to beg for alms from the wealthy. Beggars, pickpockets, criminals and undesirables form sprawling guilds, staking out turf and brawling with one another over it.

Pavtlow's sudden evacuation has placed the urban poor into an odd place. On one hand, the rich whose wealth they hoped would trickle down are gone now. On the other, they left a lot behind them. Food is still scarce, but housing is easy to get now as many handsome residences have emptied. The people tear some down for parts, and others become guild houses for new thieves' or beggars' guilds. Now that they have reliable housing, they are starting to create new economies for themselves: growing crops on mansion roofs or specializing in crafts or services.

## The Pavtlow Kremlin

The Czar's palace, or kremlin, is a sprawling fortified compound, built hundreds of years ago and renovated in fits and starts ever since. Each face of the structure represents a different period in, and set of influences on, Ussuran architecture. The fortifications are technologically unimpressive. Thick stone walls with a walkway on top and some cannon towers left unfinished after Ketheryna's departure; but the streltsy's Old Guard, a few sections of veteran gunners, hold the kremlin as if the Czar still draws breath.

They number few and can't defend the whole kremlin themselves. Instead, they hire neighborhood urchins to run patrols through the compound, notifying the Guard of looters. The streltsy then roll out their famous mobile barricades and open fire on the bad guys from behind them, hopefully driving them away.

These streltsy prioritize defending Musorga Hall. This royal art museum brims with paintings, sculpture, ceramics and other artworks from across Ussura and beyond. During the chaos of Ketheryna's departure, the Old Guard assaulted many rich folks' abandoned dwellings in order to capture artwork to stash in Musorga Hall. Now, one of Théah's richest troves of priceless artwork remain under the guard of a few dedicated but harried old veterans. They cannot defend it forever.

## Crime Families

The Sokolovskayas were one of many small thieves' guilds in Pavtlow until the power vacuum opened up, and now they are the biggest thing in town. In the old days, the established crime families and thieves' guilds fought one another without end. The Sokolovskayas, though, realized there would be more for everyone if they divided up business fairly. So they began to organize meetings and broker deals. Now a guild handles robbery, another handles assassination, a guild for corruption, a guild for fraud...and the Sokolovskayas provide administration and take service fees. Safest and steadiest job they have ever had. Knowing what the Old Guard hides in Musorga Hall, they plot a massive multi-team assault and heist on the kremlin. Selling the art hidden there will make them legendarily rich—if they can prevent the participants from backstabbing one another in the process

## Veche Province

Veche is Ussura's second-largest province after Molhynia, but the least dense. Once larger, its rulers have spread themselves too thin. Somojez Province invaded and conquered a great deal of the territory on the Eisen border.

Veche has a long history of tension with the Sarmatian Commonwealth. Many boyars on the southern border have long hungered to expand their territory southward. When they got word of Golden Liberty, many of them reasoned that without the old aristocracy's strong leadership the Nation would be easy to take. Yet, their own lack of organization prevents them from moving in on the Commonwealth.

General Winter has based himself in Veche for the past two years, although he has a scary knack for showing up in far reaches of the country at a moment's notice, lending to rumors that he travels via Leshiye magic. He has ingratiated himself with the prince of Veche…or perhaps the prince of Veche has ingratiated himself with General Winter. General Winter has already cracked down on several of the most powerful boyars on the southern border, forcing them to swear fealty to him or die.

## Siev

Veche's seat of government is Siev. Situated on a main road leading to the Sarmatian metropolis of Stanisławiec and the Sejm River, Siev was key to moving Ussuran goods south. Originally an important diplomatic hub, the city had envoys coming from all over the Sarmatian Commonwealth, Vodacce and the Crescent Empire to meet with Ussuran interests. But after General Winter took up residence in the hills east of Siev, he froze the Sejm. Someone must ask him to relent so Veche's already troubled economy does not worsen…but so far, no one has successfully asked General Winter for anything.

Siev has a reputation as a boring place, all business and no fun; but it remains Ussura's toymaking capital. Businesslike its craftspersons may be, but if you want to delight your children (or Ussuran adults) with pewter soldiers painted or unpainted, wooden dolls and dollhouses or chess sets, Siev has the best quality at the best prices.

With General Winter came the members of the Rilasciare who support him. Most of the city functions normally, business as usual from most standpoints, except for the lack of trade and the diplomatic envoys abandoning the city in favor of Bashanta or Sousdal. In the outer edges of the city, the Rilasciare have taken hold and installed a democratic commune. The people work, provide goods and support each other all based on a collective vote.

For the most part, they ignore Prince Bogdan and the other boyars in the area, content to guide themselves. As long as General Winter stays, few would dare challenge their sovereign right, but he is a lousy defender otherwise.

## Bashanta

Just a couple of years ago, Bashanta was a small village. Despite its desirable location on a major river, its swampy terrain attracted vodyanoi and rusalki and repulsed humans who were not Ushkuiniks. Then Ketheryna Fischler Dimitritova abruptly relocated her court and capital there, draining the swamp and inviting thousands of artisans and engineers to the city to build Ussura's—no, Théah's!—most advanced city.

She paid Prince Bogdan of Veche handsomely to construct it on an impossible two-year timetable. To succeed, Bogdan worked thousands of muzhiks to death in unsafe environments and then concealed the entire fiasco from Ketheryna. Onion-domed towers, handsome streets, spacious theaters and forbidding churches replaced mud and huts.

It is beautiful, advanced and—according to many a traditionalist Ussuran—all for show, lacking substance as anything more than a proof of concept for visiting Théans who still think Ussura backward. Those Ussurans deride the city as Ketheryna's "clockwork onion."

### Aztláni Observatory

The massive stepped pyramid perched on the town's highest point surprises many newcomers to Bashanta. The dome crowning its highest step surpasses every roof in the city. Ketheryna invited a team of Tzak K'an astronomers to design the Aztláni Observatory with the help of Alvara Arciniega, the telescope's inventor himself. The first floor is a public science museum, featuring Théah's second-largest armillary sphere (the largest is the Hierophantic Cathedral) and

dozens of the latest technological marvels, many built by Ketheryna herself. Above and below, a complex of laboratories births Ketheryna and her scientists' latest creations.

Just the other day, though, a gigantic explosion in the night blew a hole in a corner Observatory wall. It has not yet been repaired, though round-the-clock guards ensure no one outside can see what goes on within. Two rumors vie for prominence about it: one, that the Inquisition blew it up because it offended their anti-science sensibilities; or two, that a weapon tested within detonated accidentally. Neither possibility comforts those who dwell nearby.

### The Bashanta Kremlin

A kremlin is a fortified citadel inside a city. This kremlin's site on a hillside below the Aztláni Observatory is no accident; military technology labs beneath the Observatory connect to the Kremlin's testing facilities. To impress visitors, Ketheryna hired Vodacce artisans to build the Kremlin as a star fort, even though such a design offers little advantage inside a built-up city.

Her elite guard of Eisen mercenaries marches down to the plaza below every morning to drill in public and then marches back up to the Kremlin. But the training grounds connected to the Observatory's sub-basements contain Ketheryna's strangest, most advanced inventions.

They are not entirely her creations. She recruited experts on Ussuran folklore and mechanical engineering everywhere she could find them. The inventions started out as an experiment on the domovoi, the tutelary house-spirits occupying nearly every Ussuran household. The same domovoi often remain within a house torn down and rebuilt, so long as the stove where it slept remains intact. If the family moved, and the stove moved with them, that same domovoi followed.

So Ketheryna's research team took abandoned stoves and placed them in increasingly outlandish homes. Churches. Taverns. Even Tamatama-style caravans. As long as he still received offerings of food and liquor, the domovoi stayed and continued to defend the home against misuse and neglect, even moving objects around the house to make noise or frighten off vermin and other intruders.

The latest experiment places a compact stove housing a domovoi in the chest of a clockwork automaton, essentially a gigantic toy soldier, like the ones Ketheryna played with during her childhood in Eisen. When exposed to a threat—a dangerous animal, perhaps—the domovoi animates the clockwork soldier, making it walk, moving its limbs to fight off that threat.

Perhaps Ketheryna lets her fascination with this development overcome her. Could this be the newest frontier in home defense or even soldiering? She has not revealed them to the public yet, but the Czarina has already installed these toy soldiers in various halls in her own palace. The question remains, though: might Ketheryna's nutcrackers face down human soldiers as well? And are the domovoi willing fighters or trapped and enslaved?

### Imperial Palace

On the other side of the Observatory, the Imperial Palace is a comparatively humble structure amidst blocks and blocks of lavish apartments, linking to it with bridges and skyways. Ketheryna's dwelling connects to her courtiers' to keep the political powerhouses in town close. Many of these apartments' outer hallways have large glass panes for walls on their outer hallways: expensive and lovely, convenient if you like to spy on your neighbors, but not so good at keeping out the Ussuran cold. Still, they made it through winter hail without shattering.

The palace and the surrounding apartments host a year-round series of balls, salons and more public entertainments such as opera or dance. Ketheryna recognizes that the entertainments and spectacles she has designed mean nothing unless people talk about them.

The Imperial Theater also lies on the edge of the upper-class residential district. While many of Bashanta's amenities seem to have only nobles in mind, the theater is accessible to nobles and commoners both. This structure features state-of-the-art mechanisms for trick entrances and exits, quick backdrop changes and other stagecraft marvels.

# Somojez Province

Somojez Province occupies northwestern Ussura and much of the border with Eisen. Its namesake city actually lies on an island far to the north. Somojez reaches deep into Ussura, and once occupied most of the northern mountains until Novgorov conquests carved Rurik from its shores. Now Somojez pierces the heart of Ussura deep into the mountains, but no one lives there. As for Somojez city, the island has been separated from its original province, and the people there live alternating under Vesten and Ussuran rule. Currently, Vestenmennavenjar owns the island, and the Pscov family has better things to do rather than take it back.

Ussurans generally practice an old form of religion dating back to the First Prophet, which is called Orthodoxy. They have long combined their religious beliefs with rituals to respect and honor the Leshiye and domovoi found in their lands.

Metropolitan Lyuba's reforms threaten to split every city in the province in two. The middle and upper classes largely support the reforms, which centralize power in the cities and purge the Church of its "backward elements"—both superstitious peasants and the superstitions they believe. The muzhiks, on the other hand, see the reforms as unnecessary and classist.

Somojez's issues threaten to spill into other provinces. Schismatists (that is, reformers) have secured the support of wandering priests and sent them elsewhere in Ussura to drum up support. The traditional Orthodoxy is now starting to do the same. So far, Pavtlow seems sympathetic to the Orthodox Church, especially the corps of streltsy; whereas much of Bashanta leans towards the Schismatists. Neither candidate for Czar has made their feelings known yet.

## Veche

Ironically, Somojez's largest city is Veche. This town and the surrounding region used to be the capital of Veche Province, until a once-minor boyar from the Borovoi Forest region named Vsevolod assembled an army and expanded his province by force. Lord after lord, region after region fell to Somojez's conquering armies until a tour through the northern mountains' monasteries exposed Vsevolod to the Orthodox Church. After that, he experienced a change of heart. He ceased his conquests and turned his attention to establishing and protecting the Ussuran Church. But to Veche's great consternation, he refused to give up his new possessions, citing his "Theus-given duty" to Orthodocize the people therein (never mind that most of them were already Orthodox). Depending on whether you ask the Somojez or the Veche, Grand Duke Vsevolod was a religious hero or a hypocritical tyrant.

Located just south of the Borovoi Forest, Veche attracts strange people. Poems hold that Princess Nadzeya, the most famous of the legendary Ussuran bogatyrs, was based out of Veche. She frequently adventured in the forest to the north or the Velde Hills to the south and east (though in truth every region in Ussura has Princess Nadzeya stories). The armored drachen in Somojez's coat of arms reputedly lived in a lake east of Veche and north of Tebizond. Many of Veche's citizens claim to be partially descended from Leshiye, goblins or other strange creatures from the surrounding countryside.

## St. Anderson

The city of St. Anderson is named after Toivo Anderson, a Vesten raider who converted to Orthodoxy after arriving in Ussura. After his conversion, he journeyed south through Somojez Province, atoning for his sins as a raider by defending Orthodox Ussurans against aggression. The stories they tell nowadays say the aggression all came from Eisen, but in that period of Ussuran history, they likely suffered aggression from other Ussurans to the east. St. Anderson, an important port town, has easy access to the ports of Vendel and Pösen. St. Andresgorod, in the south of Somojez, is named after the same saint. That city was the last one conquered in the wars between Somojez and Veche, before Vsevolod relented and took up a religious life.

St. Anderson once again saw action in the War of the Cross' last years, when an Eisen expeditionary force under unscrupulous mercenary Captain Regula Gerver struck at St. Anderson unprovoked, thinking the chaos of the War would grant her all the cover she needed to plunder a rich port. The local boyar, the eager but inexperienced Lady Yesfir, rode out to meet Captain Gerver in battle and was immediately defeated and captured. Unwilling to ransom her, the townspeople fortified St. Anderson for a long siege, receiving supplies from Ushkuinik blockade runners.

When she could not starve them out, Captain Gerver headed home to Eisen, taking Lady Yesfir with her. After nearly twenty years of captivity, Lady Yesfir finally won her freedom when Captain Gerver died in a Horror attack. The boyar walked from Eisen back to Ussura, the land welcoming its long-lost daughter home by keeping her safe in the harsh weather. She wants her town back, as is her ancestral right—but the townspeople, unsure of this woman and confident in their ability to rule themselves, refuse to give it back. How will Ketheryna respond when Lady Yesfir's complaint reaches her? How will Ilya respond when the townspeople's plea reaches him?

## Tebizond

Tebizond, just east of the Velde Hills, is called "the holiest city in Ussura." Spanning the river called commonly by its Eisen name, der Rotstrom, this city is an important pilgrimage site for Orthodoxists. It is the gateway to the mountain range to the northeast that hosts famous reliquaries and monasteries, many of which defy the very laws of nature as they stretch through the space between mountains. Occupying ancient Syrneth dwelling sites, rumors say the religious orders here have knowledge about the Syrneth which no one else in the world understands, but keep them secret as a matter of their oaths to the order.

## Borovoi Forest

Borovoi Forest lies just north of the city of Veche. A ring of light and relatively normal forest surrounds a dense core of the weirdest, most complex ecosystems in the continent. Lumberjacks, hunters and trappers serve as the de facto guards on the wall, warning travelers of the dangers within. Yet outsiders keep coming to Borovoi Forest.

Some are bogatyrs seeking adventure. Some are explorers or treasure hunters who want to claim the forest's literal or figurative fruits. Some are traders, bringing magical curiosities or other riches to the goblin market they have heard lurks within. Some are Matushka's enemies, whether human or otherwise, so desperate to flee her wrath or her retribution that they tried their luck among the walking trees. Many of the largest and oldest trees are awakened, animate beings, capable of pulling up their roots and moving from place to place.

## Borovoi, the Leshy

This forest is the home of Borovoi, the Leshy with teeth and beard of grass and moss, perhaps the most alien of the major Leshiye active in Ussura. He is a massive, towering creature, easily mistakable for a tree or perhaps a mass of trees, when not moving.

Trunk, bark and vine wind together in his shape, atop prehensile roots that writhe free from the loam and carry him forward, plunging into the earth before him. His trunk is so wide, two persons could not stand on either side of him, reach their arms around the trunk and have their hands meet. His dozens of branch-hands reach down from the top of his trunk, tipped with claws of twigs and leaves. Countless animals live within him, and when he deigns to talk, which is rarely, a mouth full of soil opens in the trunk, speaking in a voice like trees creaking in the wind.

Borovoi is not just the spirit of his forest. Borovoi is the spirit of every plant and fungus in Ussura. He feels each blade of grass grow and die. In spring and summer, vibrant, even playful (in a slow way), he poses riddles and speaks fondly of healthy crops. In fall and winter, he grows somber and serious. Prove yourself a friend to Ussura's growing things and Borovoi speaks to you of the secrets only plants can know. On what grasses has General Winter's army trod? Among what marsh reeds is Lazavik of the Ushkuiniks' home? What oak hides Koshchei the Deathless' heart? Borovoi knows.

Borovoi Forest is one of two places in Ussura where Matushka has no power, Vir'ava Forest being the other. If her little hut on chicken legs walks there, or she flies there in her magical mortar and pestle, the trees rise up and repel her, lashing her with thorny vines or beating her with heavy branches until she flees. The Leshiye confined to Borovoi Forest once roamed all Ussura freely, but Matushka wanted exclusive access to the Ussuran people.

She fought, cursed and tricked every Leshy she came across until they removed themselves to places where they could be safe from her wrath. Borovoi rallied the plant-spirits of Ussura around him and brought them to the Borovoi Forest, where they could band together and resist the killing winter. Their influence suffuses the plants of the region and the land itself.

Borovoi Forest abounds with bizarre trees. For example, there are two species of apple tree identical to one another, one of which causes you to grow a horn every time you eat an apple from it, the other of which makes you more beautiful every time you eat from it (and makes any horns you may have grown fall off). Another tree's apples can restore the aged to youth.

Coffer-oak trees naturally grow with beautiful treasure chests, elaborately carved, entangled in their branches or bound up in their roots. As the trees get older, they grow to surround the treasure chest, eventually swallowing it up and leaving it invisible to anyone who does not know exactly what to look for. If you brave the Forest, you might be able to escape with a coffer-sapling and stash something in it before the tree grows and hides it away for you forever.

## Secrets of the Forest

Borovoi Forest has two great secrets. One is a path leading from the depths of the forest to the Vir'ava Forest far on the other side of Ussura. In the very center of the forest, hidden amidst the wild overgrowth, a strange market appears. Magical creatures—long-nosed goblins who can change their shape, and talking animals full of cruel tricks and sage advice—live in this oasis of light and speech. Every night, one stall—and always a different stall, with its own idiosyncratic price—sells a fare from Borovoi Forest to Vir'ava Forest.

The other secret is that Borovoi Forest moves, slowly and surely. Borovoi and his trees walk with slow, deliberate steps, and they move only a few meters every month all told. All the plants gathered here originated somewhere else. In a time long past, Matushka forced them out of their homes, and they collected in the far northeast corner of Ussura after long journeys and many privations.

But Borovoi remembers a time before Matushka reigned supreme, before the tectonic plates crashed together on the border of Molhynia, when dense forests full of magic reached into Ussura's center. He yearns for that time to return. And Veche, orderly urban Veche, is so close. For the trees of Borovoi Forest, the day when they climb over Veche's walls and reach their vine-fingers through its windows, reintroducing growing life to the sterile city, is so, so close. Then Matushka will learn her lesson: what you take from the trees, the trees take back.

# Gallenia Province

Gallenia's ruling Riasanova family ensures that the province, while Ussura's smallest with but one major city, has the country's most active trade network. The Crescent and Cathayan merchants who cross the Szabla River are hardly numerous by Vodacce standards, but their trade relationship with Gallenia is as old as Gallenia itself. Crescents first settled the province, with western Ussurans arriving after the Knias Douma appeared and outlawed battle between provincial leaders. Western Théans with pale skin seeking ranchland and farmland eked out a living amongst the steppes, and the Khazari drifted slowly northward out of anxiety that the Crescent Empire was hot on their trail.

The Riasanova family has a busy schedule of trade fairs and festivals, coinciding with the most convenient times for merchants to arrive from outside Ussura. Locals trade honey and ore for silk, high-quality steel, foreign herbs and other substances rare in Gallenia.

A combination of natural features and territories administered by militarily inclined boyars define the borders of Ussura. To combat destructive internecine wars, the first Knias Douma forced, coerced or bribed many inland warlords to relocate to castles in the marches, refocusing their violence outward.

Cossack patrols ride from castle to castle, hunting smugglers sneaking across the border. Only certain Czar-sanctioned toll roads can be crossed in this way. These toll roads prevent Lady Arzu from opening as many supply lines as she would like, but if she could trade her abundant mineral resources with Curonia and Cathay unrestricted, Gallenia would be rich.

Matushka lives in a little hut on huge chicken's legs that wanders Gallenia's western wastes, though by flying in her magical mortar and pestle she can cross Ussura faster than a song can leap from a singer's mouth. In this realm, you find no other Leshiye, for Matushka forbids their presence. Just as other Leshiye are creatures of the wood, mountain or rain, Matushka considers all humanity her domain.

In the old days, Leshiye lived everywhere. A human could make deals with them in exchange for powers like what Matushka offers. But Matushka did not like how that worked. In those days, valiant bogatyrs, sneaky princes and common fools tricked her and confounded her at every turn. She caught one person who deserved to be eaten, but he revealed that some animal he had met taught him how to turn into a falcon. When she caught another person, she revealed she had knocked three heads off a drachen with a mace and found Matushka's secret weakness hidden in an egg, in a duck, in a hare, in a treasure chest.

So Matushka began to chase down other Leshiye in her flying mortar and pestle. If she could catch them, she ate them. If not, she chased them far away from humans. Soon, the message got around to all the Leshiye of Ussura: if you make deals with humans, if you protect them in your lands, really if you do anything except scare them away, eventually, Matushka will come and take from you what was rightfully hers.

## Sousdal

Lady Arzu makes her home in Sousdal, the only city in Gallenia with proper structures and walls. Situated in the eastern steppes at the base of a mountain pass leading to rich ore mines, Sousdal is not as isolated as it would seem. Just south along the river lies Curonia and trade with the Sarmatian Commonwealth, and to the east through easy mountain passes, a traveler can make her way into Vir'ava Forest and further into Cathay. The city itself is mostly just a sturdy keep surrounded by shops and houses, but for Gallenia it might as well be a palace.

South of Sousdal, on the Sousdal River, lies one of the few toll crossings into the Sarmatian Commonwealth. Anyone working, living or traveling through Gallenia makes his way through Sousdal at some point. It is a city of transients, filled with traveling merchants, traders and shop keepers passing through the city to or from parts further east and south. Gallenians who do live there service travelers, making it one of the most open cities in all of Ussura. The city boasts a cultural fusion of Ussura, Sarmatian, Crescent and Cathayan influences.

Many rural Gallenians view Sousdal as a bit of a challenge to their way of life. In his eyes, the city is far too metropolitan for his liking, and Lady Arzu's dealings with foreigners makes him fear that she intends to have Gallenia leave Ussura altogether. Of course, that doesn't stop him from traveling to Sousdal during the warm months to take part in the spring fairs and sell his wares to those selfsame foreigners.

## Vir'ava Forest

A long time ago, Matushka tried to eat a girl, as she frequently does. The girl in question fled eastward across Gallenia, with Matushka in hot pursuit in her flying mortar and pestle. But the girl had a trick up her sleeve: a magical towel and comb a talking cat had given her. She threw down the towel behind her and a wide river sprang up, mystically barring the pestle's passage; Matushka had to go get her oxen to drink up the river so she could cross. Then the girl threw down the comb behind her and a sprawling, dense forest sprang up. Matushka tried to gnaw through it with her iron teeth, but failed.

Where Borovoi Forest is wild, dense and overgrown, Vir'ava looks like an illustration from a book of Færie tales. Sun-dappled paths through the forest, just wide enough for two humans to walk hand in hand, lead to flowered glades with sphinx-moths fluttering from blossom to blossom. Plants here are not alive and mobile, as in Borovoi, but the animals tell a different story.

## The Magic Forest

In Vir'ava, you can find a bear with a wooden prosthetic paw, which he attached to his foreleg after a woodsman chopped it off, a woodsman whom he challenged to a fight and whom he later ate out of spite. Here, a spider knight who weaves webs to catch the most annoying creatures, flies and mosquitoes, enlists the aid of crickets and beetles to help him trick and trap them. Here are a cat and sparrow who live as humble woodchoppers, but who helps any bogatyr who opposes Matushka. Vir'ava Forest even has a hare who can swallow a duck and a duck that can swallow an egg and an egg which you can open and close and place anything inside, even an idea.

Vir'ava herself, the girl of legend, and the forest mother, lives by the garden at the forest's heart. She is physically small, not like the towering, inhuman mass of her "husband" Borovoi. But she is the butterfly to his blossom.

From a distance, she looks human in shape. From up close, you realize black-and-gold fuzz like a bee's rather than normal hair covers her head, with two long feathered antennae extending from her forehead. Two of her wings are a butterfly's, delicate and mismatched; the other two are stabilizers like a fly's, sticks with balls on the end. A tough, jointed carapace covers her upper torso; and her lower body tapers into a long abdomen with a pointed stinger. She also has four arms instead of the normal human two.

A court of pollinators—flies, bees, butterflies, little red hummingbirds—attends her at all times, moving in patterns through the air matching her moods and gestures. Delight her, and butterflies alight on your clothing. Enrage her, and face her bees. As frustrating as Vir'ava is to Matushka, Matushka dares not molest her when she walks abroad. If Vir'ava really is the soul of all the pollinators in Ussura, her death will wither the crops and starve the people.

Second only to Vir'ava, but abounding in power, is the Swan Maiden. A tall woman, her limbs and her neck all stretch just a little longer than expected for a human of her size. She is all lean muscle covered in downy white feathers, and her arms extend into gigantic wings, from which she can summon artisans to build her anything she desires. The Swan Maiden might be Vir'ava's daughter, though few enough see her to ask.

## Leader of the Opposition

Vir'ava and her forest stand as proof that Matushka is not the only game in town. While Matushka herself is extremely powerful, capable of granting all the powers collectively called Dar Matushki, she is not Ussura's only source of these powers. Many other Leshiye can grant one or two of the Gifts commonly associated with Matushka. They just don't, for fear that Matushka will find out about it and come down on them.

For those brave or foolhardy few who break Matushka's unspoken rule and make their own deal with an Ussuran, Vir'ava Forest provides one of the few places they can go to escape her. All Leshiye and humans in Vir'ava Forest must kneel to the Forest Mother herself, observing her court's etiquette and paying her homage with gifts and praise.

Those who comply find Vir'ava Forest a safe haven. It is one of the only places that a shapeshifter whose power does not come from Matushka can train to use his powers in relative peace and safety, getting advice from sympathetic folks.

Vir'ava welcomes even a person touched by Matushka, as long as he observes Vir'ava's laws and pays her homage. Only Matushka herself cannot enter. She has sent spies into Vir'ava to uncover the Forest Mother's weaknesses, but their efforts have been inconclusive so far. Some of them returned to announce that Vir'ava has no secrets: her court of magical animals and shapeshifters remain loyal and healthy. Any successful attack on Vir'ava will have to lure her or the Swan Maiden out of her sylvan place of power.

# Molhynia Province

Molhynia's windswept steppes make up Ussura's largest, strangest province. Much of the country, though navigable by boat, requires long overland treks to finish a journey. The terrain is hilly or mountainous, occasionally desert or taiga. Temperature varies wildly.

## Breslau

Molhynia's largest permanent city, Breslau, situated amidst the northern steppes, is a walled, fortified city. Its highest point is Koshchei the Deathless' own kremlin, which no one from the city below may enter or exit. Secret passages under the earth link his castle to the world outside. Only Koshchei and his "brides" ever enter or leave by these.

Koshchei expects Breslau's entire able-bodied population to serve in the militia, maintaining the fortifications and manning the walls and pickets against Crescent invaders or bandits from elsewhere in Ussura. This tradition dates back to Breslau's first settlement as a mining town.

The mines near Breslau produce demantoid gemstones, gold, copper, diamonds and small amounts of iron. These resources keep the town rich so long as trade with southern provinces and Cathay continues. The mines run on an uncommon system: a worker-run commune, owned in equal parts by everyone, contributes to the efforts. The idea came from the early history of Ussuran Orthodoxy, a far less hierarchical and authoritarian time when people lived and worked in groups for the common good. Koshchei collects a portion of their profits as taxes, but otherwise leaves the mine alone.

The problem with this system? It is technically illegal by Ussuran law. A few hundred years ago, boyars pressured the Czar to outlaw peasant communes after muzhik revolts ousted several boyars and replaced them with systems like Breslau's. When visitors come from other provinces, Koshchei comes down from his castle and administrators dress up in fancy clothing so everyone can pretend boyars own the mine like anywhere else in Ussura. But it is only a matter of time before the truth gets out. Some boyars would love an excuse to sweep in and steal Koshchei's lucrative mines. Others personally fear or hate Koshchei. Worst of all, added attention might clue the outside world into the women Koshchei hides in his castle.

## Saranbaatar

Saranbaatar is Molhynia's largest Khazar city. Like many Khazar settlements, Saranbaatar is mobile. Three to five times a year, the entire city breaks down in less than a day, rides to its next location and then sets up just as quickly at its new site.

Scouts range ahead of it, identifying oncoming threats and relaying information back to tribal elders who decide on a new location for the town. Sometimes they choose the location based on the motions of enemies, the spirits and their premonitions about weather or a resource surplus that pushes the town towards trade with another settlement.

## Animals

Animals outnumber humans in every Khazar settlement. Each family maintains enough riding and pack animals—horses, camels and yaks—to move them, their *ger* and possessions from place to place when Saranbaatar migrates. The family also has at least one *bankhar*: a large, sturdy, fluffy dog to guard and accompany the family.

Bankhars are a landrace rather than a breed, naturally adapted, rather than bred over thousands of years to thrive in Ussuran climates and watch over flocks and errant children. Many large flocks of sheep and a few goats also travel with Saranbaatar. A hunter relies on raptors, primarily golden eagles, to help him take in game.

Surplus wealth is traditionally measured in extra horses; Khazari generally think of value in terms of how many horses (or what fraction of a horse) something rates, and horses feature in at least half of all Khazar songs. The horses tend to be compact and sturdy, suitable for roles from labor to combat to providing milk for fermentation, but specialized for few.

## The Khazar Ger

A ger is a large, sturdy tent. It consists of a wooden lattice, doorframe, support poles, roof beams and a circular crown, over which the inhabitants stretch felt made of sheep's wool. Gers vary in size from single-family dwellings to giant tents used for public meetings and the like. A ger usually takes a family about two hours to set up, but comfortably defends against the Ussuran cold and elements once in place. When broken down for transit, camels or yaks bear the ger's individual pieces towards the tribe's next destination.

## Stupas

After a life of adventuring, the great Sarangerel Bogatyr settled down (by Khazar standards, anyway) and took holy orders, becoming a Madhyamika nun. Founded by a Cathayan sage, Madhyamika seeks freedom from human suffering through compassion, moderation and non-attachment. She originally founded the city now called Saranbaatar as a nomadic Madhyamika monastery, although it rapidly picked up clergy and followers from every religion in Ussura.

The favorite locations at which Saranbaatar typically sets down have two permanent structures: a bath house and a *stupa*. A stupa is a dome-shaped mound of rock or other earthwork containing the relics of deceased Madhyamika monks and nuns. In Khazar territory, stupas often have a syncretic function, becoming bases for Turăist shamanism, Yachidi temples or whatever other religious structure passing Khazari may need.

Saranbaatar is large enough to have dedicated clergy for different denominations, but like most Khazar clergy, they happily muddle through some other denomination's rituals if, for example, you need to talk to the ghost of an ancestor interred at the stupa right now.

After Saranbaatar fully sets up at a new location, a religious festival highlights the teachings and interests of those interred at the local stupa. The festival also venerates and illustrates the local spiritual landscape, describing which deities and other figures inhabit the countryside as well as how they might be respected and propitiated.

For the past few years, though, Saranbaatar has found many traditional stupas in the wilderness despoiled or desecrated. Even after the townsfolk pitch in to reconstruct and revitalize the stupa, many of the ghosts and spirits who once attended do not return and shamans' calls go unanswered. They have not yet discovered the truth, but Matushka is behind the stupas' desecration. She herself cannot approach a stupa consecrated to other spirits. Yet her drive to marginalize every other spirit in Ussura has led her to bewitch humans to despoil stupas after Saranbaatar or another moving city has visited it.

## Sports

In and around a large and colorfully decorated tent at the edge of town, athletic competition teaches young Khazari many crucial life skills, most importantly sportsmanship. When you and your neighbors constantly raid one another, you have to know how to set aside personal antagonism in case, for example, a giant empire attacks your territory and you must band together to drive them off. Every Khazar physically able to do so learns archery, horsemanship and wrestling. Less universal but still important are hunting (usually with eagles, occasionally with smaller raptors) and the use of traditional hand-to-hand weapons including the knife, spear, axe, saber and shield. Khazari working as mercenaries sometimes carry pistols, but muskets and crossbows are unpopular compared to the famous recurved composite bow of the steppes.

For practical and religious reasons, the spirits forbid mortal combat between Khazar and Khazar within a radius of a few kilometers extending out from a stupa. Break this rule, and a spirit conveys his displeasure with unseasonable squalls or animal stampedes. Offend a Khazar near a stupa and she will probably challenge you to wrestle a few rounds at the athletic tent instead.

The latest athletic craze is *chogān*, a sport invented the Crescent state of Persis to train cavalry. Two teams of four riders each use mallets to knock a ball into a goal at their opponents' end of the field. Khazari have gone predictably mad for this exhilarating intersection of riding and tactics, even going so far as to invent camel and yak variants because why the hell not. This year, Saranbaatar has chosen a site further south than usual in hopes of attracting Gallenian chogān teams, currently the best in Ussura, to attend their yearly invitational games.

## Military Defenses

During more restive times, mobile cities underpinned Khazar war efforts. Enemies struggled to strategize how to attack or occupy Khazar territory when their cities' locations were mere guesswork. Half-completed enemy fortifications littered the steppes during times of war as cities like Saranbaatar turned into siege machines alarmingly fast.

Like in Breslau, every able-bodied Saranbaatar resident fights in times of war. A soldier, typically mounted, maintains a herd of around sixteen horses to stay fast during times of intense warfare. These horses also provide milk or occasionally meat. A soldier protects herself with lamellar armor and a conical helmet with a neck guard. She mostly relies on the bow and arrow as her primary weapon, with a basket-shaped shield and axe, spear, mace or saber in case things get close. A section leader wears a banner bearing his clan's *tamga*, or sigil, to identify himself. He issues battle orders as song lyrics, easy to remember and recognize, backed by percussion instruments such as drums or bells.

## The Crystal Mountain

Molhynian mountains are among Ussura's tallest, including the largest, the Crystal Mountain, a gigantic peak more notable for the width of its base than for its height. It is made entirely of a translucent crystal, blinding to look upon while the sun shines. A twelve-headed dragon once occupied a lake nearby, concealing all the treasures (and people) he stole inside the mountain. Only by transforming herself into an ant, using powers she had learned in the Vir'ava Forest, could Sarangerel Bogatyr free them.

Inscriptions on rock and crystal faces in the crystal foothills warn travelers that atop the mountain dwells Chernobog, a spirit and a mystery even to most Ussurans. They have heard of him, of course: the great black horror atop the highest mountains, flinging lightning from on high, cursing anyone who disturbs him. As a god of mountains and storms, he is associated with Molhynia, a province few non-natives visit.

The funny thing is, though, no one actually knows anyone Chernobog has cursed. It is always just rumors, none of them particularly old: an acquaintance of a friend of a relative who went up on a mountain and got the pox…or was he forced to wander the wilderness forever? No one can remember. Truth is, Chernobog has not actually cursed anyone, because Chernobog is not actually Chernobog—he is someone much older, in disguise.

In northeastern Ussura, people worship a far more popular storm deity, Tură, the ancient sky-god of the Khazari. But Tură is not just god of the sky: he is the very sky and the weather. When you walk out of your ger and feel the wind and the spray of fog on your face, when you see the distant lightning or feel the summer sun's heat emerge from behind a cloud—that is not just Tură's purview, it is Tură.

Tură once loved Matushka. Together they ruled over the steppes, Tură in the sky and Matushka on the earth. But humans fascinated Matushka, so much that she could not let them be. Matushka wanted to get personally involved in human life, to help or hinder them as they matched or transgressed against her laws. Tură could not countenance such a choice, and so he left. Since then, he has watched Matushka's icy grip tighten over Ussura. She terrifies the other Leshiye, drives them into the wilderness and keeps them away from the humans she sees as her children, and her children alone. But she is domineering and cruel. Tură, who left because he did not want to get involved, now feels an obligation to do so. He is not just a weather deity, however, he is the weather and cannot take human form. From atop the very highest mountain in all Ussura, a climber can hear something inaudible: the voice of Tură himself, words rolling and crackling from dark clouds like thunder.

Tură needs his secret kept. If Matushka knew he was back and meddling in the affairs of humans, she would kill him, or at least try to. The Chernobog story cuts down on the number of adventurers who would otherwise climb the mountain at night to hear the god's voice: why make the effort when all it will get you is a curse? A Khazar shaman knows the truth, but to keep it from Matushka, he swears to secrecy. Thus, only a formidable and foolhardy bogatyr climbs the Crystal Mountain to challenge the unchallengeable Chernobog. Once she summits, she finds something older and wiser waiting. These bogatyrs hear the truth from Tură's own voice as he recruits them to resist someone he once loved.

Tură's chosen are still mostly Khazari, but a steady trickle of Heroes from outside Molhynia have joined their ranks. This new generation of bogatyr now wanders Ussura, telling others that "Chernobog has cursed them." Little do others know, and little does Matushka know, these new bogatyr collect friends, resources and power, preparing to stand up to Matushka and make Ussura a safe place for other Leshiye again.

# Dar Matushki

A woman had two daughters, one beloved and one despised. One day the woman sent her despised daughter out into the snow to gather berries. As the daughter despaired over her task, she met and gave kindness to an old woman. She returned home with berries and gold beside. The next day the woman sent out her beloved daughter, certain the girl would earn an even better prize. But the girl was cruel to the old woman and returned home with snakes twisted around her arms. The snakes squeezed and pinched her, just like she did to her sister. The girl vowed to make amends. Once she did and for as long as she remained merciful, the snakes were hers to command.

Matushka guards Ussura from outsiders, from other Leshiye and from Ussurans themselves. She seeks out those in need of correction, the humans who poison Ussura with their cruelty, fear, excess and lies. An Ussuran who passes her tests returns with whatever he had sought and an additional gift, such as a warm coat, a bit of gold or new boots, for being so good. Those who fail earn a Lesson.

A Lesson forces a person failing the Mother's tests to face his weakness. The Lessons are usually painful, all the better to stick in the memory. A girl may speak toads and snakes until she stops speaking lies. A fox may accompany a boy, committing him to terrible tasks until he stops running from everything that scares him. A woman may thirst no matter how much she drinks until she sets all alcohol aside. A man may lose all he owns or holds dear until he learns to give away what he can to those in need.

Once a person who failed his tests learns his Lessons, he receives two Gifts. A person who forgets her Lessons, lose her Gifts. This loss is not a punishment, but a warning. If she persists in her forgetfulness and does not repent, she receives her Lesson again. This time the Lesson will be more painful than before and much more difficult to forget.

## The Test and the Tested

Matushka's tests are always easy to pass and easy to fail. She goes into the world disguised as an old woman or as a child, whichever her target is more inclined to ignore. In this guise, she requests help. The request is always minor, for example, some bread, guidance home, a bit of money or a toy fetched down from a tree. She asks for food, money, time or a bit of endangerment, but never for more than her target can give.

Matushka tests three types of people. The first shows behavior she believes harms Ussura, but has the ability to learn and the potential for Heroism. Matushka does not waste her touch on those who cannot or refuses to contribute to Ussura. The second person includes those who, having learned one Lesson, request another. Matushka smiles on one who wishes to better himself, but her pleasure does not make his Lessons any less terrible or Restrictions less binding. The third bears undue hardship with patience and cheer. For this unfortunate, the test presents a potential reward for her good behavior. She receives a gift, but not Matushka's Touch. She does not require Lessons, nor does she receive one.

## The Lesson

Matushka's Lessons hurt, no exception. The pain may include physical, mental or social sources (persistent wounds, nightmares, ridicule), whatever is most effective case by case.

The Lesson targets and reveals a vice: cowardice, spitefulness, mendacity, cruelty, indifference or over-indulgence. It requires that a person who failed his test understands why he earned Matushka's attention. The Lesson concludes when the sufferer demonstrates this understanding. These demonstrations are usually personal and not as demanding as the penance required for breaking a restriction. For example, a liar might confess his lies and undo a harm his dishonesty had caused. A coward could brave a task that scared her. Someone cruel could apologize to whomever he hurt and show her unqualified kindness.

On rare occasion, a person refuses to learn her Lessons. For her, the Lesson never ends.

## The Gift and Restriction

Once the Lesson concludes, Matushka revisits the tested, in person or in dream, and gives him two Gifts and a Restriction. She explains the Gifts and everything required of him in return. No one has the option to refuse. They call a person who completes his lesson *Poluchatel* (recipient). The Gifts he receives are extensions of the Mother's own power, her command over the land and its fauna and expertise with mending.

Each Gift carries a restriction that reinforces the Lesson. Liars must be truthful. Hedonists must practice restraint. Whoever breaks a restriction loses access to his Gifts and must do penance to regain it.

The combination of Gift and Restriction is called a Lesson so that the Poluchatel never forgets what he has learned. One who does not do his penance must undergo his Lesson again. It is less easy the second time.

## The Exception, or The Seeker's Test

The exception to the above is one who seeks Matushka out on her own. Matushka watches her seekers and decides which may find her and which may not. Those who find her receive three objects: one to destroy, one to protect and one to give away. The seeker must determine which is which and treat each object appropriately. This test requires discernment, intelligence,

obedience and command over personal desires as the most desirable items are often those which he must destroy or give away. Whether the objects are only items or symbols of something greater, such as a child, wealth, safety or love, only the seekers know.

If she succeeds, the seeker receives two Gifts of her choice with the Restriction easiest for her to keep. The naturally kind must always show kindness, for example. To those who fail, Matushka offers a choice: freedom or a Lesson.

## The Czars

Matushka pays special attention to the Czars and Czarinas of Ussura. She tests each leader repeatedly and extends her blessing as long as they continue to pass. These tests are secretive and do not follow a predictable pattern. Only once a leader has failed does Matushka reveal the test.

One famously failed test involved an apple tree. Every night someone stole apples from the tree. Rather than investigating himself, the then-Czar sent his sons. The thieves killed one son and injured the other. Matushka berated the Czar for laziness and cowardice because he refused to go on his own and removed her blessing. After that, the injured son died and the Czar's wife left him for fear that Matushka's curse would taint her as well.

Each Czar and Czarina knows that they must always be their best and to be the best leader for Ussura. Without Matushka's blessing, retaining power demands terrible sacrifice and personal loss.

Many wait for either Ilya or Ketheryna to fail Matushka's tests so they know who to support, but whatever she has put before them, they both seem to have passed without incident.

## The Poluchatel in the Community

An Ussuran regards the Poluchatel with wary respect: wary, because he knows very few become Poluchatel without cause, and respect, because he knows the Gifts require strong self-control to maintain. Additionally, several famous Ussuran Heroes were also Poluchatel. Their early encounters with Matushka and how they transformed from bad children to heroic adults remain popular stories in Ussura, especially among children.

# Tură's Touch

Just as Ussura has its mother in Matushka, it has its father in Tură. He approaches this role differently than Matushka. Instead of restrictions, he gives freedom and responsibility. Some say he is less cruel than Matushka, but he demands just as much in the end.

To better understand the difference, imagine that someone asks you to bake a cake. Matushka would give you a recipe and demand that you follow each line exactly, swatting you with a wooden spoon each time you made a mistake or forcing you start over. Tură would give you every ingredient you needed or requested and a kitchen to work within, but let you figure out the steps for yourself. In the end, both require the cake.

Tură is not necessarily against everything Matushka stands for; instead he does not like her methods, and he is less than pleased with how she treats the other Leshiye.

Tură and Matushka once loved each other and shared in one another's power. Matushka allowed Tură to use and gift Regeneration, while Tură allowed her to use and gift Storm. Now, however, they regard one another as a danger to Ussura. Matushka is, as yet, unaware that Tură has begun to actively work against her. He has used Matushka's own transformative powers to hide himself as Chernobog and remains high in the mountains, closer to his own realm.

When a person finds Tură, he offers her Gifts in exchange for a Task and a Mark. One who refuses his offer awakens in the mountains without any memory of Tură or her time with him. Those who accept become Chernobog's Cursed.

Tură tasks his new charges with righting the wrongs he perceives Matushka has perpetrated throughout Ussura. Namely, he seeks to free the other Leshiye from Matushka's prohibitive restrictions.

When a Cursed leaves the mountains, he weaves fantastic stories of how he disturbed Chernobog and earned his ire. The Cursed are united in their campaign against Matushka's control and keep Tură's secrets. Only when they find someone who could add to their cause do they quietly share the truth.

## How It Works

Tură does not seek anyone out, but waits for seekers. You may have found Tură by accident while exploring the mountains, or maybe you heard of his hiding place from one of the Cursed. When you acquire the Sorcery Advantage, Tură gives you two Gifts and a Task. He also leaves a black mark about the size of a large thumbprint on your face, neck or hands. Once you have Tură's Mark, he can give you additional Gifts and Tasks through your dreams.

### Gift

This is a supernatural power. Where Matushka's power focuses on mending the land and its fauna, Tură's Gifts focus on the sky and weather. You can use your power by spending a Hero Point.

### Task

Your Hero gains a special Story—"Tură's Task"—that details just what Tură wants from you. You may complete Steps in other Stories as normal, but the Hero cannot write any new Stories until you complete Tură's Task. Once completed, you can write new Stories just as normal.

## Gifts

Tură's Gifts are very similar to Matushka's, but are sky and weather flavored. From the list of example Matushka's Gifts in the **Core Rulebook**, Tură only offers Illuminate, Purify, Storm and Regeneration.

The following is a list of additional example Gifts that only Tură provides. You can create your own with the Game Master's assistance. All Gifts require a Hero Point to use.

### Language of Birds

You can speak to any birds in the Scene. You may ask them about what they have seen or heard before you arrived or earlier in their travels. You may also request aid from the birds in Tură's name. Even birds who have never been to Ussura try to fulfill your request. If the request requires a Risk, the bird rolls 5 Dice, but you decide how it spends its Raises. It gains 2 Bonus Dice if the request is particularly well suited to it.

## Lightning

You summon lightning to strike your enemies. While you can summon lightning no matter the weather, you must have clear access to the sky. If you are indoors and all the windows are closed, you cannot summon it. With lightning, you deal Wounds equal to your Ranks in Scholarship. Wounds caused by lightning cannot be defended against.

## Read the Wind

The breeze brings you quick images from wherever the slightest wind can touch. This can be a quick way to check for anyone following you, an ambush up ahead or anything interesting nearby. If you concentrate, however, you can focus on one or two events near or far. This is a Notice Risk. For each Raise, you can ask a question about what is happening in the scenes. Each question may only involve one sense, that is, what is visible, audible or smellable, not two or more at a time.

## Wind Walk

You, and anything directly touching your skin, become air. You should probably ask a friend to watch your gear. While wind walking, you are invisible and intangible, but if you talk or make some other noise, you can be heard. Also, someone may notice a slight breeze when you walk past. You may travel as an air current can, meaning you cannot go through liquid or solid objects, but you can move through cracks or small holes.

Wind walking is a dangerous endeavor. You must take care to remain whole and not get trapped in someone else's lungs or in a small, unbreakable container. If you do, you cannot turn back to your corporeal form. If you remain as wind for more than 15 minutes, you start to lose yourself. You can sustain this form for one Scene. Each Scene after that costs 2 Wounds. These Wounds are taken at the start of the Scene and do not heal until you become corporeal again. If you take a Dramatic Wound while Wind Walking, you immediately become corporeal again, unless trapped. If trapped, you continue taking Wounds until free. Once free, you immediately become corporeal again.

## Tasks

When you first meet Turǎ, he asks if you are willing to keep his secret and to spread the myth of the terrible Chernobog. If you agree, he gives you two Gifts and a Task.

The number of Story Steps for the Task depends on the number of Gifts you have. Each time you purchase the Sorcery Advantage you gain two additional Gifts and two additional Steps to your Task. These Steps can be separate one-Step Stories or combined for a single two-Step Story. Therefore, if you take the Sorcery Advantage once, you can choose between taking 2 one-Step Tasks or 1 two-Step Task. If you take it twice, receiving four Gifts, you have four Steps to distribute among one to four Tasks.

### Spread Turǎ's Message

At one Step, this requires simply telling a story that reflects well on other Leshiye, it doesn't have to be Turǎ, or poorly on Matushka. The Cursed have earned a reputation as storytellers across Ussura because of this common task. At two Steps, you must tell stories to three different communities. At three Steps, you must identify a good candidate for the Cursed and send a message back the mountain near Turǎ. At four Steps, you must approach the candidate yourself and give directions to the mountain. If he refuses Turǎ's Gifts, he won't remember you.

### Undermine Matushka's Message

At one Step, you must help someone by teaching her how to take care of herself. In this way, you remind others that they must take care of themselves to help others. At two Steps, you must invite strangers to join you for a rousing evening of new friendship, food and overindulgence. In this way, you demonstrate that indulgence can be positive rather than always a vice. At three Steps, you must convince people to work together to build walls to keep out the dangers of the wild. In this way, you teach people that a healthy amount of fear bears rewards. At four Steps, you must find someone planning to seek out Matushka and convince her that she either does not need sorcery or should seek Turǎ instead. In this way you either help someone understand her own power or, at the least, ensure Matushka has one fewer Poluchatel.

## Stop Matushka

At one Step, Tură gives you a specific Task as part of a much larger plan he does not share. The Task may be delivering a letter, standing outside of a house for several hours, opening a window or singing a certain song loudly in a certain bar. At the second Step, Tură asks you to perform two small, seemingly unrelated tasks. At three Steps, Tură asks you to answer a question that requires some investigation. At four Steps, Tură asks you to answer a question that requires spying on one of the Poluchatel, the Czar, the Czarina or on Matushka herself.

The following are two examples of possible Tasks, the first at one Step and the other at four:

### Spread Tură's Message

**Ending:** Children share the story you told them.

*Steps*
- Travel to a small village and tell a story of a fantastic Leshy who grants wishes.

### Stop Matushka

Tură has asked you to discover how a popular Poluchatel healer came to the city.
**Ending:** The healer is disgraced.

*Steps*
- Travel to the city and ask around about the healer.
- Track down the inn where the healer first stayed when she came to the city
- Meet with the priest who delivered the healer to inn and convince him to share the healer's confession.
- Smuggle what you have learned to another of the Cursed to take to Tură.

If you take the Sorcery Advantage at character creation, you can claim you have already completed up to half of the required Steps for your Task(s), round up. If you do this, you and the GM decide together what you have done so far and name someone you affected with your deeds. You may also choose to start the game with Tură Tasks as your initial Story.

## The Mark

When Tură gives you your first Gift, he marks you with his thumb. This Mark appears as a black splotch on your skin. The splotch appears on your face, neck or hands and is always cold to the touch. If you have the Mark, you can tell if another's Mark is true or false. The Mark also allows Tură to bestow additional Gifts on you without requiring you to visit him in the mountains again.

## The Cursed in the Community

How an Ussuran treats the Cursed depends on whether or not he knows about the Mark. If he does not know, he assumes the Cursed is one of the Poluchatel and treats her accordingly. This is true even if he sees her use a Gift only offered by Tură.

If he knows about the Mark, though, he knows she belongs to Chernobog's Cursed and treats her with suspicion and pity. Suspicion because he has heard the stories the Cursed have spread about themselves and Chernobog. Pity because he believes that every Cursed is doomed to die a violent death.

If an Ussuran knows that you are one of the Cursed, any action you take in a Dramatic Sequence involving him requires an additional Raise to overcome his suspicion.

## The Cursed and the Poluchatel

Generally, the Cursed and the Poluchatel treat one another well. The Poluchatel tend to treat strangers kindly regardless, and a Cursed cultivates friendships she may later exploit for information. Once Matushka learns that Tură has been meddling, however, the dynamic among the Cursed and Poluchatel is certain to change.

# Dueling in Ussura

Ussuran dueling has always favored an unarmed style of combat. Some say that only in a fistfight can one learn the true measure of her worth as a warrior. Because of this, formalized styles of fistfighting are taught all across Ussura, regardless of social class. Many Ussuran boyars favor their native fistfighting styles over the sword-based duels popular in Théah's other countries.

Because an Ussuran duelist needs relatively little in the way of gear or equipment to practice these arts, even the smallest village in the Ussuran tundra boasts a handful of duelists. An Ussuran duelist prides himself on teaching and training the most promising youths. He drinks vodka and quietly watches as his village's children engage in the normal scrapes of childhood, afterward seeking those who displayed the greatest instinct for brawling. He trains these youths rigorously, ensuring the children master the art.

In cities there are formal and prestigious dueling academies such as the Schola Vani (School of War) in Ussura's capital of Pavtlow. Unlike their more rustic counterparts, these schools are actively courted by parents seeking admission for their children. The schools typically limit admission to the children of boyars or others with the means to pay for attendance; however, they may allow an especially talented muzhik child to train on scholarship. Although these scholarships are few and far between, they provide hopes to an Ussura's muzhik child that someday, through sheer will combined with strength of arm, she may one day rise above her station.

Ussuran dueling is on full display during holidays and Winter Fairs. There, boyars host dueling contests in honor of Matushka. In preparation for these contests, messengers carry word across their region, seeking out the most promising duelists to attend and perform in public. Depending upon the holiday, fair and the hosting boyar, one of many different forms of duelist competitions may occur. However, regardless of the kind of duel, one rule takes precedence: never hit a duelist once she has fallen to the ground.

The first, and most common form of the duel is the one-on-one fistfight. One-on-one duels come in two forms. In the first, known as *perestrelka* (skirmish), a duelist dodges and weaves, avoiding attacks and hitting the other when she can. The second form, known as *povoroti* (turns), practiced by only the most stout and sturdy, requires the fighters to take turns hitting one another.

When one of these duelists receives a punch, dodging is against the rules. All she can do is defend herself with her arms and wait her turn.

The most popular of duelist competitions at festivals are known as wall-on-wall matches. Providing the greatest form of entertainment in Ussura, they involve anywhere from dozens of participants in small towns to hundreds in large cities. These bouts can last for hours. Participants form teams known as "walls," and

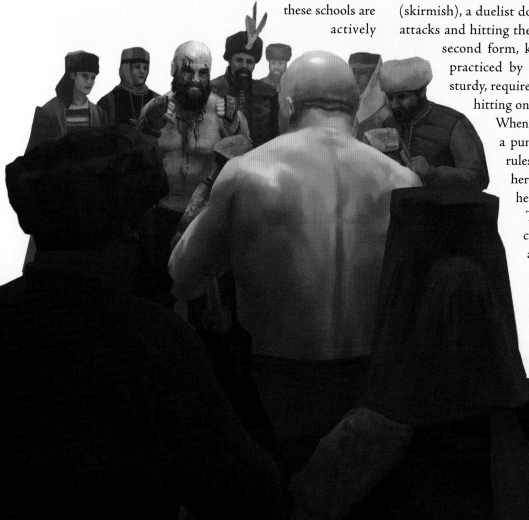

each wall has a chief fighter who serves as a tactician and commanding officer. Each wall is composed of a tight formation of duelists, three to four ranks deep. The goal is to attack the other wall and push it out of the match area.

Wall-on-wall fights often employ basic tactical approaches to the fights. Teams try to breach the opposing wall by using their heaviest fighters, or they may try to encircle a wall and force it to defend attacks from all sides, thereby wearing down each individual duelist. Walls may often use false retreats or other tactics designed to lull the opposing wall into a false sense of complacency. However, as a general rule, each wall does their best to ensure that they never break formation during the games. To do so risks giving the opposing side an advantage that might be decisive to the match.

Whether one-on-one or wall-on-wall, a duelist in these contests fights with bare arms—that way he demonstrates to all watching that he uses only the strength of his own muscles without the need for steel or iron reinforcement.

In Ussura, the bare-knuckled duelists are every bit as respected as their blade-wielding counterparts in Théah. That is not to say, however, that Ussuran duelists never use swords and other traditional bladed weaponry. A true duelist master realizes he must sometimes meet an opponent on his own terms. Such masters are eager to learn the bladed duelist arts of other schools.

Knowledge of bladed techniques has also been necessary in times of war, as Ussurans are ever the pragmatists. Though less common amongst Ussuran duelists, bladed dueling is most often found in cities where dueling schools teach bladework as part of the curriculum. However, amongst kin and fellow Ussurans, the bare-fisted boxing duelist techniques reign supreme.

## NEW YEAR'S EVE

The grandest festival for Ussuran duelists occurs on New Year's Eve. Cities and villages alike celebrate and feast, slaughtering hogs to eat and uncorking the finest winter ale. Children go to bed early, eager to receive presents from Grandfather Frost and his granddaughter Snegurochka. Public squares host dueling exhibitions amongst these festivals at both the individual and wall-on-wall level.

Ussura's finest fighters gather to compete for the entertainment of each community and to gain favor and notoriety amongst the boyars. The ultimate dream for duelists is to be invited to the rare Pavtlowan one-on-one match for New Year's Eve, when even the loser of such a match shall know fame and fortune!

## Kulachniy Boi

The most widespread of Ussuran fistfighting duelist techniques, *kulachniy boi* (fist pugilism), focuses on punching and boxing. Kulachniy boi duelists practice these arts for both practical as well as ceremonial purposes. During Ussuran holidays, duelists meet and fight for sport with no intention to do any lasting harm to one another. After all, everyone is gathered in celebration.

This changes when a kulachniy boi duelist goes out into the world, where her knowledge can mean the difference between life and death. The specially made gloves and metal arm guards known as rukavitsa provide a kulachniy boi duelist with the ability to inflict far greater damage, while still maintaining the appearance of being unarmed.

### Style Bonus: Iron and Velvet

When wearing rukavitsa under her longsleeves, a Kulachniy Boi Duelist may use her Ranks in Brawl in place of Weaponry when she performs Duelist Maneuvers. While wearing the rukavitsa, the duelist gains one free Raise to keep her weapon concealed.

# Legendi of Ussura

Despite some Church factions' best efforts, the Ussuran people know better than to abandon their belief in the strange and wondrous. Their wintry crucible of a home is a haven for spirits, magic and the inexplicable. The minute an Ussuran stops making her yearly offerings to Matushka or tills land that belongs to a wilderness spirit, she forfeits her right to the Leshiye's protection, and many brand her an outsider. Outsiders don't fare well in Ussura's punishing winter, so an Ussuran continues to heed tales like these and views efforts to dissuade her with suspicion.

## Chervona Ruta, the Fern Flower

On the mountain slopes of Ussura, a rare yellow fern flower grows, the *chervona ruta*. Legend says that once a year on the summer solstice, the setting sun lends its colors to the flower as it blooms, turning it red just for one night and enchanting it with the summer's own luck. Picking it brings magic and danger into your life, as those who take such magic for themselves almost certainly die afterward.

A red fern flower brings fortune to the one who carries it. This fortune may take the form of wealth or luck, but as long as the flower is alive, its magic works. Some people have tried drying the flowers to keep the luck going, but this seems to have no effect.

Gifted from one who plucked it from the ground to another, it can forge the bonds of love where none existed before, though the bonds wither and die when the flower does. Some people say the love forged through a fern ensures a bond of hatred when the flower's magic fades. Others insist that the love forged through the flower sparks a natural love that persists beyond the magic of the flower. These people say that the red fern forged love is stronger than any other.

Woven into a crown or bracelet and worn, the red chervona ruta grants the gift of animal speech. It only works in the area where the flower grows, but all manner of animals have great wisdom to share upon the Ussuran slopes.

But beware—evil spirits stand guard where it grows, and those who take it for themselves must kill or outsmart these guardians to lay hands on the crimson bloom.

## The Truth

The legends about the chervona ruta's enchantments are true, but the spirits that guard it are not evil. They are hirelings of the Leshy Poludnitsa, also known as Lady Midday. Poludnitsa, a cruel and pessimistic spirit of summer who loathes humankind, views agriculture as an attack on the land. She afflicts farmers and travelers with heat sickness if they cannot solve her riddles and uses her scythe to cut down those who cross her.

She enchanted the chervona ruta with the solstice's power to win a wager with Matushka. Poludnitsa insists that humans, greedy by nature, always put themselves first. She made the fern's leaves to yield a tea that can grant a weaker, more temporary version of the flower's magic; but to benefit from its full power, one must pick the flower, uprooting and killing it.

She bet Matushka that nine times out of ten, a human would pluck the flower instead of brewing its tea and leaving the enchanted bloom for others to find. Her spirits guard the flower not to stop anyone from picking it, but simply to question a visitor about his intentions and report back afterward.

Those who kill the flower for selfish ends meet death by Lady Midday's scythe. Those who pick only the leaves for tea, or who take the flower only out of selfless need on someone else's behalf, escape unscathed.

A Hero who learns the truth can trick or persuade Lady Midday to end her wager by proving her wrong about human nature. A Hero could get drawn into the affair by someone on the run from Poludnitsa's judgment or he could end up on her bad side himself. Matushka could even involve the Heroes in an attempt to win the bet, if one of them possesses her Gifts and maintains her favor.

Lady Midday is a Strength 9 Monster with the Elemental (Heat) and Relentless Monstrous Qualities.

## The Firebird

Few have ever seen the Firebird, but many claim that honor. Few possess one of her magical feathers, but many possess mundane imitations.

Tales of the wondrous miracles the Firebird can perform vary from region to region. Here, rumors say she heals the sick and resurrects the dead. There, stories say she grants wishes but at the price of shortened years, and she stores up the unused years in her tail feathers to distribute among the worthy. Elsewhere, fables say she can tell truth from lies and burns up a liar who uses her silver tongue to take what is not hers. All the tales agree that the Firebird is a beautiful bird with bright plumage in flame colors, and that her feathers provide warmth, light and good fortune to whoever holds them.

Just enough people have encountered the Firebird or run across one of her lost feathers to prompt dozens of Heroes, bandits and the desperate to travel far and wide searching for her. Boyars with something to prove send champions to cage her and bring her home. Merchants, thieves and the hopeless poor quest to collect her feathers and make a fortune selling them to kings and sorcerers across Théah. Adventurous children pursue her aid to cure ailing parents of incurable diseases, and heartbroken lovers want to beg her to bring their dead paramours back to life. Some even seek to worship her.

The Firebird is an elusive and dangerous prize that nonetheless attracts pilgrims from all walks of life who expect her to fulfill promises she never made. The problem is, no one knows where she can be found. Some legends claim she can only be found in the far north in the frozen mountains near Breslau. Others say she makes her home in Vir'ava Forest amongst the talking animals. Despite both these places being common hunting grounds for the Firebird, few still catch sight of her.

## The Truth

The Firebird was once a young woman named Stasya. Her family was oppressive and cruel, forcing her to work long hours in their mine with little respite. She went hungry and thirsty most days, pulling red rubies from inside the mine. Koshchei the Deathless heard of her plight, and rescued her, as he often does.

Yet, inside his castle, Stasya had a hard time fitting in. She longed to be truly free, roaming the Ussuran countryside. Koshchei could not let the girl go, because it would endanger the rest of his charges. She yearned for freedom, but Koshchei could not let her leave.

So, she made a deal with a fire Leshy, who transformed her into a bird of fire and light. She flew away from castle, seeking her freedom. Yet, even now she is in a different kind of prison, for the fire Leshiye refused to return her to her human form.

Koshchei, for his part, seeks the girl, afraid she will reveal his operation and endanger his charges. Reports of his interest in the Firebird has drawn other interested parties, assuming she has some kind of magical properties he wants. From there, the legend of the Firebird took on its own life and has grown ever since.

Many boyars—the Deathless included—routinely offer significant rewards to any who can track down the Firebird and hand her over to them. She, in turn, seeks someone willing and able to help her transform back into a human, or at the very least to protect her from the grasping hands of Ussuran greed. She does not want to be anyone's prisoner, no matter how well-meaning or desperate her jailer may be, but she also fears disappointed retribution from those who discover her warm, fiery glow is her only magical power. Until she knows someone truly wants to help her, she fights for her life if found or caught.

The Firebird is a Strength 4 Monster with the Elemental (Fire) Monstrous Quality.

## Mstitel the Night-Haunt

In a blue dusk, the crunch of horses' hooves in fresh snow and the jingle of their tack ring out above the wind's dire susurrus, and a silent shape follows where they lead. It knows the flash of coin by torchlight, exchanging hands to pay for meat and wine. It can smell a boyar from a mile away. And soon after, it destroys him.

Mstitel the Night-Haunt is the bedtime story a grown adult tells in the dead of winter, safe in his lofty fortress towers behind comforting lines of pikes. He tells of its uncanny ability to spot boyars, its trickster nature and its steely claws that rend and tear apart its unsuspecting victims.

The muzhiks have nothing to fear from this nightmare; it hates the nobility but leaves the peasantry alone. No one knows why, but a boyar from Gallenia Province knows not to travel at night or, if he must, to hide his riches and to dress in plain wool to confuse the great Avenger. Even boyars traveling in groups are not safe from the Night-Haunt, as it seems capable of taking on several men at once.

It comes out after dark to ambush any noble it finds on the road or in the wilderness, first showing itself only in eerie acts of malicious mischief—scattering a campfire's wood, tipping over a wagon or disturbing a flock of bats to swarm the traveler in a shrieking mass. It may trail the boyar for hours, terrorizing her until she can take it no longer.

Once a boyar grows sufficiently terrified, running for his life or brandishing lanterns in tenuous shows of bravado, Mstitel strikes. It drives idle swords through fleeing victims, pushes boulders down from ridges to crush people or spooks horses into plowing over cliffs or bridges into ravines, taking their riders and carriages with them. The few survivors of Mstitel's attacks say that just before the chaos began, they spotted a pair of furious red eyes watching from the shadows.

## The Truth

Once, a vast and sprawling estate crowned a mountaintop in Gallenia Province, home to the household of Lady Kveta Masalsk Radkova v'Riasanova. Her many children and grandchildren lived with her there, the tenth and eleventh generations of the family to grace its halls.

The estate's domovoi grew fiercely loyal to the family over the years. When a rival boyar family fell to Villainy and brought soldiers to murder Lady Kveta and all her kin, the domovoi was left alone in a house turned empty tomb.

The depths of its grief at losing its purpose and its people drove it to tap into reserves of will and power no domovoi should possess. It became something *else*, something darker and bigger, and its guardian instincts warped into a need to "protect" the land from the boyars who abuse it. It became Mstitel the Night-Haunt.

When it comes upon a traveler, it watches her to determine her noble or common heritage. It listens to her speech, gauges her wealth from what luxuries she carries and occasionally poses questions or riddles with the wind's voice to see how she responds. If it sees anything that displeases it, it succumbs to its rage and plays with her before it kills her, in a horrible mockery of its once-friendly attitude.

If a Hero learns Mstitel's history, she might be able to appease it through vindictive deeds against the family who killed Lady Kveta's brood or funerary rites that put the spirit's vendetta to rest. Perhaps she could even find Lady Kveta's last remaining relative and convince Mstitel to commit itself to his service.

Mstitel is a Strength 7 Monster with the Fearsome, Nocturnal and Shadowy Monstrous Qualities.

## Rusalki and Vodyanoi

All fishers and river travelers in Ussura know the dangers of setting off in a boat without protections from the beauteous rusalki and the hideous vodyanoi. The mere presence of a human who has not placated these creatures with offerings or promises angers them, and when angry, they drown people and break things.

The rusalki were living women once, but linger in their watery graves to haunt anyone with the audacity to survive. The vodyanoi are half-human children born to those who dally with Leshiye of the deep and resent humanity for its ability to travel far and wide while they remain mostly water-bound. People consider the two types of creatures a single cooperative threat.

Some say the rusalki and the vodyanoi enslave humans so they can build a vast army of amphibious soldiers to one day emerge from the lakes and swamps to drown all of Ussura, freeing their malevolent masters to rule it as a vast underwater kingdom. Bogatyr and other armed forces kill or banish these creatures when they can, particularly now that the Ushkuiniks use their relationship with them to strongarm anyone who dares put rudder to river.

Some families whose livelihoods depend on living on a riverbank or lakeshore make long-term deals with the spirits. Such a family might agree to give up its firstborn of every generation to the local rusalki or allow a vodyanoi to spend every thirteenth month under its roof as one of them.

## The Truth

The rusalki and the vodyanoi work together when it pleases them to do so, but their cooperation, a mutual agreement based on shared territory, remains fraught with competition and backstabbing. The Ushkuiniks and others who have figured this out leverage it to their advantage, playing on the spirits' pride and spite to pit them against one another or manipulate them into joining forces for a time.

These creatures entertain no grand plans of armies and conquest, though occasionally a vodyanoi with delusions of grandeur might try to take over a single lakeside estate or fishing enterprise. The rusalki generally lack the imagination or motivation to meddle in land-dweller affairs beyond the shoreline.

The vodyanoi keep underwater fiefdoms in a twisted reflection of surface life. When they "drown" someone, he does not die—instead, the frogpeople curse him to breathe water instead of air and force him into servitude. Tales of daring rescues rarely make it to the fireside; the victim is dead as far as anyone who saw him drown is concerned, and even if someone could rescue him, how would he breathe? But Heroes could bargain with the vodyanoi for the return of loved ones or earn the favor of a more powerful Leshiye who could break the curse.

The rusalki care little for servants or wealth, and, contrary to popular belief, they are not dead and were never human. A rusalka is a water spirit, and watches over a particular area of a waterway and considers it her property. If she seduces, drowns or attacks someone it is because he trespassed in her domain and deserves punishment. If she tricks or convinces a vodyanoi to make someone breathe water so she can take him as her slave, it is because she thought him pretty and wanted him for herself. Rusalki are possessive and jealous creatures with little regard for other people's wishes, which makes them selfish and combative but relatively easy to bribe. A Hero dealing with a rusalka must take care to determine whether the spirit he faces is a true rusalka or a ghost pretending to be one, as the tactics for getting what he wants or ridding the waters of the threat vary greatly between the two.

Rusalki and vodyanoi are Strength 6 Monsters with the Aquatic Monstrous Quality.

## Upir

Among the more dedicated Ussuran Orthodox Church crowd, legends of the *upir* take on the tone of a cautionary tale. Take care, says the Church, not to engage in witchcraft or worship false gods. Do not die of unnatural causes and do not bring corruption or shame upon your family. If you do any of these, you may become upir when you die: a walking corpse that never grows old, thirsting for human blood and killing to survive. They walk among us when the sun sets, drawing a victim away from her safe hearth to drain her and leave her stiff, cold husk lying in the town square for the morning light to reveal.

Those who subscribe to the older tales reject the Church's idea that upir result from sorcery or damnation, instead believing that the upir carry a contagious disease that transforms people into bloodsucking creatures of the night after death.

In places where this belief persists, tradition requires immediate cremation for the bodies of those who die from illness or unknown causes, lest they rise again to become monsters. Some believe an upir can be cured of his condition as long as he does not die first, and each region has its own idea of what signs indicate that someone is upir. Some think the infected person loses the ability to see colors or the ability to eat anything other than meat. Others view erratic or antisocial behavior as symptoms, while still others posit that upir can walk in the bitter cold without protection and come through unscathed.

A third tale puts the blame for the upir condition on a botched reincarnation. By chance or through witchcraft, two souls reincarnate in the same body. While one dominates the waking personality, the other roams free at night while the body sleeps, to deliver nightmares to children and consume their life force.

When the upir dies, the second soul escapes the body as a butterfly or a moth and finds a new host, continuing its murderous escapades. Thus, in communities where this belief holds sway, people kill butterflies and moths on sight in case they house an upir's second soul.

Regardless of the specifics, few Ussurans doubt the existence of the upir. Occasionally, when rumors of sightings fly with greater frequency, small bands of bogatyr seek specialized training from die Kreuzritter

## CAN I PLAY ONE?

Since not all upir are Villains, a player might express interest in playing one. After all, the ability to keep playing the same character even after she dies is appealing. A campaign that includes an undead upir character will veer into a horror story mode relatively often and the player should be prepared to explore the constant struggle against Corruption, but if the GM and players agree that is the sort of story they want, go for it! Use the Befleckte Seele Background (found on page 203 in the *Appendix*), and gain the Nocturnal Monster Quality from the Dark Gift Advantage.

It is also possible to play a living upir for the duration of the campaign, in which case the character's heritage can be a source of story hooks without imposing too much extra temptation toward Villainy.

to become upir hunters and ride to rid the land of these unnatural predators. Scholars from other nations compare the Ussuran upir to various other kinds of blood-drinkers. In some cases the similarities are inarguable, but in others the upir hunter who tries to vanquish her foe by means that should kill an Eisen vampir finds herself in big trouble when they don't work.

## The Truth

The origins of the Ussuran upir lie in dark sorceries of the distant past, when an old patriarch could not bear the thought of dying and meddled in necromancy to save his own wrinkled hide. He won the prize of immortality, but at a terrible price, passing his newly inflicted bloodlust down to his children and his children's children, all the way down the family tree to the present day. The bloodline is far-flung and diluted today, spread thinly throughout Ussura, and not everyone who carries the blood of the patriarch becomes upir.

A person with enough of the blood, born under the right moon—this is a true upir. While he lives, he suffers from strange appetites: raw meat, perhaps, or the company of crows or exposure to the cold. He might even crave blood, but he does not need it to survive. He ages normally and dies normally. Once he *does* die, though, he transforms into an immortal creature that looks and acts just like a human, but hungers for human blood and cannot survive without it.

He can only be killed with fire or by certain rituals or Leshiye-blessed weapons. He is not nocturnal by nature and he only has one soul, but because an upir's soul *does* walk the world without his body while he sleeps, manifesting as a butterfly or a moth to drink the blood of another through her nightmares, a upir can choose to sleep during the day to minimize the harm he can cause.

Not all upir are Villainous, though it is easy for them to become so. The upir condition is not contagious, nor is it caused by practicing sorcery or performing Evil Acts. That said, someone who dabbles in dangerous necromantic magics runs the risk of accidentally (or purposefully) recreating the original ritual and turning himself and his whole family into upir.

Most upir are Monstrous Villains with Strength 7 and Influence 5. They have the Powerful and Regenerating Monstrous Qualities and the Extended Family and Fascinate Advantages. Some exceptionally old upir might have higher Villainy Ranks and more Monstrous Qualities.

## Strannik

Just north and east of Tebizond, high in mountain ranges rarely traversed by people, resides the legendary Strannik.

Some say the creature is simply a human; having been abandoned at birth and raised by bears, she has no knowledge of human society. Some believe she is a Leshiye, more powerful than Matushka, but more elusive, making it difficult to interact and gain a blessing from her. Some believe she is an evil spirit, taking the lives of those who trespass in her mountain passes. Others say she is a terrible serpent, given a humanoid form to trick the heartsick into her lair so that she may suck the warmth from them. Still others believe she is the lone remaining Syrneth, capable of terrible and wondrous acts.

Every story is different except for one thing: she appears as a tall woman, dressed in dark furs and seemingly untouched by the cold of the land. Some stories attribute great power to Strannik, explaining how she reshaped the moutain to better suit her needs. Some describe her as viscious and monstrous, killing any who dare tresspass in her lands. Others say she gives blessings to those who can find her.

### The Truth

The truth is that no one has actually ever seen Strannik. The origins of her legends are as varied and disparate as the legends themselves.

The most common story tells of a young girl lost in the mountains and raised by bears. Even those stories that say Strannik is a Leshiye or Syrneth start somehow with a girl lost in the mountains. Maybe she gained her power through a Leshiye and somehow surpassed her benefactor, or maybe she found a magical artifact in the mountains left by the Syrneth and was subsequently possessed by an ancient spirit.

Everyone in the Somajez Province has a story about Strannik, always involving a friend, acquaintance or even a relative who saw her. This unfortunate soul may have lost his way and was guided to safety by her, or maybe she killed him in a fit of rage (of course, if that were true, how would the storyteller come to know of the incident?).

She may not even exist, but the stories persist, and people spend long nights telling ever more unbelievable stories about Strannik and her wonderful and terrible power.

At this point, the telling of the story is almost as important as the story itself. Any storyteller worth his salt in Ussura has at least one Strannik story, if not several. Sometimes people get into games of one-upmanship, contradicting each others' stories, or telling tales that come from increasingly more credible sources, but always once or twice removed from the storyteller.

Chapter 4

Dodacce

# VODACCE

*"The most extravagant thing a prince can own are
his principles—all too often, their price is his life."*
—Cristoforo Scarovese, *Discourses*

*"For every martyr whose voice carries beyond the
grave, there are ten thousand quiet corpses."*
—Giovanni Villanova

To strangers, Vodacce is a baffling mixture of honor and depravity. Men exercise power over land and kin with impunity, while women warp the strings of destiny.

In Vodacce wicked words will get a man killed, but a wicked action could see him to the heights of power. Here, destiny serves ambition, inaction is sin and ruthlessness merely pragmatism. Male and female, young and old, noble and peasant, all dance on the spider's web called the Great Game, though only a few prowl the center.

## The Great Game

The long, level roads that connect the cities and provinces of Vodacce are a remnant of the Old Empire, a silent testament to the peninsula's last unified days. In the long twilight of imperial glory, ambitious men came and went, each seeking to claim a fraction of its power and prestige for his own.

The precise number of these pretenders has waxed and waned over the centuries; once there were three, today there are seven. But few or many, the stratagems and subterfuges employed by these so-called Princes have weathered the centuries and today are known by a single sobriquet: the Great Game.

Among the defining characteristics of the Great Game are its ruthlessness and omnipresence—the Vodacce say that only Theus sees more and forgives less than a Vodacce Prince. From a bacchanalian revel to the quiet of the confessional, the threads of the Game insinuate themselves into every aspect of life in Vodacce. In truth, the only place to shelter from a Prince's anger is in the court of one of his rivals, and such safe harbor always carries a price. In this manner, even someone seeking safety and security from a momentary slip of the tongue finds himself reduced to little more than a Prince's plaything.

The Game's ruthlessness, in contrast, is little more than pragmatism. In a Nation where well-bred women can ruin a man's fortunes and twist his very nature, a grieving mother, daughter or sister can be every bit as dangerous as an assassin. Early Princes learned, often to their sorrow, that the only sure way to victory is to be thorough in the destruction of one's rivals.

Thus, even the limited niceties of warfare do not apply to the Great Game. A rebellious cousins infant daughter, spared out of momentary sentiment, may grow into a powerful Strega and pass her gift on to her own daughter. So tightly do the ties of family and honor bind that this child may use Fate herself to avenge the death of her grandfather. Should the guilty party go to an untroubled grave, his heir may inherit the hatred of his enemies along with his father's fortune.

For this reason, a wag of the Old Empire once remarked, "call no man happy until he is forgotten," and with typical Vodacce pragmatism, the Princes of old deduced that the easiest way to induce amnesia in their rivals involved regular and thorough blood-lettings. In addition to bringing the cycle of revenge to a close, such displays often have salutary effects on an uninvolved party, who may find his ambition lessened by the potential extermination of everyone he loves.

Sadly, this system of casual brutality perpetuates itself. A Prince who can no longer credibly threaten the swift, sure and comprehensive destruction of his enemies finds them multiplying beyond his reach. In turn, his bloody successor quickly finds himself bound by the same system, becoming both Prince and prisoner in one fell stroke.

# Le Streghe

*"There are no coincidences in Vodacce."*
—Marcelo, called "Il Pazzo di Potenza"

In Vodacce, you do not say that a man has fallen; you say that he was pulled. So all-encompassing is Sorte's reach that people deem almost every occurrence with intention and motive behind it. The Vodacce presume that a temperate man who suddenly turns to drink experiences not a personal crisis, but rather has offended a powerful Strega. Similarly, a Vodacce accepts outrageous turns of fate and wildly improbable coincidences without so much as a blink—when fate can be bent to serve a man's ambitions, expectations based on the normal course of events no longer apply.

A peasant may believe that nailing seven spiders to his lintel keeps the Princes' Fate Witches from cursing his harvest, but the proliferation of folk practices and superstitions that have sprung up in response to Sorte's power conceal a deeper irony: a Fate Witch herself is nearly defenseless. The power of Sorte does not extend to its practitioners; a Strega cannot use her powers to benefit herself.

As a result, these formidable sorceresses are servants in their own homes. Cloistered, barely educated and shackled to their husbands by their marriage vows, the renowned Fate Witches of Vodacce serve the ambitions of their husbands against their will, be they brutes or gentlemen. What is more, convention requires each Strega to test all her daughters for the gift, condemning the next generation of women to the same fate.

Countless travelers from the other nations of Théah have wondered why women who wield the power to shape destiny itself tolerate such grim circumstances. The answer is as unsatisfying as it is simple: survival. Powerless to protect each other and possessing only the rudiments of an education, these women have little choice but to rely on others to shelter them from those they have wronged at their husband's behest.

Complicating the situation is that the status of Streghe remains the one issue—perhaps the only issue—that all seven Princes agree on. Whatever an individual nobleman may think of his wife, no matter how much he may love her or admire her natural intelligence and ready wit, he knows in his heart that should she go unveiled or be seen at study, the agents of all seven Princes would descend on his family with all their customary thoroughness and brutality. From the first Prince to claim the title to the current seven, each has understood that his wealth and power relies upon the subjugation of these powerful women.

This tragedy, centuries in the making, may be entering a new phase. Morella Alouse Giacinni, wife to l'Empereur Léon Alexandre of Montaigne, and Domenica Vespucci, the wife of Stanisław II of the Sarmatian Commonwealth, both Streghe, *left their homeland with the good graces of their Princes.* Whatever the short-term gain these alliances bring to their allies in Vodacce, they have also provided these women with a taste of freedom and privilege unheard of in their native land.

## The Women of Vodacce

Men hold all the power in Vodacce, and yet the women could be all powerful. Through a few cleverly crafted laws in past centuries, women remain trapped in the hands of the men who wed or fathered them, unable to rise up and claim control over their own lives. A noble keeps his women on tight leashes, controlling what they learn, how they act and who they interact with, as much as he dares. Even a noble-woman who is not a Strega finds herself at the end of a gilded chain. A commoner has an easier time of things. For the most part, a common woman can do

anything she wants, barring the necessity of reading or writing, forbidden even to the peasantry. Only a woman who trains as a courtesan may seek out higher education, and even then, those who learn to read are rare. One could say a courtesan has more power than any other woman in Vodacce, even the Streghe. While she may not control fates, she keeps her ear to the pulse of the Great Game and even dabbles in the politics of the Nation. Yet, the number of women who work and fight in Vodacce is no less than any other Nation. You would be hard pressed to convince a master Duelist that she possesses less power than a preening courtesan.

No matter what a woman does, the people of Vodacce often frame her by the men in her life. Her father's name is sometimes more important than her own accomplishments. She is supposed to be demure, and her husband keeps her in check. Vodacce women live in a world of double standards. Men enjoy the company of courtesans, but it is scandalous for a woman to do the same. Men stay out late drinking and dueling casually, and yet a woman who challenges someone to a duel must be sure she does not break the Duelist Guild's rules, or be punished. Men can sit around all day philosophising, yet if a woman attempts to do the same, she breaks the law. Women must step carefully in Vodacce, but all learn the song and dance and perform it with ease.

## Important People in Vodacce

## Prince Alcide Mondavi

The ancient Mondavi family traces their ancestry to the noble families of the Old Empire in an unbroken line of rice brokers. While possessed of the fine features of his forbears—chestnut hair, a strong jaw, sharp cheekbones and pale blue eyes—Alcide, his people say, loves books more than women and farming more than fighting.

If he does not love fighting, he certainly excels at it. Few have challenged the young Prince, and none lived to tell about it. In contrast to the braggadocio of many Vodacce *bravos*, Alcide destroys his enemies with phlegmatic indifference. Whether against an assassin's blade or in a duel to the death, combat seems to be just another obstacle between the bookish Prince and his studies, one that he prefers to dispatch with haste.

This public face is a construct, a fiction the Prince's rivals discover only too late. If Giovanni Villanova prefers to wear his mercilessness on his sleeve, so to speak, Prince Mondavi chooses to conceal his brutality behind his family's reputation for

complacency and diffidence. Make no mistake: Alcide Mondavi is a monster, and la Montagna di Cacciatori, his hunting lodge, a mute testament to the Prince's psychotic cruelty.

The Prince keeps his lands orderly and free of undesirables through an effective, if immoral, policy of kidnapping and murder. Upon his accession, the Prince's game wardens—in reality, a handpicked squad of remorseless killers—abducted the town of Elemosina's scofflaws, racketeers and outlaws, and released them within the Prince's private game reserve. There, Prince Mondavi hunted them down like animals, ending each life in an intimate whirl of blades.

Only this form of hunting still provides the Prince with any sense of accomplishment: to gaze into a man's eyes in his utmost extremity, to witness his dawning realization that he is nothing more than an animal and then to end him. The predatory animals that prowl the mountain no longer concern Mondavi;

they merely help conceal the aftermath of his hunts since all have developed a taste for the flesh of humans.

Recently, the Prince's ambitions have grown. No longer content to pursue his mad passions in private, he steers Vodacce toward a violent future. Quietly, he and his agents have begun to heighten tensions between the other Princes, all the while using his rice exports to buy the loyalty of bloody-handed Eisen mercenaries and the Inquisition's most ruthless agents. If his plan succeeds, he will provoke a war among his rivals, grow rich selling rice to both sides and then unleash the worst his brutal allies have to offer on his exhausted Nation.

He plans to drown Vodacce in blood, and if it brings him a crown, so much the better.

## Portraying Alcide Mondavi

Though never unkempt, Alcide dresses with little regard to the latest fashions, favoring plain garments and utilitarian cuts. In public, Alcide carries himself with an aloofness bordering on disinterest and has little time for social niceties. Few of his associates know of the monster that dwells inside Prince Mondavi, and those who find out usually do so on the wrong side of the hunting lodge.

## Story Hooks

+ The Heroes encounter a group of bloody and exhausted commoners just beyond la Montagna di Cacciatori. In terror, they relate a wild tale of kidnapping and abandonment on the mountain. While they initially feared an attack by animals, they soon realized people hunted them, people who trapped and killed several of their number and pursued the survivors down the slopes. They need the Heroes' protection in order to escape the Mondavi lands.
+ Rosa Esposito, a bravo, challenged Prince Mondavi to a duel to protect the honor of her charge, a young noble from Caligari. He refused the duel and now won't accept her requests for correspondence. She worries about what happens to those who threaten Prince Mondavi, and asks the Heroes to help her protect her ward in case the worst happens.

# THE PRINCES

Each of Vodacce's principalities are ruled by a single Prince. Not every Prince is a true Villain, like Alcide Mondavi; some can sometimes be downright Heroic. Some of the Princes are definitely Villains, enacting plots to assassinate, undercut and subjugate their fellows.

Gespucci Bernoulli is a man of wealth and excesses. He is a ruthless leader who believes that a show of force is a necessary first action when threatened. Vincenzo Caligari is a spy and smuggler, and completely fixated on Syrneth artifacts. He is a changed man, and many argue that he's no longer a man at all. Giovanni Villanova might be the worst of the lot. He is pragmatic and ruthless, showing zero regard for friendships or family relations when in pursuit of a goal. He is the wolf the other Princes throw their enemies to. He is also the biggest threat to the other Princes and one of the few things that keep them all at bay.

On the other hand, a couple of Princes are unwilling to go to extremes to undermine their neighbors. They stand on the strength of their wealth and power, but do not abuse those things. With a little push, they may even see the merit in helping the Heroes along.

Donello Falisci is a jovial man, if a bit wine-sotted. He may trade in secrets, but he is more likely to pick and choose where to sell those secrets than others with such power. Michele Lucani is a man of honor, refusing to force his wife and daughters to use their powers over Fate for his whims, instead working side by side with them. Alessandro Vestini is probably the weakest of the Vodacce Princes, even if his lands are prosperous. His wife runs his principality, and women have made great strides within his lands. He often feigns ignorance about which forms of scholarship the women in his principality choose to pursue.

Additional information on the various Vodacce Princes can be found in the "Places" section, starting on p.174.

# Anacleto di Rinascita

Foreigners who visit the library in the tower of L'Edificio find its keeper, Anacleto, to be almost preternaturally intelligent, willing and able to discuss topics as diverse as theology, natural philosophy and celestial mechanics at the highest levels.

The Bibliothecarius proves an attentive listener, quick to ask probing and insightful questions about lands beyond Théah or the ruins of ancient civilizations. From time to time he has even helped a frustrated archæologist unravel the secrets of a baffling artifact, provided the owner allows him to document anything she discovers for L'Edificio's collection.

Though not widely known, the Invisible College has approached Anacleto numerous times about membership, only for him to rebuff them again and again. A devout Vaticine, Anacleto finds the anti-intellectual turn the Church has taken repulsive, seeing it as the inevitable influence of Castillian prurience on the dynamic and inquisitive faith he cherishes. Nevertheless, he refuses to associate with those the Church denounces, no matter how much sympathy he may have for their cause.

Only two topics frustrate the aging scholar's curiosity: the origin of Théah's Syrneth ruins and the nature of divinity.

In the first case, L'Edificio's accounts of murderously complex traps, inhuman architecture and strange materials from the ruins seem to point to something outside Theus' plan for his children. The fascinating artifacts the Caligari family has hoarded do not seem to belong to any chapter of humanity's history.

To the Bibliothecarius' mind, they seem to be something parallel and apart, devised by bizarre minds to suit outlandish hands. His sedulous pursuit of this topic has drawn Anacleto closer to the reclusive Prince Vincenzo Caligari, a man thirty years the scholar's senior who moves with the strength and confidence of a man ten years his junior.

For the second, the reports of heathen gods walking Aztlán in the New World shook the elderly librarian to his core. If tangible, numinous beings indeed exist in lands beyond the sea, by what logic do scholars rule out their existence—either past or present—on Théah?

The deeper Anacleto and his scholars probe, the greater the sacrifices required to unravel the mysteries unfolding before them. In the furtherance of this research, both the *Eruditi*, the order of librarians, and their chief regularly perform acts that have indelibly tainted their souls, decisively wagering their hope of salvation against the promise of an earthly apotheosis.

## Portraying Anacleto di Rinascita

Portly, with lively eyes, tightly curled gray hair and a bushy salt and pepper beard, Anacleto is a fatherly presence. He frequently peppers his discourse of esoteric subjects with earthy analogies and often interrupts a high profile lecture to deal with a wayward godchild's problem.

He is a knowledgable man, When one of his interlocutors brings up Aztlán or the Syrneth, his eyes light up, and he presses her for any details she may have to offer, happily bartering his own knowledge if required.

## Story Hooks

+ A Hero comes across a Syrneth artifact that defies his efforts to understand, with ad hoc attempts to activate it leading to injury or death. Since his usual contacts refuse to deal with it, he must take it to Anacleto and risk carrying a device of unknown power into the heart of Prince Caligari's demesne.

+ A book has gone missing from L'Edificio. Anacleto realized the tome was missing only after a visiting scholar came seeking information on some of the oldest Syrneth ruins in Vodacce. Anacleto has asked around the city, but no one has borrowed the book, and his records are suspiciously empty surrounding all books from that section. He needs someone to track down the book before the visiting scholar realizes it is missing.

# Desiderata, Mistress of La Passione

A striking woman of indeterminate age, Desiderata is Vodacce's farthest-famed courtesan. Mistress of La Passione, the Vestini family's courtesan academy, she claims no kinship to that noble lineage. Indeed, unusual for any powerful Vodacce woman, little is known of her past—she meets any attempts to pry with courteous and charming deflections.

What people know obscures more than it illuminates: Desiderata arrived at the gates of La Passione as a girl and paid her tuition in full from a bag of mixed gold and gems of uncertain provenance. As the years progressed, she matured into a handsome young woman. Much sought after by the noble scions of Vodacce's first families, she could never quite conceal her contempt for the loudmouthed and empty-headed noblemen. Paradoxically, this attitude made them pursue her all the more fervently, and Desiderata quickly extracted favors and finances from her besotted paramours.

She used these favors to secure La Passione's independence from Prince and priest alike. A dalliance with the young Prince Marco Vestini established the school in perpetuity, while carnal knowledge of a Cardinal secured the school a writ of exemption from ecclesiastical persecution. When the school's mistress grew too infirm to continue in her position, Desiderata, though quite young for such an honor, was the only choice to succeed her.

Since she assumed the title of Mistress of La Passione, Desiderata has played merry hell with Vodacce's endless litany of double standards. She has openly taken lovers both male and female and refused to chastise her students for doing the same. One of her protégés was found abed with the wife of a Lucani nobleman. Desiderata conducted a brief inquiry into the wife's situation. Upon finding that she had paid the courtesan for her time, Desiderata announced to a stunned Lucani that he should either satisfy his wife or reduce her allowance.

Desiderata has also modified La Passione's curriculum, adding courses in self-defense, shooting and physical fitness. She managed to draw the ire of the Duelist's Guild by teaching her students an unsanctioned style of knife fighting, which uses a stiletto—a weapon easily concealed in a courtesan's elaborate costume—to attack the neck, abdomen and groin. The students of La Passione, often led by Desiderata herself, walk the gutted streets of Bassifondi, distributing food and checking in on the indigent population that resides there. On a number of occasions, Desiderata has offered a precocious young girl from the slums an education at La Passione, free of charge, fueling speculation that her own past may be entangled with the blighted district.

## Portraying Desiderata

As Vodacce's foremost courtesan and a high-ranking member of Sophia's Daughters, the Mistress of La Passione's charm is professional, but so deftly practiced that even those who know the game well are taken aback by her seeming sincerity. She diverts conversations to discuss her interlocutor's favorite hat, presses him for the details of his haberdasher and praises his sophisticated taste. Among those who have earned her trust, however, she turns plainspoken, goal-oriented and ruthless.

## Story Hooks

- Desiderata has heard rumors throughout Pacatezza of a nobleman who hurts his wife. The woman was once one of her courtesans, and, acting through intermediaries in Sophia's Daughters, Desiderata hires a Hero to look into it. When he arrives to rescue her, she refuses to leave her husband, because he will not release her daughter, a Strega, putting the Hero in a difficult position.
- Prince Vestini is snooping around La Passione. One of his favorite courtesans has not returned to his estate, and he searches for her. The girl overheard a conversation she should not have, and she fears he wants to make her disappear in a more permanent sense. Desiderata asks the Heroes to smuggle the girl out of La Passione in the night, making sure she has no knowledge of the details.

# Marcelo, il Pazzo di Potenza

Something of a talisman for the people of Potenza, Marcelo has been a fixture of the city's life as far back as anyone can remember. His ravings outside the gates of Prince Bernoulli's palace earned him the moniker *il Pazzo* (the madman). From his lank gray hair to the bunions infesting his bare feet, Marcelo looks every inch the crackpot people purport him to be.

Among the citizens of Potenza, stories of Marcelo's rise and fall vary as much as the cadence of his rants. The conspiratorially minded claim that he was a Bernoulli cousin, tortured and broken for some heinous crime in the distant past. Others say that he was a *somozzatore* (frogman), who found something beneath the city so abhorrent that it shattered his mind. Among the Potenza's merchants, called *colonelli*, it is an article of faith that a vengeful Strega cursed him for reasons unknown, inflicting Marcelo's current condition.

He spends his days ranting, raving and speaking in tongues, yet occasionally his words come out perfectly clear and concise. Sometimes he speaks of his past: the feel of his daughter's hair between his fingers, the sunset along his favorite canal or the smell of his wife's perfume. Other times, he speaks prophecy to whomever passes by. Whether prophetic or banal, these moments of devastating clarity surprise onlookers and capture their imagination.

Marcelo's oracular moments have turned him into an unlikely soothsayer. Ship captains consult him before a dangerous voyage, hoping for a prophecy of perils to come. City fathers and guild leaders question him on topics so clearly beyond the disheveled beggar's experience that it would be comical if they did not swear up and down that he had saved the city from catastrophe countless times. Even rascals and ragamuffins huddle with the flea-bitten prophet, seeking his advice on their petty conflicts.

By popular agreement, there are three forbidden topics: the Bernoulli family, artifacts salvaged from Syrneth ruins and the origin of his abilities. If someone mentions any of the three in his presence, he either lapses into a catatonic state for days or falls into a howling fit, spitting and scratching at anyone who disturbs him. In either case, his madness renders him at best useless and at worst dangerous to those who rely on his counsel.

## Portraying Marcelo

Marcelo il Pazzo is not that old, though his unkempt grey hair and grizzled beard would convince you otherwise. He is aged beyond his years from his brush with Fate. His voice is sonorous and light; even when rambling incoherently, he sounds friendly and reasonable.

Marcelo suffers under a terrible burden: whatever caused his condition forces him to see all possible futures. The terrible strain of following the skeins of Fate as they twist and turn through the hands of Vodacce's Streghe slowly cost him his family, his occupation and his very sense of self.

Beneath his disheveled appearance and behind his words lie an entreaty—always ignored by those who depend on his counsel—to return his life to him. He sometimes appears as a man trapped in a nightmare, while other times he seems blissfully unaware of his condition.

## Story Hooks

+ After encountering Marcelo and benefitting from his soothsaying, a Hero happens across an artifact she believes can lift his curse. Potenza's merchants, politicians and rabble want to preserve Marcelo's curse as a benefit to themselves and refuse to allow the Hero near him. What can the Heroes do to help Marcelo?

+ As one of the Heroes passes by, Marcelo stops him. Completely lucid, Marcelo has a pleading look in his eyes. His daughter, long lost to him, is in grave danger. He knows not where she is, and only has a random set of visions to lead him there. If the Heroes would only take him to see her, he could save her life.

# Ippolito Malandrino

There is no more famous outlaw in all of Vodacce than Ippolito Malandrino, at least as far as he is concerned. An equal opportunity killer-for-hire, highwayman and pirate, Malandrino plies his trade by land and sea, from one end of Vodacce to the other. The high politics of Vodacce's Villainous princes disinterests the bandit, who busies himself with pedestrian crimes, like armed robbery and kidnapping. Nevertheless, the dashing rogue rarely misses an opportunity to promote himself, often hiring local urchins to tell tales of his knavery before he arrives in town, hoping to make his targets more tractable.

Something of a peacock, he has been known to let his horse—the melodramatically named "Bucefalo"—go hungry to pay for a particularly fine cloak. Those who have suffered Malandrino's attentions wonder why the Princes allow him to raid across their lands, speculating that he may have an arrangement with one or more of them, acting as a proxy when they need a villain who cannot be traced back to them.

Those of a more romantic bent tell a different tale: people say that one of the Princes murdered Ippolito's lover when he wouldn't betray his beloved Malandrino, and that his death broke the brigand. Blinded by rage and grief, the purportedly less depraved outlaw began a lifelong quest for vengeance, and his descent into villainy continued apace. These rumors never quite specify which Prince, the victim's name or when any of this occurred, and given Ippolito's penchant for self-aggrandizement and rumormongering, they are probably best discounted. Probably.

## Portraying Ippolito Malandrino

The brigand cuts an elegant figure. Lithe and dark of hair, with twinkling green eyes and an easy smile, he both adeptly picks pockets and melts hearts.

Few live life with more brio than Malandrino, and his allure is undeniable. He can play the dashing rogue, the grieving lover and the anti-hero with ease, depending on which pose more likely gets him what he wants. At his core, he is deeply selfish, more focused on his own pleasure and leisure than any moral or metaphysical concerns. A Hero seduced by his easy charm finds herself left in the lurch when his goals diverge from hers.

## Story Hooks

- Prince Villanova has hired Ippolito to scour the Lucani lands in pursuit of an artifact of the Old Empire, which allegedly contains proof that the last Imperator of the Numanari intended a Delaga to succeed him. As the last princely descendent of that ancient family, Giovanni Villanova intends to use it to make a claim on the throne, forcing the hands of his rivals and throwing the Nation into chaos. Can the Heroes stop the dashing outlaw before he achieves his goal?

- The stories of Malandrino's quest for vengeance hold more truth than fiction. Malandrino seeks to end Prince Mondavi's hunts, but does not have the wherewithal to do so by himself. His goal is to kill the Prince, but would the Heroes go so far?

# Mother Superior Teofila di Tamamello

Courteous to a fault, Teofila di Tamamello welcomes all women of good heart within the walls of St. Dorothy in Agony. A good heart is not necessarily a restrained one, and families, both noble and common, have used Mother Teofila's generosity as a means to offload daughters who could not, or would not, abide by the stifling codes of Vodacce society. Once forced to take orders, these women could be forgotten by their relatives and ignored by society at large.

Mother Teofila has done much to break down barriers between sisters and novices of different social classes, forging a community out of a collection of scorned and abandoned women. Teofila's drive to create commonalities among her charges stems from her childhood in Tamamello, a border town in far northwestern Vodacce. There she saw brave women from the Sarmatian Commonwealth inveighing against the evils of war and preaching the gospel of suffrage. Enthralled by their message, she resolved to bring the same progress to her own Nation, taking orders at a young age to provide a modicum of protection and privacy for her efforts.

A true woman of the people, Mother Teofila is considered considered dangerously progressive by the priests of the Vaticine Church, who consigned her to the crumbling church of St. Dorothy in Agony, hoping that life in a Vodacce backwater would teach the priest her place. Instead, she surprised them by taking in Vodacce's unwanted women and bringing them to the Church, a tale of redemption that even the most conservative priest could appreciate.

Within the church walls, Mother Teofila subjects her novices to a grueling curriculum that emphasizes all aspects of a Vaticine education, including those out of favor with the current Church hierarchy. The academic grind, more than any individual student can handle, necessitates the formation of strong bonds among novices, so that the strengths and weaknesses of one offset the complementary aptitudes of another.

Currently, the Mother Superior is caught in a dilemma. Her relationship with Donello Falisci has brought material temptations and divided loyalties to her church. His donations have bought the church the best food and materials for lessons, which she appreciates, but it seems that some of her wards— though scorned by their own families—still long for the material comforts of nobility and status. Now she tries to distance herself from him without raising his ire.

## Portraying Mother Teofila di Tamamello

Mother Teofila's warmth and courtesy do nothing to blunt the force of her intellect. Despite her age, she quickly susses out deception, insincerity and ulterior motives. Clad in the humble vestments of a Vaticine priest, she projects an aura of calming authority wherever she goes.

Decades of caring for Vodacce's forgotten women and advancing the cause of Sophia's Daughters have made her levelheaded and decisive in a crisis, and it takes a great deal to ruffle her feathers.

### Story Hooks

- Mother Teofila needs a reason to distance herself from Prince Falisci without harming her charges, and she sees the Heroes as a likely cat's-paw. She asks them to procure an embarrassing document from a Falisci nobleman and deliver it to a contact of Desiderata's in Sophia's Daughters, knowing her rival will make it public. The resulting furor will give her the pretext she needs to distance herself from the family, while bringing the ire of the Falisci to bear on Desiderata and the Vestini who protect her.
- Mother Teofila has secretly started teaching her wards how to read, a practice strictly forbidden in Vodacce. As long as it remains a secret, she is fine. Except, one of Falisci's guards caught one of the girls with a book. Now Mother Teofila needs someone to convince the guard to keep her secret or find some way to silence him.

# Orlando Rabbioso

On the night of Voltadi, 3 Corantine 1666, the townsfolk of Baccante beheld a strange sight: a man, as naked as the sword in his hand, brawling with the town guard on a bridge over the Fiume di Vino.

Whether due to the ferocity of his swordplay or his state of dishabille, the nude knight appeared to get the better of the guard. When the light of the rising moon seemed to return the interloper's wits to him, a guard settled the matter by using the lull to hazard a leap that carried them both into the river.

In the interrogation that followed, the bemused authorities received a tale delivered with more conviction than the outlandish circumstances ought to permit. In a thick Montaigne accent, the naked stranger explained that his last memory was of holding a pass in the mountains north of Buché against an irregular force of Castillian soldiers that had cut him off from the rest of the army.

Stranger still, his stilted speech and archaic manners appeared to support his claim that he was the chevalier of Montaigne myth who single handedly held off an army of Crescent invaders until his king could arrive with an army, though this would make him many centuries old.

After a brief audience, Prince Falisci declared Orlando a harmless eccentric and set the would-be knight free. Seemingly beyond the influence of Sorte, and rumored to appear wherever the greatest need, this ingenious gentleman has seen off bandits, pirates and worse. In one notable engagement, he saved the mayor of Sedilo from a pack of assassins, fighting with such puissance and passion that it earned him the epithet *rabbioso* or "the furious."

While Rabbioso's interventions are not always welcome, they arise from the sincere conviction that he is a legendary knight-errant charged with protecting the poor and helpless from the depredations of the honorless and tyrannical. In one case, he disturbed the solemnity of a wedding because he believed the bride coerced.

Naturally, this notion has made him quite unwelcome in certain parts of Vodacce. A bounty rests on his head in Villanova lands, and to the extent the Mondavi and Caligari families tolerate Orlando in their provinces, it is because he has done nothing specific to earn their ire.

However strained Orlando's relationship with the Princes may be, for the first time in decades the downtrodden and forgotten have a champion, a novelty as uncommon as it is dangerous in a nation accustomed to autocratic rule.

## Portraying Orlando Rabbioso

Tall, blonde and brawny, Orlando Rabbioso seems to have emerged from a particularly implausible fantasy. Between his formal, antiquated patterns of speech, his adherence to ancient codes of chivalry and his truly atrocious accent, he seems nearly a caricature of the questing knight.

Whatever the truth may be, no doubt Rabbioso believes to the bottom of his soul what he claims to be. He is honorable to a fault, and will help any who have a grievance worthy of his attention.

### Story Hooks

+ Recently, Orlando took to the battlements of L'Aquila and announced that he would not rest until he brought the outlaw Ippolito Malandrino to justice. The two have played a game of cat and mouse that has captured the popular imagination, with stories—both real and fictional—appearing in fishrags up and down the peninsula. Orlando mistakes one of the Heroes as the infamous vagabond and does not let it rest until he proves him wrong.
+ Orlando was brought from his time into the present by a powerful Syrneth artifact under the control of Prince Caligari. For his part, the Prince has no idea he is responsible for Orlando's presence, but Orlando knows that his only way back to his time requires access to the Caligari museum. Will the Heroes help Orlando infiltrate the old Prince's home to find the artifact?

# Vittorio Ribaldi

There is scarcely a man in Vodacce who has seen or done more than Vittorio Ribaldi. Born into a poor family in the outlying ghettos of Potenza, Ribaldi took to the sea at a young age. After finagling his way into the captaincy of a small barque, Vittorio began a life of adventure that continues to the present day. After cutting his teeth smuggling fruit into freezing Ussura, he moved on to blockade running.

Vittorio's illicit cargoes of food and medicine brought hope to the starving peasants of Eisen and the embattled partisans of Castille during each Nation's time of war. When the Inquisition began to choke the life out of Vaticine scholarship, Vittorio and his crew commandeered an Inquisition caravel carrying a cargo of so-called heretics to the stake and released them on the shores of Vodacce.

When his exploits grew too numerous for the Church to ignore, Ribaldi and his crew took their captured ship, which they renamed *La Fortuna*, and set sail for Aztlán. There, if the tales are to be believed, Vittorio was shipwrecked, fought in a doomed peasant uprising against the Empress of Runakuna, defeated a Nahuacan Eagle Templar in single combat, then claimed his weapon and feathered cloak and wed a Tzak K'an princess.

That last appears to be beyond dispute, as the Aztláni woman resides with him in Fontaine, answering to the name Allegria, and doing her best to keep up with their three young children, all of whom seem to have inherited their father's casual disregard for danger. Nor were his exploits limited to Aztlán, but the accounts of Vittorio's later voyages to far-off Cathay and the Crescent Empire take days in the telling.

Whether the tales portray truth or not, Ribaldi retells them with a great deal of vim and has attracted quite a following as a result. When his acolytes ask why he abandoned a life of exotic travel and adventure to return to the mountain fastness of Fontaine, the old campaigner becomes enigmatic and withdrawn.

## Portraying Vittorio Ribaldi

Vittorio Ribaldi is a middle-aged man with a magnificent silver beard and mischievous hazel eyes. People know Fontaine's most colorful resident for his outlandish style of dress. He is never without his beloved striped poncho, a garment favored by the Runakuna of Aztlán, or his *macuahuitl*, an obsidian-studded war club beloved of the Nahuaca.

A raconteur to the core, Vittorio embeds political lessons into his tales and peppers them with hints about the ability of brave men and women to change the world. Ribaldi's cell may contact those who show an interest in the Rilasciare.

By appearing to be little more than an incorrigible flirt and harmless old-timer, Ribaldi ensures that he never exposes himself until the rest of his cell has vetted any potential recruits.

## Story Hooks

- Ribaldi plans to shake the foundations of Vodacce politics, recruiting an army of liberators to return the Nation to the democratic traditions of the Numanari. He has not decided whether to make common cause with Donello Falisci or simply wait for the Princes to exhaust themselves and strike. Through his cell, he employs Heroes on missions designed to test their loyalty and capabilities, sow discord between the Princes or probe the character of Prince Falisci.
- Ribaldi's past has caught up with him. An angry woman, the jilted lover of one of Ribaldi's flings before his marriage, has finally tracked him down. It would be fine if she wanted honorable restitution, such as a duel or a nice conversation. Instead, she is stalking him and leaving unpleasant gifts for him to find, insinuating a gruesome death. Can the Heroes help Ribaldi track the woman down before she does something extreme?

# Ronan Lehane

Ronan Lehane was born and raised in rural Inismore, the son of a half-Montaigne and an Inish lighthouse keeper. His grandfather taught him sword use at an early age. His sword skill was good enough to earn him entry into the Valroux Dueling School, and he spent most of his early years as a duelist-for-hire.

That is, until he met Edward Cranna, an Avalonian playwright looking for a leading man in his newest play, "The King of Blades." Ronan impressed the playwright with his mastery, and Armistead just had to have him in the play. The gig paid well, and Ronan fell in love with the stage after his first performance. That, and he fell in love with his leading lady, Lenora, a blue-eyed Marcher with a fiery spirit.

After the first season with the acting troupe, Ronan and Lenora were married, and Ronan had solidified his position as the best Hero actor the troupe could stage. His most famous role was as the King of Blades, but he took on every heroic, sword-swishing, swash-buckling role Armistead could come up with.

Ronan's career on the stage ended abruptly when during the final act of a traditional Vodacce tragedy, a masked actor actually stabbed Lenora, killing her on stage. Ronan was unable to catch the culprit, and he left the troupe in search of whomever had assassinated his beloved.

Lonely, broken and without much hope, Ronan tracked the assassin across Théah. He left Inismore and made his way to Castille, where he finally found the assassin as he was boarding a ship to Vodacce. Ronan faced the woman, asking for answer, and ready to kill her. The story she told him earned her her life, but left him with even more questions.

She had been hired by an agent of Prince Alcide Mondavi. She didn't know the reason, but it seemed the man wanted Ronan to come to him. She was to lead him there, upon pain of her own death, but only after killing Lenora. She had insinuated herself into the troupe almost two years before the assassination, which bewildered Ronan as to why Prince Mondavi would be so interested in him.

Now Ronan is in Mondavi lands, attempting to untangle a plot that runs deeper than just himself and his lost love.

## Portraying Ronan Lehane

Ronan Lehane has pale skin with brown hair and eyes. He keeps his hair cut short, to keep out of the way while fighting. His athletic arms are covered in thin white scars from his dueling days. He favors muted colors and practical clothing for travel and practicing with the sword.

In his youth, Ronan was a happy man, smiling and flamboyant—traits he picked up from his mother. Now, he is quiet and driven. Every now and then, you may catch a smile or a quirk of his lips that shows his old self, but his grief over Lenora is such that he rarely lets himself feel anything other than a burning revenge.

He is not a fan of Vodacce in general, but especially despises Prince Mondavi and any who bow down to him. He is likely to help the Heroes if they ask, though he may ask for favors in return.

### Story Hook

- Ronan has uncovered information about a powerful Streghe in the employ of Prince Mondavi. Apparently, she has foretold Ronan's destiny and is the primary reason for his current situation. Prince Mondavi keeps her locked away in la Montagna di Cacciatori. If Ronan could get to her, he could find out what is going on, and deal a significant blow to the Prince. Will the Heroes help Ronan infiltrate Prince Mondavi's hunting lodge?
- Lehane has insinuated himself close to Prince Mondavi, and was just about to enact his final plan when he received a letter from his old acting troupe. They claim to have new information about Lenora, they too troubled by her death. He can't go meet them and take out Mondavi at the same time. Will the Heroes help him?

# Gregorio Zambelli

Gregorio Zambelli is a name feared and reviled all across Caligari lands. He serves as Prince Vincenzo Caligari's chief assassin and wetwork specialist. Sure, sometimes he's just coming by to pick up an artifact, from inside your locked vault. But more often, he is employed as a spy and assassin, ensuring the loyalty of those who get close to Prince Caligari.

Gregorio is a mystery, and has his own secrets. The first and foremost being that he was born as Lucrezia Constantina Iolande, the youngest daughter of a famous courtesan family. Gregorio always struggled as Lucrezia, enamored by the tales of Vodacce Bravos and the stories of derring-do. Lucrezia was supposed to be a good girl, trained as a proper courtesan and companion. Yet, she always wondered why the courtesan simulations never ended in "and that's when you save the other women from the Villain and run off with his money."

Lucrezia ran away from home as a teenager, and made her way in the streets, but as a non-noble, non-courtesan woman, the going was tough. She taught herself the sword after stealing a dagger, but feeding herself was difficult. That is when Gregorio Zambelli was born. Gregorio could go places Lucrezia could not, and could even learn to read and write. Gregorio's life wasn't easy, buy after a few well-placed kills, using his alternate identity as Lucrezia to lure unsuspecting victims, he earned a reputation.

Gregorio quickly found himself in Prince Caligari's employ, and now serves as his most trusted agent. Of course, if Prince Caligari knew the truth about Gregorio, he might not be so forgiving.

## Portraying Gregorio Zambelli

Gregorio Zambelli is petite with raven black hair and dark skin and nearly golden eyes. He is young for his rank and position, barely cresting his early twenties. He is boyish in appearance, and his voice is soft and light, when you can get him to talk.

Gregorio is loyal to Prince Caligari, and would do anything for him. His life depends on the man's good graces, and he wishes to do nothing to disrupt the life he has created for himself. If the Heroes cross his path, they can expect a dogged foe who does not give up easily.

*Secret Societies*

## The Brotherhood of the Coast

Those few Vodacce inclined to ethical piracy have already made their way to the Brotherhood's ships, leaving only the worst scum to ply the islands off the peninsula's southern tip. In truth, the Brotherhood has no allies in Vodacce waters, as the Princes resent their intrusion as much as the pirates do.

Between the Inquisitorial galleons in the Vaticine Gulf and the pirates and Princes' marines everywhere else, the Brotherhood prefers to stay in the wilder waters of the Widow's Sea. A Brotherhood captain has been known to take on passengers delivered to him by agents of Sophia's Daughters or to pursue a particularly villainous competitor, but these always remain matters of individual initiative rather than Brotherhood policy.

## Die Kreuzritter

In Vodacce, the acolytes of die Kreuzritter occupy a few remote holdfasts at the edge of civilization. To the extent that agents interact with Vodacce society, it is to trace lost dracheneisen carried south by Eisen who fled the War of the Cross or gather information on monster attacks reported by locals.

Currently, Vodacce members of die Kreuzritter push to have all wayward Streghe declared "dark sorcerers," while foreign acolytes resist the definition. What impact this debate will have on the activities of Sophia's Daughters remains to be seen.

## The Explorer's Society

If anything, the Explorer's Society would like to be *more* active in Vodacce. It maintains chapterhouses in Potenza and Baccante at the sufferance of Prince Bernoulli and Prince Falisci. Efforts to make inroads into Caligari lands and find out exactly what the Prince does with his hoard of artifacts have met with disaster and tragedy.

Furthermore, the patron Princes occasionally remember that the Explorer's Society exists and press members for artifacts and information in exchange for their continued toleration. Forestalling these powerful men—or giving up only the minimum required—has become a full time occupation for the heads of each house, limiting expansion opportunities.

## The Invisible College

As the Inquisition expanded its campaign of persecution of scholars across Théah, the Invisible College began to look for havens beyond the reach of Verdugo and his thugs. Though the deliberations were mysterious to most members, Serafino was selected as a natural home for scholars under threat from the Vaticine Church.

Giovanni Villanova vowed to destroy the agents of any power—secular or religious—interfering in his affairs, and the city housed a major university of which the Prince was a benefactor, a sure sign of his commitment to science. Finally, the city's notorious black market provides an ideal place to procure everything from new identities for fugitive scholars to rare reagents for further study.

# The Philosophi Sanguinis

In practice, the Invisible College's foray into Villanova lands has worked out a bit differently than the Secret Society intended. While most scholars simply passed through Serafino, entering as a fugitive and departing under a false identity a few days later, a few elected to stay. These scholars, many of whom secured appointments at the University of Serafino, find the lack of ethical or material constraints quite freeing.

Devoting themselves to the higher mysteries, these Philosophi Sanguinis, "philosophers of blood," began to dabble in the occult: sorcery, unnatural creatures and particularly grisly artifacts became their specialty. Needless to say, Prince Villanova supports their work enthusiastically. He funds their projects, and in return they share their discoveries with him.

To the average citizen, however, the presence of these natural philosophers has been nothing but good. The advancements they have been able to come up with far outstrip those coming from Castille since the Inquisition's reign. And if their methods are a little unethical, you won't hear the commoners complaining when it means food on the table and a better quality of life.

An Eisen by the name of Rehor Heinzdorf has developed a rough theory of heredity, and his research into hybridization has allowed farmers to harvest greater yields from more robust crops. Thanks to medical research carried out in Serafino, several conditions previously believed untreatable can now be managed or prevented, and infant mortality has fallen dramatically.

Herr Doktor Heinzdorf has taken up a new avenue of inquiry. Noting that sorcery tends to follow noble bloodlines, he remains determined to understand the relationship between the two. If sorcery is a disease of the blood, he could undoubtedly formulate a cure, freeing Vodacce's noblewomen from servitude.

What use Prince Villanova would put such a "cure" to is best left to the imagination, but the Philosophi Sanguinis have begun to interfere with both die Kreuzritter and Sophia's Daughters in the pursuit of sorcerers to study.

## Favor with the Philosophi Sanguinis

The Philosophi Sanguinis concern themselves with natural sciences and new discoveries, though they rarely care about the costs of such. They do not shy away from dangerous or taboo subjects, as long as it is in the name of discovery.

A Hero who belongs to the Philosophi Sanguinis may earn Favor in the following way:

- Delivering a forbidden reagent, dangerous artifact or unnatural creature for study by the Philosophi Sanguinis is worth 4 Favor.
- Smuggling a fugitive scholar into Vodacce is worth 5 Favor.

A Hero who belongs to the Philosophi Sanguinis can call upon them for aid in the following ways:

- Procuring a new identity for the Hero or another member of the Invisible College requires 3 Favor.
- The use of a forbidden discovery costs 10 Favor. The Philosophi Sanguinis dole out the fruits of their research sparingly, as they are hazardous to both body and soul. They may include—but are not limited to—a poison distilled from the essence of an unnatural being or an artifact capable of unleashing a ruinous curse. Whatever its nature, the effects of such an item are both dramatic and corrupting, something to be called upon only by Heroes in direst need. The player should work with the GM to determine the effects of the discovery. Whatever the item is, is one use only, and the Philosphi Sanguinem expect a full report on its effects once the Hero has used it.

## Knights of the Rose & Cross

A generation ago, the members of the last Rose & Cross chapter house in Vodacce died by poison during their evening meal, and the culprits disappeared into the countryside. Though rumors state that the Society still counts some benefactors among Vodacce's noble families, the Knightly Order of the Rose & Cross prefers to leave the cause of chivalry to lone actors like Orlando Rabbioso rather than risking Knights.

Knights are in no way forbidden to travel within Vodacce, or even to act as their code dictates. Instead, agents are warned that Vodacce is not a welcoming home, and maybe they should take a page from the other Secret Societies and remain innocuous while traveling there.

## Los Vagabundos

While Los Vagabundos do not operate openly in Vodacce, the Nation remains an important part of their activities. Los Vagabundos make use of the prosperous Castillian community in L'Aquila to hide members whose activities in Castille have garnered too much attention.

In addition, donations from L'Aquila's Castillians make up an important source of income for Los Vagabundos, and more than a few of them willingly look the other way when it comes to smuggling goods across the Vaticine Gulf.

## Močiutės Skara

Grandmother's Shawl remains quite active in northern Vodacce, where its presence helped ameliorate the worst impacts of the War of the Cross and the war between Montaigne and Castille. It owns a sprawling manse in Fontaine, which members use as a transshipment point for supplies traveling up the Sejm to Eisen and points westward.

The Society has a cordial relationship with Prince Vestini, who knows that without the Shawl, refugees would have surely overrun his lands.

## The Rilasciare

The Free Thinkers of Vodacce are a persecuted bunch, residing primarily on the margins of princely power. Profoundly influenced by Sarmatian political thinking, Vodacce's Rilasciare work to expand the rights of the common people, curtail the influence of Sorte and weaken the Princes' prerogatives and power.

Writers, intellectuals and common folk, tired of oppression at the hands of Vodacce's Princes, envision a future where a republic allows every man and woman a say in how they are governed and guarantees them a voice in the Nation's major decisions.

### Favor in Vodacce

A Hero who belongs to the Rilasciare may earn Favor in Vodacce in the following ways:

* Publicly exposing a Prince's agent is worth 3 Favor. Common methods of exposure include pamphleteering, soapbox harangues or whispering campaigns carried out in the market or other public spaces.
* Humiliating a Prince or thwarting his goals is worth 5 Favor. Unlike exposing an agent, this humiliation need not be public—if the Prince knows and the Rilasciare know, that is enough.

A Hero who belongs to the Rilasciare may spend Favor in Vodacce in the following way:

* Causing a major disturbance costs 6 Favor. Whether inciting a bread riot that draws the guards away from a noble's residence or organizing a demonstration that clogs the streets near the gate and allows a Hero to escape her pursuers, agents of the Rilasciare's pull with the common folk is unmatched. A Rilasciare Hero should note that such disturbances usually invite retribution from tyrants and must be careful not to put those he champions in harm's way too often.

# Sophia's Daughters

Those who champion the rights and freedoms of Vodacce's women are torn between two strategies for making these dreams a reality. The first, clandestinely advanced by Desiderata, Mistress of La Passione, claims women must seize their rights, by force if necessary. To that end, she has worked to ensure that the women of La Passione train in the "manly arts:" armed and unarmed combat, shooting, conditioning and other such physical pursuits.

In opposition to Desiderata's dreams of insurrection and armed struggle stands Teofila di Tamamello, Mother Superior of the Church of St. Dorothy in Agony and close confidant of Prince Donello Falisci. She believes that she can advance women's causes without throwing the Nation into chaos. To that end, Mother Teofila schools her charges in politics, history and law, the better to advance the cause of reform from within. She plans to start a school for young noblemen within her church, in the hopes that early exposure to women of such talent and intellect will shape their sympathies in the years to come.

Neither side has been able to overcome the other, as each has the support of one of the founders of Sophia's Daughters. Juliette stands by Desiderata, her teacher and mentor. Intimately acquainted with the amoral cruelty of Giovanni Villanova, she knows that only force prevails against him and his ilk. Valentina, while no less aware of her husband's inhumanity, believes that open rebellion will lead to the deaths of thousands of innocent women at the hands of their husbands and lovers, a cost she is not yet willing to condone.

While the identities and relationships of those involved remain unknown to most rank-and-file members, the disagreement is very much in the air, and each Daughter finds herself drawn to one approach or the other.

## Favor in Vodacce

A Hero who belongs to Desiderata's faction of Sophia's Daughters may earn Favor in the following way:

- Defending a Vodacce woman from violence or oppression at the hands of a man is worth 2 Favor. This defense is worth an additional point of Favor if it involved giving the man a violent message.

A Hero who belongs to Desiderata's faction of Sophia's Daughters may spend Favor in the following way:

- She may purchase the aid of a Strength 10 Brute Squad for 4 Favor using the same rules as the Rilasciare entry in the *Core Rulebook* (page 269). The squad is composed of masked Sophia's Daughters, and unlike their disorganized Rilasciare peers, the squad may be given specific and detailed instructions as to what to accomplish. For an additional 2 Favor, the Brute Squad may be given a single special type and ability (see **Core Rulebook**, page 192) that the Hero may activate using her Hero Points. The squad lingers until defeated or the Scene ends, at which point it departs.

A Hero who belongs to Teofila's faction of Sophia's Daughters may earn Favor in the following way:

- Providing help to the downtrodden is worth 2 Favor, or 3 Favor if the recipient of this aid is a woman. The aid in question must be non-violent, something along the lines of advocacy, helping to find a permanent shelter or providing a source of food or money.

A Hero who belongs to Teofila's faction of Sophia's Daughters may spend Favor in the following way:

- She may call on a fellow Daughter for aid at the cost of 4 or more Favor. Her ally has all Traits at 3 and single Skill of your choice at 3 Ranks, though you may not select Aim, Brawl or Weaponry. You may increase her Ranks in that Skill by spending an additional 3 Favor per Rank, or give her additional Skills, subject to the same limitations, at Rank 3 for 2 Favor per Skill, but you may not do both. Her services end with the Scene.

*Places*

# Bernoulli

Prince Gespucci Bernoulli controls a series of enclaves running along the eastern coast of the Vodacce peninsula. Protected from landward invasions by swamps, mountains and shallow coastal waterways, these cities and towns live and die by the sea, depending on it for food and trade and subject to its whims in all matters. Currently, the cities of Pioro, Porto Spatia and Saint Andrea pledged themselves to Prince Bernoulli. He also claims the loyalty of the town of Orduño, whose odd name stems from nearby Lake Orduño, if you believe the Prince, or a lost bet with a Castillian admiral, if you believe the inhabitants.

## Potenza

The first and greatest of Prince Bernoulli's holdings is the ancient island city of Potenza, which guards the mouth of Lake Rosa and controls all seaborne trade with the lands of the Caligari and Falisci families. The ability to inspect and tax cargoes coming from two of Vodacce's richest families, combined with the

Bernoulli family's exclusive license to trade with the Crescent Empire, have made Potenza a wonderland of wealth and excess.

As one of the oldest cities on the Vodacce peninsula, Potenza has grown from a hamlet into a formidable trading power, and its layout reflects this confused trajectory. The streets near the ancient center are cramped and twisting—an ideal location for late night assignations or assassinations—while farther out, grand boulevards reflect the city's later prosperity. A rise above the great harbor once supported a fortress that later converted into the Bernoulli manse.

A sprawling complex of grand frescoes, white marble and gilded tracery, the palace leaves its visitors with no illusions about Bernoulli's wealth and power. However, like the marines concealed within an opulent Vodacce carrack, the palace contains armaments every bit as deadly as those borne by the fortress that preceded it. In Gespucci Bernoulli's lifetime, no enemy ship has stood against the guns of the palazzo.

## Il Arsenale

Much of Potenza's wealth and status derives from its skilled craftsmen and artisans, called *colonelli* in the local dialect. Nowhere is this reality more apparent than in Potenza's secretive guild of shipwrights. Plying their trade alongside an artificial lagoon, and protected by thirty-foot walls patrolled by armed guards, these men and women can produce a barque in a day or a carrack within a week. The mysteries of this complex, known as il Arsenale, have proven difficult to unravel. Most people know that membership in the guild is hereditary and permanent; they forbid marrying outside the guild.

An enormous longhouse constructed in the form of an overturned hull, il Arsenale's guildhall is a thing of wonder. Called il Bastimiento, it provides a workplace, where everything from delicate ornamentation to major ship components are finished before installation. Cantilevered decks extend into the nave, providing work surfaces for a colonello, while a system of tracks, pulleys and platforms allows her to move pieces not only up and down, but also fore and aft. A colonello who cannot be bothered to wait for the next platform often navigates the interior by climbing on the rigging that operates the system.

Daylight enters il Bastimiento's cavernous interior through oversized portholes along the keel and sides, while adjustable mirrors hung throughout the nave catch the light and reflect it wherever the colonelli need to focus during working hours. At night chandeliers of wrought brass, glass and gold filigree supply light for meals and celebrations.

## Gli Ghetti

Among the more peculiar features of Potenza are its outlying districts, known as *gli ghetti*, ghettos. In 900 AV, the city's population began to outgrow the sliver of land it had been founded on. With their usual ingenuity, the city leaders simply made more land. Using lumber cut from mainland forests, Potenza's carpenters and engineers sank thousands of wooden pilings deep into the muck surrounding their island and then constructed stone platforms on these supports. Atop these foundations they erected homes, piazzas and palazzos, driving the supports further into the depths, where a combination of time, salt and silt have transformed them into something closer to rock.

Today, the outlying ghettos of Potenza display an architectural wonder unmatched in Théah, where opulent houses tower over the canals that lap at their front doors. Here, the streets are made of water, and people navigate these tangled arteries using narrow boats driven by a single oar fixed at the back. Flooding is a frequent occurrence, and even the wealthiest of Potenza's residents shrug their shoulders at a little high water, wading through their parlors when necessary.

## La Città Sommersa

The artificial expansion of Potenza's boundaries has inevitably involved pitfalls, sometimes literally so: in the nearly 800 years since Potenza built its first ghetto, war, storms and the occasional earthquake have sent parts of the city to the depths. Few have the time or inclination to clear this detritus, with new construction rising atop the ruin of the old, giving rise to what residents call "la Città Sommersa," the Drowned City.

Whether starting from the edge of the city or a nearby canal, divers—called *somozzatori*, or frogmen—swim beneath Potenza, navigating the dense forest of pilings in search of treasures lost to the sea. Among Potenza's poorer citizens, it is common enough to see young people goading one another to take longer and longer trips beneath the water, driven by the need to prove her bravery to her peers or simply in search of a trinket for a sweetheart.

The activity is dangerous in the extreme. What little light filters down from the canals quickly fades, leaving a somozzatore to grope his way from piling to piling, navigating by touch and memory more than sight. These would-be treasure hunters guard the locations of air pockets jealously, because once these vital way stations are depleted, they rarely if ever refill; even a room full of air can quickly become a death trap if enough rascals visit it.

Finally, the waters beneath the city serve as a dumping ground for everything from sewage and garbage to dead bodies. In addition to being wildly unsanitary, this refuse attracts both local sea life, from catfish to sharks, and worse. Potenza's wealth means that a great many somozzatori return with valuable trinkets, but maimings and deaths constantly occur among the city's frogmen. Many simply vanish: drowned, devoured or otherwise returned to the sea.

## Carnivale

The origins of Carnivale, the oldest and most beloved festival in Potenza, have been lost to history. Some claim that it celebrates the triumph of a Prince over his rivals, others a religious event connected to the life of the First Prophet, while a few claim it a pagan rite dressed in modern clothing. Whatever the origin, Carnivale is celebrated by everyone in the city, young and old.

But what clothing! All winter long, a citizen of Potenza works to produce a costume of surpassing extravagance, which she debuts during the days of Carnivale. Custom and tradition expects a true celebrant to make her own costume, but in recent days, a wealthy and well-connected citizen simply hires tailors to make up for his own lack of talent. This sort of behavior is particularly scandalous because it goes against the key tenets of Carnivale: anonymity and equality.

A secretive guild of colonelli provide the former by producing the masks for the event, called *mascherari*. To advertise their wares, these men and women stand on corners wearing their finest masks, while an interested customer may approach them to set an appointment for a home consultation. At the appointed hour, a masked personage—perhaps the same person, perhaps another, because mascherari traditionally wear different masks at each stage of the process—appears at the customer's doorstep to discuss the finer details of his purchase.

Finally, the mascherari delivers the mask in a locked box to the client, to protect his identity during the festival. From time to time, the mascherari gifts a poor client with a far finer mask than she can afford, the better to confuse the issue of class during Carnivale. Of course, creating a substandard mask for a rich patron is completely unheard of.

Accordingly, only the mascherari can identify the revelers during Carnivale, and this makes the guild one of the most powerful in Potenza. The licentious nature of the festivities means that the mascherari end up knowing the secrets and shames of Potenza's upper crust, a fact they are not shy about using to protect their business or advance their interests.

## THE PRINCES' LANDS

The Princes have divided much of Vodacce between them, centering their domains on a few rich settlements and parlaying that wealth into allies, armies and trade agreements. They jostle and squable, pulling at each other's holdings and trying to find the cracks in whatever armor each has devised.

Whether his lucre comes from harvests, tariffs or taxes, each Prince knows his position to be as precarious as it is powerful. A few burned fields, a port aflame or proof of a rogue Strega, and each would find himself a peasant as base as any other, should he even survive his fall from grace.

This combination of power and vulnerability makes the Princes such dangerous men and explains why each is a law unto himself within the borders of his demesne. Any who cross the border lines find themselves in a different world, and better be ready to crush his opponent, or be crushed himself.

During Carnivale, anyone may approach anyone else, and the festivities are open to all. Participants construct their own costume in secrecy, ensuring equality despite a person's status. Thus, a poor but talented seamstress may find herself the belle of a nobleman's ball, while a wealthy merchant who has never held a sewing needle in his life may find himself friendless and alone if his costume does not measure up.

Whatever the costume, Carnivale gives a Potenza citizen a license to behave as he wills. Epidemic drunkenness and fornication abound, and the more harmless sort of plotting comes to the fore: an officious participant who does not give himself fully to the spirit of the festival may find himself tossed in a nearby canal. The city even permits Fate Witches to take part, exchanging their translucent lace veils for a more concealing fall of black silk.

# Falisci

Prince Donello Falisci controls both banks of the Fiume di Vino, from its source in the mountains, north of Sedilo to its mouth on the northern shores of Lake Rosa. While old Vaticine records give the river's name as Fiume Divino, the River of God, the peasants and nobility both agree that Fiume di Vino, the River of Wine, fit both ruler and land better.

Without doubt, the grapes that grow on the hills of the Falisci lands are the reason why the family's holdings reckon among the richest estates in Théah. Such is the quality of Falisci wines that lesser gentry have beggared themselves for a rare vintage, while even Théah's noblest count their cellars empty if they do not contain a few bottles of the eponymous wine.

## Baccante

Where the Fiume di Vino makes a lazy loop to the east before winding its way the last few miles to Lake Rosa lies Baccante, the foremost city in Falisci lands. This is the Vodacce of Théah's imagination: a city of marble amid rolling hills, dotted with olive groves and vineyards protected by rows of narrow cypress trees. The city itself is famed far and wide for its wine, and while many of the finest vintages price beyond an average citizen's means, even the meanest table wine ranks several steps above its equivalent in the rest of Vodacce.

If wine is Falisci's most famous export, it is hardly the only one. Located in the center of the Vodacce peninsula along a major arterial river, Baccante does a healthy trade in goods from across Théah. Ores and gems from the mountains north of Sedilo find their way downriver, exchanged for Lucani lace, Mondavi rice, Crescent goods imported by the Bernoulli family and fabrics from far off Montaigne and Avalon.

Falisci prides himself on open attitude of his cities and gives price breaks for imports and exports, as long as the seller does his business inside the city. The forum in Baccante rings with the shouts of hawkers from every Nation, each pushing the latest wares from their corner of Théah. In the space of an afternoon, a wanderer in Baccante can spend a year's wages among its stalls.

All of this appears exactly as its ruler intends, for Baccante is a carefully constructed lie; the Vodacce of Théah's imagination is exactly that, imaginary. The Falisci family may practice a gentler form of politics than their peers, but they are no novices when it comes to the Great Game. Powerful men and women—lulled by Falisci wine and the comforts of the city—are prone to wagging their tongues, and the family always keeps informants close at hand.

Baccante's carefully manicured appearance is the work of decades, and the highly professional bureaucracy that runs the city knows exactly which family pays their wages and to whom they owe their allegiance. The warmth and courtesy Baccante offers comes from that of an actor, not of a friend.

By creating the illusion of neutral ground and looking after such niceties as public safety, sanitation and commerce, the Falisci family has created a formidable clearinghouse of intelligence from all over Théah. The other Princes understand the perils that go along with a visit to Baccante, though they know the value of it as well. Where else in Vodacce can one catch up on the latest palace intrigues in Montaigne or hear the most appalling enormities about life in distant Ussura? The pull of the city is magnetic, and in the end, few choose to resist it.

## Il Bugiardo

Tucked away in the ancient Numanari catacombs beneath Baccante hides the city's worst kept secret: il Bugiardo, a seedy watering hole popular with expatriates and agents of rulers both foreign and domestic. Seated at rickety tables abutting ossuary niches, spies, revolutionaries and outlaws drink, argue and exchange news.

The proprietor, a handsome young exile from Potenza by the name of Lelio, is famed for his outlandish lies, many of which contain a grain of truth. His stories are like puzzles, everyone trying to suss out the truth from the lie, and people take great pride in deciphering his secrets. Of course, for his part, he just likes to tell a good story.

Lelio strictly forbids combat within il Bugiardo, claiming it disturbs the sleeping dead, whom he has taken up a personal responsibility for. More than one scoundrel who disregarded Lelio's policy has "taken a wrong turn" in the catacombs, never to be seen again.

## La Vigna

While Baccante displays the most visible demonstration of Falisci power, it is not the center of it. That role belongs to the estates at La Vigna, where the Falisci family lives and plays. A half-day's ride north of Baccante, among fields of the family's oldest vines, the compound encompasses ruins dating back to the Old Empire, which have been tastefully integrated into the more recent construction. The Falisci are masterful entertainers, and even the court favorites of Charouse covet an invitation to a gala at La Vigna.

Such is the wealth of the Falisci family that every half-dreamt vision of excess a partygoer might imagine becomes reality or close to it. Gilded fountains pump Falisci wine, while lovely courtesans entertain noblemen with their wit and beauty, and servants tempt guests with delicacies from across Théah. In contrast to the egalitarian debauchery of Potenza's Carnivale, the revels at La Vigna invite only the select few.

Here, men exchange favors, conclude treaties and broker noble marriages that set the course of future events. It was at La Vigna that Morella Giacinni's hand was proffered for L'Empereur Léon Alexandre du Montaigne, a match that threatens deeply held Vodacce beliefs; anywhere else, it would have been impossible.

Indeed, the design of the setting itself facilitates such difficult conversations. Built alongside the villa of an imperator of the Old Empire, the compound includes numerous ruined courtyards and ambulatories where dignitaries can hash out the troublesome details of an agreement over a glass of wine.

When it comes to matters that Prince Donello Falisci believes to be of particular importance to his family's fortunes, he invites the parties to take a personal tour of the Falisci cellars and to sample rare vintages directly from the barrel. The honor is keenly felt and rarely bestowed; if the parties leave with an agreement in hand and perhaps the touch of a hangover as a result, it all benefits the Falisci.

## Postumi

The Church of St. Dorothy in Agony was established a generation ago as a home for dishonored women. Located on the northern outskirts of Baccante, it quickly became the dumping ground for families whose daughters had failed to live up to the oppressive codes that govern Vodacce womanhood.

Here, for the first time, noble and commoner mixed freely under a shared burden of scorn and rejection. In addition, the church afforded these women all the benefits of a Vaticine education, schooled in mathematics, history, literature, languages and law. The church claimed to read the lessons to the women, but if they were caught reading a book or writing a letter, no one was really around to care too much about the indiscretion.

Touring the church upon his accession, Prince Donello Falisci soon realized that the sisters and their charges were some of the most intelligent, unconventional thinkers he had come across. He dawdled for a time discussing the nature of Theus and the history of Vodacce with some of its least valued citizens, and his visits quickly became commonplace.

After several years, the Mother Superior broached the idea of formalizing the relationship, and shortly thereafter Falisci clerks arrived bearing piles of business records, legal documents and some of the family's less sensitive diplomatic correspondence. The results astounded the Prince—the analysis carried out at the church uncovered several merchants cheating the family and a number of troubling inconsistencies in the reports received from those the Falisci considered close allies.

Nicknaming the church *Postumi*, "the hangover," for the clarity and pain its residents lent to his family's affairs, Prince Donello began to solicit their opinions on more sensitive topics, eventually recruiting several of the brightest to serve as agents of the Falisci. The relationship has continued to deepen over the years, with the Falisci family providing for Postumi's material needs while the women, abandoned by their own families, have found a valued and essential place in another's.

# Villanova

Across Vodacce, parents use the name Villanova to terrify children into doing their chores or to invoke as a kind of talisman against lesser evils. There is scarcely a family in Vodacce that more perfectly encapsulates the ruthlessness, pragmatism and indifference to ethics or morality than the Villanova.

Sheltered between the mountains and the sea, the Villanova estates are the scorpion's sting at the end of the Vodacce peninsula, and none of the other Princes make a move without first considering how Prince Giovanni Villanova might respond.

## Serafino

At first glance, Serafino is nothing short of angelic. Set in a deep natural harbor against the sapphire blue of the open ocean, with fertile lands stretching for miles behind the city before fading into a picturesque mountain range, the city makes a convincing case for paradise. The city's architecture only enhances the impression, as soaring marble spires and bridges lend the city a sense of verticality and grace.

While prosperous and well maintained, the city is neither a trading hub nor renowned for its crafts. The ships stop at Serafino because they carry the sort of exotic—and largely illegal—goods that might interest the Villanova family or its patriarch. From exotic toxins and unusual weaponry to stolen goods simply too hot to fence anywhere else, the black market of Serafino never lacks for activity. Nor is it particularly illicit, occurring on market days a few short steps from the more traditional market.

Of course, what is illegal in other lands is free game in Villanova. Prince Giovanni's laws serve only to protect himself and his holdings. The activities that might get you put into prison in the neighboring princedoms are rarely noted in Villanova lands: from murder to possession of drugs, poisons, and dangerous weaponry. But, don't pay your taxes, or fail to show respect to a noble and you'll lose your head post-haste.

Ultimately, Serafino prospers, like all endeavors in Villanova lands, because it serves the interests of the Villanova family. Should they decide that the city threatens their plans, the family would not hesitate to burn it to the ground.

## L'Universita dei Serafini

Serafino's true wealth lies not in goods, but in knowledge. L'Universita dei Serafini is a testament to what brilliant men and women can accomplish when utterly free from moral or ethical constraint.

Whether the rumors of vivisections and other darker acts are true or not, the medical science coming out of the university leaps far ahead of its peer institutions. A team of students claims to have cured the painful and deadly side sickness by cutting a living man open on a table, while others tout advances against typhus, cholera and even the white plague.

There is a darker side to this experimentation, as none of the students or teachers swear to avoid harming their patients. Whenever a new toxin or chemical comes to the attention of the Villanova family, they use the university as their testing ground. In most cases, a convicted criminal serving a long sentence is hauled out of jail and subjected to a number of tests; if he survives, his sentence is halved, and if he doesn't he reaches a different kind of freedom.

In one particularly efficacious demonstration of such a compound, Prince Giovanni Villanova is said to have remarked, "What use are armies when a man can command death itself?" That saying, if anything, ought to replace the university's motto above the school's grand entrance.

Not everything is sinister experimentation at the cost of human lives. Much of the natural sciences practiced at the university occurs in chemistry laboratories, and relate to creating compounds to combat a wide variety of ailments. Of course, the only way to test those compounds is to administer them, but often any chance at a cure is better than suffering with a life-threatening illness. At least, that is what the reserachers and doctors at the university claim whenever anyone asks any pressing questions.

Then there's the post-mortem dissections, where scientists learn about organs and whole body systems from cutting open the dead—a practice frowned upon nearly everywhere else in Théah.

# Caligari

The lands of Prince Vincenzo Caligari encompass the fertile eastern shore of Lake Rosa and the mountainous eastern coast south of Porto Spatia. This quirk of geography forces trade, bound for Caligari lands through the narrow strait at the mouth of Lake Rosa, to frequent "inspections" by ships belonging to Prince Gespucci Bernoulli.

As a result, blockade running and smuggling have become specialties of the Caligari family, enabling their illicit trade in artifacts and antiquities.

## Il Bosco Grigio

A spine of young mountains guards the eastern coast of the Vodacce peninsula, rising thousands of feet in the air, with the highest peaks sporting snowfields through the heat of summer. Warm, wet air rising off the Numanari Approach to the east and the Vaticine Gulf to the west cools as it hits the mountains, falling as snow on the northern end of the range and cold rain on the islands to the south. In the Caligari lands, this phenomenon has given rise to a sprawling forest known as "il Bosco Grigio" or the Gray Wood.

While united by a single name, il Bosco Grigio is in fact two forests. To the west of the mountains, it is a deciduous wood of beech, chestnut and oak, where a citizen of Rinascita, Caligari's main city center, is wont to stroll when she needs to escape the oppressive architecture of her city. The Caligari family owns the forest and has exclusive rights over any and all game and fowl hunted therein, but a citizen is free to explore the forest and gather fallen wood as he wills.

Over the centuries, the harvesting of deadwood and the wanderings of Rinascita's citizenry have hampered the growth of the understory, giving the forest an open and airy feel. Today, it remains a favorite of young lovers and others who wish to talk far from prying ears, though those who use the privacy to plot against the Prince and his family have been known to suffer "hunting accidents" within the forest's confines.

The forest is also where Prince Caligari houses his collection of Syrneth artifacts. Deep in the forest lies a mausoleum-like structure with only one door, reportedly made of solid dracheneisen. The door is locked with a mundane key lock and a locking mechanism clearly Syrene in nature. No one but the Prince knows what treasures lie inside.

## Logana Cliffs

The other forest lies on the eastern side of the mountains. As the forest climbs into the mountains and descends their eastern side, it truly comes into its name. Here, evergreens take over as stands of pine, fir and spruce carpet the ground with a muffling layer of fallen needles. Clouds and fogs quick to burn off at lower elevations linger in the valleys, lending the forest a haunted air.

As the mountains reach the sea, they drop off in vertical cliffs to a thin, pebbled strand guarded by granite sea stacks. This denotes the realm of the legendary Longana, beautiful women with the legs of a goat who live in the storm-tossed coves where the Numanari Approach meets the Vodacce peninsula. According to local folklore, any man who can convince one of these women to cross the mountains and marry him will know prosperity for three generations, and a few sailors lose their lives each year searching for them.

Whether these women exist or not generates much debate in Caligari lands, and a more prosaic explanation for the deaths in this area can be found in the wrecker groups who work this stretch of the coast. Preying on ships cast about on the sudden storms that break as the sea air hits the mountains, unscrupulous people lure ships onto the rocks with false beacons or signals of safe anchorage.

Once they smash the ship and drown the crew, they scavenge what they can from the cargo that washes ashore. Never a people to let a mysterious death go to waste, the citizens of Rinascita believe the fogs that linger in the eastern forest to be souls of those drowned by the wreckers, who must await the embrace of either Theus or Legion before permitted to depart.

Few people spend time in the haunted forest, or the cursed shores, fearing to catch the ire of the dead. This makes the wooded area ideal for bandits and thieves to make camp without fear of notice, which makes the forests even more dangerous. Of course, the only people who do enter the forest are those who know full well the danger, and maybe even anticipate it.

## Rinascita

Amid the rolling plains of Lake Rosa's eastern shore, the city of Rinascita inspires both awe and oppression in equal measure. Built almost entirely of dark granite quarried from the nearby mountains, the city towers over its surroundings, while the unrelenting grayness of its construction lends a bleakness within its confines. While other Vodacce cities have a vital, chaotic urban core, much of the hustle and bustle of city life is conducted outside the walls of Rinascita, where peasants and merchants hawk their wares in a sprawling market before the city gates.

The interior of the city is another matter entirely. The cyclopean architecture seems to loom over Rinascita's residents to such an extent that even during the busiest hours of the day the city conveys a sense of emptiness. Home to antiquarians and eccentric scholars, Rinascita is famed across Théah as a place of learning, though a foreign academician frequently describes her stay as an unpleasant if necessary chore.

The streets of Rinascita follow a distinct—if vaguely alien—pattern, as if designed by a mind unconcerned with the flows of people and commerce. Long arcing boulevards connect seemingly random points in the city, bordered by stone row houses placed cheek-by-jowl as if to forbid the creation of more useful byways and shortcuts. These thoroughfares bend back on themselves in strange zig-zag patterns, so that someone seeking to visit a friend's home a hundred feet from his front door as the crow flies might have to travel half a mile along circuitous streets to arrive on foot.

The city's somber mien finds a counterpoint in its populace, who remain, by necessity, some of the friendliest in Vodacce. Since the most direct route between two points may involve traipsing through someone's home, the citizens of Rinascita are welcoming to a fault, offering hospitality to strangers and neighbors alike. This human touch helps offset the somber and confusing architecture of the city, and while the streets may seem empty, Rinascita's homes stay filled with friends and strangers lifting glasses of wine and sharing meals together.

### L'Edificio

All of Rinascita's strange, twisting boulevards emanate from a plaza at the center of the city, above which looms a strange tower of smooth rock known simply as "L'Edificio" or the Building. Aligned to the cardinal points of the compass and rising over a hundred and fifty feet in the air, the tower houses the largest collection of written work on Théah.

An order of librarians called the *Eruditi* maintains the complex and provides Prince Vincenzo Caligari with detailed information about every visitor to the library. The head of the order, Bibliothecarius Anacleto di Rinascita, is a beloved fixture of the city's life. Far from an aloof academician, he is a true scion of the city, happy to discuss conspiracy theories with loafers in any of the city's piazzas and a welcome visitor at homes both noble and common. Not above telling off a novice, he also helps researchers and other visitors navigate the library's labyrinthine collections.

Among those collections, L'Edificio boasts more works dating to the time of the Old Empire than the Vaticine Church, and the Eruditi have protected numerous "heretical" tracts from the more zealous members of the faith. Here too L'Edificio houses some of the only extant manuscripts dealing with the occult: philosophical and religious ruminations on the origins of sorcery and its relationship to Theus.

The dark corridors of L'Edifico contain everything from codices purporting to catalogue the forms and abilities of mythological beasts to wild speculations on the nature of the so-called Syrneth. Indeed, accusations dog the Eruditi that they harbor scrolls of forbidden knowledge within their walls. Never one to avoid an issue, the Bibliothecarius famously remarked that such calumnies emanate from Cardinal Verdugo, who, in Anacleto's words, "never met a book he didn't want to burn."

L'Edifico welcomes any and all who wish to peruse the stacks, though books are not allowed to leave the premises. This results in scholars spending days at a time inside the halls, poring through books, making copies of important passages and sleeping in chairs or the cold floor in pursuit of whatever knowledge they seek.

# Lucani

Precious few in Vodacce know what to make of the Lucani family's sudden rise through the ranks. Three generations ago, the head of the Villanova family granted a keep, lands and incomes at the uttermost end of the Vodacce peninsula, not including the Signore Islands, to Michele Lucani, the first of that name to claim the title of Prince.

While a Prince by courtesy only, his family's hard work and perseverance over the past century have grown their holdings to the point where any laughter at their claims of nobility is quickly suppressed. Nevertheless, as arrivistes and near-vassals of the Villanova family, the Lucani have struggled to assert themselves against their rivals, and, though something of a paper shield, a web of advantageous marriages has kept the wolf from the door thus far.

The current Prince, Michele Lucani, named after his grandfather, has made the largest strides towards solidifying the Lucani principality as a legitimate power unto its own.

## L'Aquila

The Lucani family claims noble blood by virtue of their long residence in the city of L'Aquila, once a fortified port of the Old Empire and the residence of a major noble family. From here, Lucani ships can patrol the narrow mouth of the Vaticine Gulf for pirates and quickly reach the major shipping lanes of the Widow's Sea.

Bolstering their claim to nobility is the inarguable fact that the Streghe of the Lucani family have no equal in the power and subtlety of their art. If sorcery is a gift found only among those of noble blood, then surely the nobility of the Lucani family is beyond question.

Shot through with ruins of the Old Empire, L'Aquila and many of its structures date to those ancient days. As the empire's glory faded, L'Aquila, a remnant at the end of the earth, preserved a fraction of its history and grandeur. Today, its citizens walk on the same streets that senators once trod, and the city guard practices in the barracks that held a legion of the Old Empire in days gone by. The residents of L'Aquila fiercely live up to that legacy and tend to be bluff, honest and hardworking.

In keeping with this salt-of-the-earth attitude, the city's fame, commercially speaking, comes from its handicrafts. The textile industry in L'Aquila produces the finest cloth in Vodacce, and its tailors and lacemakers turn these into the latest fashions, which nobles and merchants seek after throughout the peninsula.

One can find the city's carpenters, famed for their ornamental work, in both domestic settings and aboard ship, where figureheads from L'Aquila command high prices. Similarly, semiprecious stones from the nearby mountains support a growing number of lapidarists, while the rich clay of the lowlands supplies the city's famed ceramicists with their material.

L'Aquila produces a peculiar decorative art form known as *opere di commessi*, where small stones of varying colors are inlaid into a large slab to create intricate patterns. The rarity of master crafters who practice the technique, combined with its surpassing beauty, have contributed greatly to the city's prosperity.

In recent years, a flood of Castillian immigrants has stretched the city's resources. Fleeing first the war with Montaigne and then the Inquisition, these refugees have settled into the rhythms of life in L'Aquila and infused the city with a touch of Castillian culture. The Castillians, for their part, have developed a kinship with these unexpectedly forthright and diligent Vodacce, and commerce between the Nations has picked up as a result.

## Il Anfiteatro

In the center of town, a massive circular amphitheater rises above a piazza dating back to the Old Empire. The structure looms over nearby houses and features relief art from the ancient past depicting gladiatorial combat and other blood sports.

The well-used amphitheater plays host to an idiosyncratic tradition of L'Aquila: any man accused of a minor civil offense that threatens his reputation may challenge his accuser to a trial by combat. If he wins or his accuser declines to face him, he forgets the matter and the crime is expunged. If he loses, he may not contest the charge further in a court of law and must abide by the judgment of the arena.

Combatants fight until one participant concedes the victory, but in the case of particularly obstinate or bloodthirsty parties, the contest can be to the death if both gladiators agree. Mostly, the fights are between hotheaded young men dueling over women or people accused, justly or unjustly, of petty theft. The forthright attitude of L'Aquila's citizens means that serious crimes are rarely committed, but those that are committed reach beyond the remit of the arena.

The Castillian population of L'Aquila has brought one of their customs to the amphitheater: *el Baile del Toro*, the art of bullfighting. Initially repulsed by what they saw as the elaborate slaughter of livestock, the citizens of L'Aquila have warmed to the sport after the severe goring of several would-be *toreros* from Vodacce. Their spectacular failures convinced the locals el Baile del Toro requires more technique than they had initially believed.

The amphitheater sees action of one sort or another almost every weekend, and the social scene around these events is lively. For the lower and merchant classes, it provides a chance to see and be seen, as well as to lay bets on everything from the outcome—in the case of human contestants—to the length of time or the possibility of a goring if one of the combatants is bovine. A curious or dissolute noble attends from time to time, eager to take the pulse of the city or indulge his baser impulses.

## Le Terme dell'Imperatore

The ancient baths of the Old Empire, located on the outskirts of L'Aquila, remain an important part of the life of the city. Without restriction by gender or social class, people use the place to conduct business, catch up on the latest gossip or simply have a soak. Whatever ancient system brings the hot water up from the depths continues to function, and the Lucani family strongly discourages further exploration.

The only area of the baths off limits to the general public is a secluded pool reserved for the use of Fate Witches. This provides one of the only unregulated social spaces for a woman with the gift. Here, blessedly free of her husband or chaperone, she can take down her veil and be as Theus made her. Though there might be much to be gained by eavesdropping on their conversation, the prospect of dozens of enraged Streghe generally suffices to put off anyone tempted by the idea.

In truth, le Terme dell'Imperatore, for all its ancient marble and intricate friezes, is part of what makes L'Aquila such a pleasant place to live. The chance to mix with one's betters—or the baser classes, depending on one's position—free of any of the trappings that serve to mark these distinctions has contributed greatly to the social and economic life of the city.

Much of L'Aquila's higher level business takes place in the baths, as people who would normally never socialize interact in the baths. Merchant and nobleman, or commoner and artisan, agree to contracts in principle while both parties relax at the baths, only to formalize them later.

And, if the idea of bathing nude in the sight of the opposite sex strained a Castillian to her breaking point, once she dispensed with her prudishness and accepted the tradition, she found it easier to integrate herself into the life of the city. Even if it was a touch too licentious for her taste.

## Il Sottomarino

Deep beneath L'Aquila lies a spacious natural cavern carved from the relentless sea and incoming tides. The cavern system, only accessible from the water coming in from the Numanari Approach at low tide, is riddled with byways and long ponderous streams.

It boasts a natural harbor that can hold up to five deep bottom ships, though when the tide rises, the cavern's ceiling is not high enough to allow a full mast. water flows from the harbor into streams that riddle the countryside, carving out deep caves within the hills. Some say small creatures live in those hills, but few pay attention to such superstitions.

Only a small group of people know of the caves beneath L'Aquila, or how to find the entrance. If more knew, surely the Explorer's Society would be crawling all over the place, looking for ancient artifacts. The largest cavern is filled with remains from the Old Empire. The place is littered with ancient machinery, some of which still works.

Just beyond the main cavern are several smaller ones, and below them, even more. The waters in the deepest caverns are heated by warm air pockets from deep in Terra's crust. This is where the pumps that bring hot water into le Terme dell'Imperatore lie, and this is where the Lucani family hides their secrets.

The Old Empire used the cavern as a storage space, fully aware that access to it is limited by time of day. When the Lucani family found the cavern, undisturbed for centuries, they discovered neatly packed arms, dried foods (long disolved to near dust) and two long rowing ships, completely dilapidated from time.

Now, the Lucani have repurposed the cavern for a similar function. Inside they store food, arms and a few ships. The family spent years tunneling from the estate into the cavern, making an easy access in case the Villanova ever decide to retake their lands.

# Mondavi

The lands controlled by Prince Alcide Mondavi are idyllic and sleepy for the most part. With the Falisci family devoting much of Vodacce's arable land to the cultivation of grapes, it fell to the Mondavi family to look after the Nation's baser appetites. As a result, the low swampy land north of Bessarion and south of the Vestini River has been given over to rice cultivation.

And while being the only producer of a staple crop on the entire Vodacce peninsula has made the Mondavi family rich, the grubby nature of their enterprise has tainted their wealth with a touch of the peasant. Never one for gossip or large parties, Prince Alcide Mondavi has let the implied insult go unanswered, content to tax his lands and hunt near his estates.

## La Montagna di Cacciatori

The Prince allows himself an additional extravagance: his private hunting reserve, encompassing the entirety of the only mountain in Mondavi lands. This mountain, known—with all the imagination one might expect of the Mondavi provinces—as the Hunter's Mountain, is the eroded remnant of an ancient volcano. An elite corps of game wardens patrols the mountain's boundaries, doing their utmost to ensure that the dangerous fauna within do not escape to trouble the countryside.

Prince Alcide Mondavi has imported white bears from Ussura, a pack of wolves from der Angenehme Wald in Eisen and even a lion from the Crescent Empire, though he found it provided poor sport in the cooler, humid climes of his home. The preserve's population of deer usually suffices to see the more dangerous predators through the winter safely, but the wardens have trapped the lower reaches of the mountain heavily to ensure that winter storms do not provide wolves or other beasts with a chance to escape.

A peasant, for her part, understands the danger and gives the mountain a wide berth. Should the wolves come howling round her door, her long-standing relationships with the wardens who often winter in peasant villages provide a ready remedy.

And if no one notices the occassional person who goes missing in the reserve, or comes out with a bullet wound or cuts clearly made by manmade weapons, then all's the better.

## Elemosina

A small, quiet city on the shores of the Vaticine Gulf, Elemosina's economic life is given over to the preparation of rice for export to war-torn Castille and starving Eisen. The trade is a lucrative one, as the Mondavi lands produce a staggering amount of rice, but the details are soporific. Often deeply disappointed by the laconic speech of dockside barkeeps and the lackadaisical attitude of the local jennys, foreign sailors provide what little liveliness exists. Desperate for a way to spend her earnings that does not leave her bored or otherwise disappointed, a sailor often starts brawls with nearby crews and bets on the outcomes, though this has the paradoxical effect of doubling the wealth of a sailor without providing him with anything else to do.

Only on market days does the city come alive, with residents displaying a connoisseurship of and passion for agricultural products downright baffling to outsiders. The price of a bushel of rice often leads to raised voices, muttered imprecations and, in extreme circumstances, bared weapons. The only death related to a duel over carrots was recorded in Elemosina in 1327 AV, and the victor's grave on the outskirts of town acts as an informal pilgrimage site for farmers entering the city ahead of a market day.

The city also notably lacks indigents and other signs of extreme poverty. Upon his accession, Prince Alcide Mondavi claimed he had enough work in his family's lands to occupy every set of idle hands, and the Prince has been as good as his word, finding gainful employment for the paupers and derelicts of Elemosina. This act has earned him a charitable reputation, unusual for a Vodacce Prince, and contributed to making Elemosina one of the cleanest, safest cities on the peninsula.

## Palazzo di Agitazione

Prince Alcide Mondavi is also unusual among Princes for making his home within the limits of Elemosina, rather than retiring to an estate in the country. The vast, sprawling Palazzo di Agitazione is hardly an ideal residence, either. The Prince's demesne takes up nearly a fifth of the city's total land area, with the palazzo itself containing 2,143 windows, 1,252 fireplaces and 67 staircases. The grounds sprawl further

still and boast 1,800 fountains amidst the manicured shrubbery. Maintaining the palazzo and its gardens requires a small army of servants, and maintenance would be foolhardy if not impossible for anyone other than the Mondavi family.

The Prince does nothing without reasons, however, and the Palazzo di Agitazione provides him with an excellent one: something about the building, whether its location or its extravagance or its materials, makes a Fate Witch extremely uncomfortable and renders her all but incapable of using her gift. This discomfort, in turn, means that the Prince can receive noble visitors in his home free of the usual concerns about the manipulations of Sorte. The experience is so unpleasant that few Streghe bother with a return visit, preferring to let their husbands do their own dirty work for a change.

It also means that Prince Alcide Mondavi lives alone, as his wife, a powerful Strega, prefers to keep a modest house for her own use and that of her daughters beyond the palazzo's grounds. She spares herself the constant irritation and pain of dwelling in her husband's mansion, and her notoriously withdrawn spouse can take time to consult his books of history and law in peace. Their marriage is far from loveless, as evidenced by the Prince's three daughters, and he makes a point to consult his wife on all matters of mutual concern. He trusts her as his confidante, even if her gifts do not allow her to live in his home.

# Vestini

After the upjumped Lucani, the Vestini are the most recent family to claim a principality. Their claims to nobility are in some ways more dubious than those of the Lucani, as Vestini noblewomen rarely exhibit the gift of Sorte, and those who do find themselves weaker than their fellow Streghe.

Free of the blessing and curse of the gift, a Vestini noblewoman improves her mind, pursuing education as far as her intelligence takes her. She cannot learn to read and write, but mathematics and arithmetic require only a knowledge of numbers. Thus, Vestini women outpace their sorcerous competition in the marriage market by developing skills that few noblewomen possess.

It is said that a Vestini wife needs no sorcery to run her husband's life, merely a tally book, a schedule and a pen. Prince Alessandro Vestini is not an altruist in the matter; instead, his wife is one of the smartest women in Vodacce, and without her support, his lands would fall to ruin.

## Pacatezza

Located at the mouth of the Vestini River, Pacatezza is Vodacce's hub for commerce across the Vaticine Gulf. Pacatezza trades in Ussuran goods coming down the Boyar's River, Eisen goods shipped down Der Baueren, and exports from the Castillian heartland flowing down the Soldano River past San Gustavo. The ring of foreign languages and the allure of exotic goods add a cosmopolitan sheen to a city already justly famous for its sophistication, and a sailor is as overjoyed to make port in Pacatezza as he is horrified to find himself a berth in Elemosina.

The city is famous for two reasons: its guilds and its women. Unlike the crafters of L'Aquila, the Pacatezza are chefs, painters, sculptors, goldsmiths and jewelers; they have dedicated themselves to epicurean delights, whether it be delicious food or beautiful art.

Beyond that, the Pacatezza pride themselves on the quality of their courtesans. A Pacatezza courtesan can discuss art, literature, mathematics and philosophy. Schooled in logic, rhetoric and grammar, she speaks with an easy and practiced cadence. In short, she rises as an island of sophistication in a sea of brutishness, and her company is anything but cheap.

The allure of Pacatezza courtesan schools attracts successful jennys from all over Théah, who attend in hopes of gaining sophistication and a patron, while providing the school's clientele with a taste of the exotic and unknown. Not all jennys make the cut, as the famed courtesans of Vodacce are a cut above the rest.

## La Passione

In the northeastern corner of Pacatezza, couched among green lawns and housed in a former church lies Pacatezza's famous courtesan school. In a slightly sacrilegious nod to the school's devout past, it kept the name of the church, La Passione, which surely needs no translation.

While many Nations consider the life of a courtesan to be a shameful pursuit, in Vodacce it is anything but. The Vestini family is famous for educating women to a level unmatched anywhere else in Théah, and many of the family's ungifted noble daughters attend the school for a few years before seeking a husband.

The Vestini family neither denies nor exalts the salacious aspect of the profession; what men and women do in private is their own business. By educating the female half of the equation, the teachers at La Passione equip their charges to fend off the more brutish sort of suitor, while teaching them to recognize a worthy mate.

A far cry from the equality enjoyed by women in other parts of Théah, it ranks a great deal better than the ignorance or penury that surrounds many Vodacce women. This is mostly due to the school's Mistress, Desiderata. She encourages students to learn martial skills as well as social ones, ensuring everyone trained at La Passione is capable of defending herself both at court and on the street.

La Passione is also famous for an annual tradition called la Tarantella, or the Dance of the Spiders. In an inversion of the usual state of affairs, during the Tarantella the courtesans adopt pseudonyms and attend the ball unmasked, while suitors, noble couples and other attendees must adopt the garb, masks and mannerisms of a courtesan. The experience is both freeing for the courtesans and sobering for the other participants, who quickly realize just how much work entails keeping up a steady stream of interesting conversation with total strangers.

## Bassifondi

For all its delights, Pacatezza is not without its blemishes. According to local folklore, the thin sorcery of Vestini blood is not due to any weakness in their lineage but rather the dying curse of a Strega. As the legend tells it, this Strega of surpassing power found a Vestini courtesan worming her way into the arms of the Witch's husband. Furious with the turn of events, the Fate Witch tracked her husband to his love nest, opened her veins and cursed them both with her last breath.

Whether true or not, the area where the Witch supposedly found her husband with his lover has been abandoned for decades. Few residents willingly choose to live in the city's eastern quarter, known as the Bassifondi, and it now houses indigents, criminals and worse. Sorcerous curse or urban blight, the fact remains that people coming down the Vestini River into Pacatezza must first drift through a wilderness of collapsed buildings, open sewers and derelict, rat-infested docks.

The only people from the city proper who frequent the area are students from La Passione, who distribute food and tend to the sick and dying. While the charity may seem out of character for normal Vodacce citizens, not a single student or teacher at the courtesan school fears to go out alone in the streets of Pacatezza, either in Bassifondi or elsewhere.

# The Unbound

While the Princes of Vodacce hold much of the Nation in their grasp, a few sanctuaries flourish beyond their reach. These places act as havens for those who live without the protection of a patron or who chafe at the confining social roles of Vodacce society.

## Fontaine

In theory, Fontaine should be the coveted possession of one Prince or another. Straddling a tributary of the mighty Sejm River at the mouth of a fertile mountain valley, and possessing rights to the rich mineral deposits of the Valtulina Mountains, Fontaine has all the makings of a Prince's plaything.

Unfortunately, getting to Fontaine from the Vodacce heartlands is more trouble than it is worth. The western slopes of the Valtulina rise between 10 and 14 thousand feet in the air, with passes few and far between their snowcapped peaks. Further complicating the situation are natural hazards including avalanches, wolves, bears and rumors of unquiet spirits, or worse.

As a result, Fontaine's people possess a rugged self-reliance seldom found in the lowlands. Here, townfolk look after their own needs, and the Great Game finds little purchase in Fontaine's alleys and markets. The town practices a radical form of suffrage, where every adult (man and woman) votes for a mayor, whose few responsibilities involve dispute resolution and ensuring public safety. A far cry from the autocracy of the principalities. The implicit challenge Fontaine poses to the Princes' rule is largely ignored due to the town's remote location and small population.

It has become a haven—perhaps the only in all Vodacce—for those pursued by a Prince or his agents. Here, outcasts enjoy a life free from Vodacce society, imbibing Ussuran liquor, discussing Sarmatian political theory and comparing the theological merits of the Objectionist and Vaticine faiths.

Aside from the iron mines that produce the ore for Fontaine's exceptional steel, the Valtulina Mountains remain largely unexplored. Persistent rumors exist of Syrneth ruins above the snowline, but only one person ever claimed to find one. The man went mad shortly after and was found dead of exposure, having flensed the skin from his face with a rock. Nevertheless, Fontaine sees a steady trickle of archæologists and Caligari flunkies, who either return empty-handed or not at all.

## Joppa

The Joppa family, another powerful Vodacce family whose wealth and influence rivaled that of the likes of the Falisci or Bernoulli, once ruled the city of Joppa and its surrounding lands. Now the city stands as a testament to what happens when you play the Great Game and fail.

More than a century ago, the Joppa family made a play to unite Vodacce under a single ruler. Francisco Joppa had made alliances with the Lucani, Falisci and Villanova families to undermine the others and raise himself up as Emperor over the principalities. When Joppa made his move, however, Villanova doublecrossed them. Prince Villanova leaked Joppa movements to the Vestini family who headed them off before much became of the coup. As a retribution for the attempt, the other Princes sent military might into Joppa and overtook the city. They rooted out the Joppa family and killed them all, or sent them into hiding.

No one now claims the Joppa name. Those who might have descended from the cursed family long ago severed any tie or association with them. Ruins dominate the lands where a thriving city once stood. The city itself suffered little damage in the attack, but after the Joppa family's decline, the residents moved to either Five Sails to the east or south into other parts of Vodacce. What remained of Joppa quickly fell to disuse and ruin, allowing thieves and indigents to move in. Eventually, without workers or merchants in close proximity to sustain them, they too moved away.

In the past few years, a small enclave of Sarmatian merchants and travelers took over the old Prince's estate, refurbished the homes and restored them to their prior beauty. Surrounded by ruins, these lavish estates serve as secret vacation homes, hidden within Vodacce's boarders, but without a Prince to tax or regulate them. Invited guests can enjoy the luxury of a Vodacce Prince's home without the hastle of having to actually deal with the Vodacce. Few know of the estates of Joppa, and the merchants aim to keep it that way. From the outside, the city looks just as empty and ruined as ever, but deep inside the heart of the city, the warm glow of commerce lights the night.

# Sorte

Vodacce's Fate Witches are tacitly feared, even by the men who wed them. Every nobleman desires to have Fate work in his favor, depending on his family's ability to arrange useful marriages and secure the power of a Strega to boost his own schemes. Brought up from a young age to harness her power, a Strega exists in her own strata of society, with a tight-knit community of sorceresses. These women teach their practices to the new generations of women born into their power, aiding the political schemes of the Vodacce nobles who support them.

Most, if not all, of the noble families in Vodacce have Sorte running through their veins, and the sons of prominent Strega are often married off to other sorceresses in order to maintain viable magical lineages. Fortunately, the practice is widespread enough that the nobility can avoid the complications that arise from closely related bloodlines. The gift can lie dormant in families gifted only with sons, but even when the line "vanishes," the families cite their sorcerous ancestors as marks of pride and status.

Streghe are easily identified at birth. Daughters gifted with Sorte usually carry *il bacio de destino*: a red birthmark said to be the kiss of Fate. These most frequently occur on the child's cheek or neck, though it may appear anywhere on the body, and has a rough heart shape or one not unlike a pair of lips. Noble families often celebrate the birth of a Fate Witch with lavish feasts and parties, and the parents often betroth daughters born with such a gift within months to cement or strengthen political ties. For this reason, among others, raising a hand against Strega is a dangerous prospect; not only do you run the risk of her family retaliating, but any of their allies as well.

While most Strega are born to noble families, any female child possesses a chance to carry the gift. The nobility find and take daughters of commoners soon after birth to raise them among the upper classes, taught all the proper etiquettes of nobility and trained in her art. The loss of a daughter is not without compensation. Even the peasantry knows the value of a sorceress' power, and the tradition of bartering is not exclusive to the nobility of Vodacce. The birth of a Strega into a lower-class family all but guarantees a more luxurious lifestyle. Of course, one who cannot keep up with the myriad unspoken rules of high society quickly finds herself disgraced and back where she began.

## Training

Streghe raise new Streghe from birth to take on their eventual role in society. A girl born to nobility studies under her mother, while one born to the lower classes obtains patronage from the families she will marry into, learning from the Streghe living there. While a Strega's education extends to such things as etiquette and behavior, the men of the house frequently police her studies to ensure her education does not include anything forbidden.

As Vodacce law prevents Streghe from learning to read or write, all of their training is by rote and experience. Isolated within their houses nearly from birth, Streghe spend their early lives learning the ins and outs of Vodacce's social structure and all the proper etiquettes expected of a woman of her status.

From early on, lessons impress upon her the gravitas of her abilities. Her true training begins at the age of ten, when a Strega receives her first deck. This deck only contains the Lesser Cards, and she uses these to learn to read the Weave around her. By the time she turns twelve, when she begins her practical training in Tesse, she has a solid grasp of the Lesser Cards and can begin incorporating the Greater Cards, starting with the ones that resonate most with her readings.

Once she has mastered the basic deck, the Strega can begin learning her Tesse. As she gains working knowledge of all four Weaves over time, she receives the opportunity to decide which to pursue first. Most students gravitate toward Arcana as their first choice, the most common of the Weaves overall. Not all choose such a path, but the habit of Reading the world around them leads most Streghe to pursue a means of manipulating that information. Many Streghe strive to master the four Weaves, and those who can command every aspect of their sorcery are treated with equal parts awe and fear by any who know of the scope of their talents. If her instructor is unavailable for a time or does not know the particular Tessere a young Strega wishes to learn, she may for a time study with another family.

The education of Streghe trumps all alliances and rivalries; it is common practice to simply turn a blind eye to the practice. Streghe themselves often care little for the relationships between families and form tight friendships regardless of political lines. Unable to participate in most public affairs until wedded, and still largely isolated afterward, they have only others in their community to socialize with. More pragmatic than their hot-tempered husbands, Streghe consider the results of magic to be strictly business and very seldom allow it to interfere with their personal relationships.

While the nobility of Vodacce typically and exclusively wed Streghe, there are rumors of the middle class and peasantry keeping their daughters to marry them to other families in the same social circles.

Other rumors include Streghe serving as headmistresses to educate other young girls in schools existing near Vodacce's borders. Details on such schools are difficult to come by; some doubt if they even exist at all. Those Streghe that exist outside of the nobility carefully keep quiet about their abilities, for fear of retaliation if society discovers them.

## Social Status

Sorte, as a force, carries with it its own title and place in society. Society considers all Streghe as noblewomen, since the gift transcends her family's status. The lack of surnames in most of Vodacce culture becomes largely beneficial in these cases. Unlike nations where noble names and titles easily pinpoint their lineage, locking those born to lesser status or lacking powerful surnames into their class, Vodacce removes those restrictions. The Vodacce widely understand the gift of Sorte as a powerful blessing, and the power itself confers status. Streghe, often considered their own family, as a whole take on the adopted surname **Destine**.

While some powerful families promise their daughters from birth to cement alliances and the like, they often do not meet their intended until the wedding. Once she enters her training, the Strega lives largely isolated from the outside world, to minimize the potential fallout from her first pluckings at the strands of Fate, and if not betrothed by the time she completes her training, she remains in her family's home until marriage. While she typically doesn't remain there long after completing her training, the years she spends training means the women that raise and teach her mean more to a Strega than her birth family.

In order to properly teach etiquette, powerful families host events intended to emulate the common social obligations a noblewoman encounters when she re-enters the world. Generally open to all Witches still in training and their teachers, the galas, feasts and other celebrations offer an opportunity for Streghe to test their abilities not only to pluck at Fate, but to decipher the complex social cues and intricacies of the courts. Streghe grow accustomed to their traditional gowns and veils and can practice their Tesse in a public setting.

Of course, to practice among the nobility could mean potential disgrace for those less perceptive or still learning. The events play hosts to local courtesans, who act as surrogates for members of the noble courts. Their close ear to the nobles and comprehensive education make them excellent proxies for socialization, without the risk of losing face in a fully public setting. Courtesans also happily take on the Blessings of a learning Strega; courtesans generally accept that receiving a Curse is an unfortunate but necessary practice, with the understanding that it will not last past the evening. Older Streghe prohibit pulls at such events, as to use that Tessere in a social gathering means an egregious faux pas.

## An Unlikely Alliance

When the festivities finish, the courtesans and mistresses meet privately. Most believe they discuss and evaluate the performances of the students, but behind closed doors, the women instead go about their true business. Few noblemen know what truly goes on behind those closed doors, and even fewer admit it, but the quiet alliance between the Streghe and courtesans allows them to influence many decisions made concerning politics. Outsiders often wonder why the Fate Witches accept their lot in life as possession and tools, and the truth is that they do not fully accept it, but instead try their best to work around it.

While their husbands, fathers and employers may act protective and parental, Streghe still live a restrictive existence. These men continue to keep them under strict lock and key and under a watchful eye. An individual noble may give his wife a lot of leeway in his own private affairs, but in public, she remains demure and obedient. Not all men afford their wives this luxury in private, and those are the ones who suffer the most, and need the most help from the courtesans.

The Streghe trust the courtesans, who are often better educated and well-versed in politics, to give them sound political advice and aid. In exchange, they receive favors from the Streghe, be they beneficial to the courtesan or detrimental to her enemies. The guise of thinly-veiled disapproval and hatred between the two groups still exists in public, and on individual levels, many Streghe and courtesans do despise each other, but for the betterment of the lives of women throughout Vodacce and beyond, they willingly put aside their differences and work together for a common goal.

## Sophia's Daughters

While many of the schemes altered or put into action by the women's alliance pertain to matters within Vodacce's borders, the highest echelon of Prima courtesans and Streghe also consort with Sophia's Daughters. The group grew in numbers and spread through the trusted allies of its founders and most other members of their respective circles.

Members of the organization primarily use the rumored schools closer to the edges of the Nation's borders, and agents carefully relegate their existence to gossip and hearsay. Without the eyes of the nobles, these schools have a much easier time arranging passage for Streghe to safe houses established in neighboring nations.

While easier to transport younger girls still in the midst of their training, it is not unheard of for adult women to flee as well. Those unmarried have an easier time of it, but even a Strega married for many years and miserable knows she has powerful allies who can assist in her escape.

Even outside Vodacce, Streghe are adamant about the training of new Witches. Many safe houses also serve as schools to aid in the continuation of the next generation's studies, alongside such topics forbidden to Streghe within Vodacce's borders. Escaped Witches learn to read and write, as well as other necessities for living outside the dazzling grandeur of Vodacce courts.

The most prominent escapees from Vodacce run the schools within these safe houses. They remain underground for fear of recapture, but often know the most about Weaves. These Mistresses often have to craft makeshift decks for their students and teach literacy alongside the meanings and titles of the cards.

Additionally, this helps grown women to learn to read and write by creating a frame of reference and helps younger students learn and memorize the meanings of the Arcana by recording them for reference. Teachers encourage a growing practice within the schools to keep a written record of the proper methods of casting Tesse and ways to repay Lashes before Fate evens the scales.

## Sorte Untrained

As more Streghe escape Vodacce and start lives of their own, the possibility of one growing up either entirely unaware of her power or using it without training increases. Even after leaving Vodacce, Streghe still insist that all must receive training, and for good reason: to alter Fate, you must pay a price. Request too much without offering anything in return, and Fate Herself takes what is owed, often to terrible effect.

While a trained Strega understands the systems in place allowing her to repay Fate, an uneducated one does not understand how to repay the debt she incurs—if she knows she incurs it at all.

A Strega born outside of Vodacce may not know her heritage until too late. It does not manifest until she reaches the age of ten. Where she would normally begin her studies, she instead lives her whole life an incredibly lucky individual.

While she's young, things always turn in her favor. As she ages, if not properly trained, her luck slowly but surely turns against her. Even without the benefit of a deck, she begins to read the world around her as Fate reveals Herself. Should she choose to pluck at the threads, she learns by trial and error—condemning her targets to misfortune.

Stories within Vodacce depicting consequences of casting Sorte center on small failings. A single family falling into disgrace, a storm causing damage to a small part of town, or a duel ending with a victory for the lesser party. Accumulating excessive Lashes proves difficult within Vodacce, as Streghe can see the strands of Fate wrapped about each other; if one has too many, her sisters force her to atone to prevent tragedy.

Outside of Vodacce, the stories grow cataclysmic. An untrained Strega may go years suffering through a bout of bad luck, slowly condemning those around her. Stories of famine, plagues or entire towns swallowed into the ground all tie back to one central figure. A Strega using her power untrained and unchecked is undone by the debts she incurs, and Fate prefers over-correction rather than not taking enough.

Fate's backlash does not only effect the Strega; those she has used her power on also suffer. Tales of entire communities decimated or damned by one person's misfortune are not exaggerated, and Streghe who hear of such instances do all they can to locate and educate those who do not understand their gifts.

## Learning and Casting Untrained

Learning Sorte outside of Vodacce or without a formal teacher lowers the cost of the Advantage to one point. This cost applies for every purchase of the Advantage that is self-taught. A Strega may learn her first two Weaves within Vodacce at base cost, escape and learn the remaining two on her own at the lowered cost; she may discover her power on her own, learning her first Weave at the lowered cost and later find a Mistress who can teach her at the base cost for any others she wishes to learn. She may also learn to properly control the magic she has taught herself, paying one point to remove the consequences from untrained casting.

If the Strega has resources to help her learn (a deck, an instructor, a written record of the practice), she can do so safely; if she has none of these resources, learning her new Tesse requires taking on a Lash.

Casting Tesse without formal training is dangerous and difficult for the Strega to control. Whenever she casts, she or her teammates suffer from backlash as her clumsy fumbling with the strands of fate causes unanticipated results.

## Arcana

While she can Read with ease, activating someone's Virtue or Hubris is tricky. When the Strega casts a Minor Arcana, she rolls a die. On an even roll, she activates the target's Virtue; on an odd roll she activates his Hubris. Her Major Arcana still works exactly the same as in the CORE RULEBOOK, page 229.

## Blessings and Curses

The Strega struggles with the scale of her Blessings and Curses. She rolls a die to determine the number of Lashes she takes before determining how beneficial or detrimental her Tessere is. You may spend Hero Points to roll 1 additional die per point and to pick the die you prefer.

## Pulls

An untrained Strega often does not know how to anchor herself before she Pulls, and when she Pulls someone, she also gets Pulled. Any time her target moves, she also moves in the opposite direction. If her target takes Wounds as a result of her Pull, the Strega takes an equal number.

# Dueling in Vodacce

What is it like to be a Duelist in a land where a challenge is as likely to be issued over business as pleasure and in the blink of an eye; where both pride and passion turn the least offense into an insult worthy of a duel to the death? In a word? Tricky.

Given the Vodacce have been known to erupt into violence over the smallest of slights, dueling never became the controversy that it did in other parts of Théah. Duels have always been a part of life in the Nation, tacitly approved by Vaticine teachings that encourage acting on one's wrath and viewing inaction as the true sin. Even so, few opposed the establishment of the Duelist's Guild, and its laws are respected—to the same extent that the Vodacce respect most laws.

The Duelist's Guild in Vodacce finds itself in a position that one duelist (as quick with her wit as her steel) termed "a double-edged sword": the country produces enough skilled fighters to fill its Guild Houses twice over. Between fencers from merchant and noble families trained in top schools across Théah and courtesans looking to follow in Veronica Ambrogia's footsteps, a swordmaster has her pick of recruits. In some Nations, an excess of qualified candidates would be a cause for celebration, but in Vodacce, it leads to some unique problems—the greatest of which is rampant illegal dueling.

The amount of illegal dueling in Vodacce is such that if the Duelist's Guild managed to be involved in every illegal duel, a guildmember would never have time to do any dueling himself. Most duels occur spontaneously and in a fit of temper or passion. Taking the time to find a Duelist to issue a challenge formally is almost unthinkable to many and can be viewed as a cowardly delaying tactic. Duelists from Vodacce may agree privately, but the fact remains: the Guild must involve itself in some measure of illegal duels to keep the peace, to make money and to justify their existence.

The Guild must pick its entanglements wisely. It cannot get involved in every fight, even if it wanted to. They issue fines for illegal duels, discouraging most casual duels. The fines are high enough that many nobles engage in illegal duels simply for the thrill of the chase the Guild might give. It may seem prudent for the Guild to find and fine nobles who duel illegally, but doing so to a Prince's son could spell disaster for the Guild House's right to stay in that Prince's lands.

## The Guild's Influence

The Duelist's Guild's existence justifies itself well to a person that knows her way around a blade, however. If Vodacce is known for skilled fencers, a Duelist of the Guild is legendary, with names that strike fear into the hearts of her lessers. Even the most eager of challengers have backed down on learning a would-be opponent is a Guild Duelist. Aside from superior martial skills, Vodacce's Guild Houses teach a student how to quiet and control his emotions. While useful for any Duelist, one "blessed" with the quick temper of his homeland finds learning to tap inner reserves of calm helpful. It also can make him particularly calculating and particularly deadly.

Trading on the fear and respect the average fighter has for Duelists has provided something of a solution to the Guild's problems. Some Duelists in each Guild House have become skilled gossips, gaining a good handle on the local developments and dramas to get ahead of any potential duels before they happen. Generally, a Duelist contacts both parties in a dispute to offer her services, assuming a need for her sooner or later—and to ensure they both know the Guild is watching. Larger Guild Houses have taken the further step of sending out nightly patrols to officiate duels retroactively and collect a fee from the challenger—or the winner if she is the only one left standing. Most of Vodacce's Princes (and many of the richer merchant families) keep a Duelist on staff to ensure that

## BRAVOS OF VODACCE

A poor Vodacce rarely fights to defend his honor and more likely fights over a real slight than a perceived one. Nobles on the other hand likely challenge someone over slight insults or perceived threats. Many nobles are not classically trained as Duelists, despite their penchant for fights. Of course, when a noble gets into an illegal duel, the Guild likely gets involved just to rake in a fine. Those fines can get hefty if the noble has a hot temper.

Instead of paying loads of Guild fines, a noble employs a bravo, a fighter who serves as a bodyguard for the noble. Most often the bravo is a duelist, though she does not necessarily need Guild membership to serve her purpose. The Guild often only concerns itself with illegal duels when it thinks they will bring in a profit, so is less likely to fine a random bravo for illegal dueling, unless they find out about her rich benefactor. In some cases, the bravo situation is much more complex than hired bodyguard. Sometimes a trained combatant pledges himself to a younger family member, a trusted friend or even a lover. He puts his own reputation on the line defending those he swears to protect.

If honor can be found in Vodacce, it is in the bravo tradition. While one may act as a watchdog to her employer, she remains devoted and loyal, as long as the money keeps coming in. Another may act solely out of a sense of duty, not expecting any compensation for defending the life and honor of his sworn charge.

anything that occurs under their auspices is Guild-approved.

Rumors say that the Duelist's Guild in Vodacce quietly gives aid to any man or woman, no matter where they come from, and no matter their skill with a blade—when they come to duel for revenge. In Vodacce, vengeance is always free.

## Dueling Style: Le Strade

No one has yet been able to trace the inventor of this style, though many skilled adherents claim the title. Named after the narrow streets it was born and refined on, the style perfectly suits the twisting boulevards and tall slender spires of Vodacce's cities.

A student of Le Strade learns to view his environment as an obstacle course and an opportunity to gain advantage on his opponent. The style favors a lighter blade in the sword hand, leaving the offhand generally free to aid in vaulting over walls, swinging from bridges, leaping between buildings or rolling under a gateway.

A devotee of Le Strade takes her training seriously and often makes "runs" through new locations to judge the distance between buildings, the height of walls to climb, run up or leap over, the weight a railing can take. Better to know ahead of time than to learn in the middle of a duel to the death. When Le Strade Duelists meet, they tend to show off their newest tricks to one another—when it happens in a Guild House, it can gather quite a crowd and a number of wagers.

### Style Bonus: La Furia delle Strade

When you wield a fencing sword (such as a rapier or cutlass) in one hand and nothing in the other, and fight in an environment with a number of obstacles to climb, jump or swing from (such as a city, town or a ship), you can perform a special Maneuver called La Furia delle Strade.

La Furia delle Strade prevents a number of Wounds equal to your Ranks in Athletics, and creates an environment-related Consequence for your opponent with Ranks equal to your Finesse. This Consequence requires one Raise to overcome and deals its Rank in Wounds to your opponent at the end of the Round if left unchecked. A Duelist can perform La Furia delle Strade once per Round.

# Leggende of Vodacce

The Vodacce possess a rich tapestry of traditional stories revolving around the supernatural. After all, it is not such a strange occurrence once you consider that this Nation—and its people—are in constant contact with one of the most powerful forms of magic in all Théah. One that seems to be particularly attractive to creatures that dwell beyond the natural world.

The following entries are taken from *Lo Conto de li Conti* (*The Tale of Tales*), the most famous collection of traditional Vodacce stories, whose compilation and current presentation is attributed to the *esploratore* Loanna Bazza.

## The Badalisc

There was once a village where the people fought, stole and schemed against one another without any recourse. The local Prince had grown tired of hearing cases of one neighbor denouncing another. To remedy this, he decreed that no one could accuse his fellows, and had to tolerate one another without resorting to violence, on penalty of death.

The villagers follwed the edict, but not in spirit. As time passed, each villager found more creative ways to offer offense and take revenge on her neighbors. So much so that, after a while, just and good people abandoned the village.

One family, however, refused to give up on the town. They were the wealthiest inhabitants of the place and, to them, leaving was not an option. They had heard legends of fierce creatures in the forest, creatures they may be able to employ in bringing the town back to its senses. So they went to the woods, looking for an answer. When they returned, they brought with them a hideous monster. The creature had a big head covered with something akin to goat skin. Two small horns stood out on top of its head, while fiery eyes glowed near them. But its most bizarre feature was its huge mouth, one big enough to devour a person whole.

The remaining inhabitants of the village thought the family had lost their minds and imagined the worse. Before anyone had any chance to escape, however, the creature started speaking in an unnatural tongue. The family's daughter, a young *signorina*, started translating the creature's words.

To everyone's surprise, the monster, through this young woman, started revealing all the villagers' deepest and darkest secrets. At first shocked by the revelations, they then got angry but eventually laughed, all the tension and scheming rendered useless by the creature's denunciations.

And so this village—and the family's position of power—was saved.

## Nowadays

Few that know this story believe it to be true and, instead, choose to interpret it as morality tale. Trust that if you make a plan against your neighbor, so too will they against you; better to trust your neighbor instead.

There is a village, deep in the northeast of Vodacce (some say near Sedilo or Fontaine), where a brave adventurer may venture deep into its nearby forest. If she does so, she can find a creature with the ability to reveal the intentions and plans of anybody around it.

The creature is elusive and hard to tame. A person must lock eyes with the creature to show he has no fear and remain that way for an hour to break its will. Even after he has control over the creature, if he turns his back on it, the spell breaks. Once tamed, the creature teaches him its language and happily allows him to tell it where to go. Once he asks the creature to make use of its ability, it magically transports back to the forest.

The Badalisc is a fiercely territorial creature and attacks anyone who comes into its den. If the interested party does not lock eyes with the creature immediately, it fights until it defeats its enemies, is gravely injured (in which case it tries to escape) or is killed. The creature is not interested in any possession or gift, and only someone who has bested it in a staredown may understand its language.

The Badalisc is a Strength 6 Monster with the Teleporting Monstrous Quality.

## The Befana

During New Year's Eve, an old Strega—some say the first of her kind—travels across all of Vodacce in only one night. From afar, she looks like a fragile old lady dressed in rags covered with soot, with a broomstick in one hand and a hamper in the other. With that broomstick, however, she traverses the skies faster than any bird, and inside the hamper, she carries judgment to all people in the land.

To those who have been good throughout the year, she brings gifts. Sometimes baubles, other times money or food for the needy. To those who have not, she brings punishment. Often in the form of bad luck, but sometimes in pain and suffering. Both are doled out at the whims of Fate, and no one is immune to her judgement from the loweliest of peasants to the haughtiest of Princes.

To thank or try to placate her, most families leave an offering of a small glass of fine wine and a small plate of their best food. More than for their nutritional value, these items reflect the devotion and respect of the Vodacce towards the *Befana*: the vigorous bringer of judgment who kindles hope in the hearts of the just and puts fear in those of the wicked.

There are many stories about the Befana's origin. Some say she lost her only child and, after a long pursuit, made Fate Herself regret Her doings. Her sense of justice was so strong that Fate anointed Befana Her envoy, leaving in her hands the task of judging people's behavior each calendar year. Other stories claim that she committed a terrible mistake long ago, one that she still tries to compensate to this day. Some say that she is the first of the Streghe, so intricately tied to Fate that she cannot die. She keeps Vodacce in check, otherwise her own progeny, the other Streghe, may lose their power.

Regardless of her origins, the truth is that during New Year's Eve no one can escape the Befana's judgment.

## Nowadays

Even though originally the Befana may have been a single woman, in reality, today there is no one Befana. There are many.

In a Nation that forces women to keep silent and behave appropriately in public, many abuses ensue. The result is a long list of trespasses, offenses and injustices that would go largely unpunished—if it were not for the Befana.

Now a long network extends across Vodacce. One that registers every notoriously bad deed. These "witnesses" exist everywhere and they include people you least expect—children, unmarried women, hard-working peasants and young couriers, just to name a few. They see, hear and, most importantly, remember and inform. Through encrypted messages, they let the Befana know who deserves a gift and who deserves punishment.

And the Befana themselves? Some are Strega, it is true, but many are just normal women trained to use deception and the Befana disguise to mete out justice. Taught not to attempt to right every wrong—or reward every right—they, instead, focus on making Vodacce a better place one New Year's Eve at a time. Although Sophia's Daughters look upon the Befana's work kindly (and vice versa), both groups greatly differ when it comes to objectives and modi operandi. While Sophia's Daughters seek to help Streghe escape Vodacce, the Befana wish to make Vodacce a better place for women to live.

A Hero interested in helping the Befana has to prove her worth in front of a number of witnesses. Since these witnesses are mostly invisible, it is very difficult to falsify such an instance. If it happens, however, the Hero receives the benefit of a wealth of information regarding misdeeds in Vodacce, and the responsibility to do something about them.

# The Biscione

In Vodacce, the old blood runs strong. And among the seven greatly respected—and greatly feared—families that maintain that strength to this day, one has power and position the stuff of much gossiping and speculation. The Vestini, at least according to the *leggenda*, possesses a mighty, immortal monster they can unleash on anybody who opposes them. One that they prominently display in their coat of arms.

The *Biscione*.

The "Great Serpent" appears in the center of the Vestini blazon, an obscenely long and disproportionately big snake whose tail coils for what it seems like miles. The monstrosity possesses bright and glistening azure scales as thick as steel, with a fin-like membrane that traverses its spine. The most unsettling part of the picture, however, is its top. There you can find a profusion of red that represents the flesh and blood of a youngster being torn apart and devoured by the monster, its sharp fangs cleaving the poor child in half.

Although the vivid painting provides reason enough to be worthy of remembrance, some whisper it compares nothing to the real Biscione. These people affirm—although never in public—that the source of the family's wealth indeed comes from the beast's accumulated treasure, an unintended benefit of its depredation. Other families therefore quickly stay away from the Vestini, fearing that they could turn this monster their away if they so desire.

They say the creature hungers for human blood, often that of the young. Some say the reason the Vestini are not as powerful as the other families is because they must feed their children to the creature to sate its desires.

A parent may tell stories of the Biscione to scare his children into obedience, threatening to let the Vestini know she's been bad, and have them feed her to the Biscione.

## Nowadays

The truth behind the Biscione reveals, as is often the case with these situations, a much worse reality than any fabled story about it. Whereas most believe that the association with the Vestini is something new, the family has been benefiting from the creature's power for a long time, as long as the family's original ancestors. This association, however, has come with a price.

A blood price.

For the Biscione truly devours human flesh and, moreover, it dwells in a deep lake whose waters preserve the monstrosity. As a result, the Biscione is effectively immortal and forces the Vestini family to feed it or risk its ire. In fact, they hardly control the creature at all and have to content themselves with feeding their enemies to it.

The age or blood relation of the person to the Vestini family is irrelevant to the man-eating monster. All that matters is that she is flesh and blood. The Vestini themselves have been at odds with the creature for some years, often unable to meet its voracious demands with just enemies alone.

To defeat the Biscione, any brave—or desperate enough soul—must try first to make it leave its waters. If confronted outside those waters, a Hero has at least more than a zero chance to defeat it. In that situation, all that is left is a gigantic snake with impenetrable skin and the strength to devour a horse in one bite.

On the other hand, anybody who wants to benefit from the waters' healing and restorative properties has to indulge in the Biscione's diet as well. As such, only someone who has eaten human flesh in the past day and drinks from the waters of the lake gets its benefits. Otherwise, drinking the waters alone proves to be extremely poisonous and can instantly kill any man or woman on the spot.

The Biscione is a Strength 10 Monster with the Aquatic, Chitinous and Powerful Monstrous Qualities. The Biscione's waters have regenerative properties, and while in the water the creature gains the Regenerating Monstrous Quality.

## The Longana

Long ago a creature from the Otherworld fell in love with ours. And even though her land was magical and timeless, she longed for this world. On the Other Side, wishes turn into reality through sheer will, so the creature entered our material dimension.

With her, she brought others of her kind. In the material world, they all looked like women from the waist up and like goats from the waist down. Since they arrived, their favorite dwellings have been the harbors and cliffs on the coast of Vodacce. In these places, they live and remain hidden, observing the mortals and trying to discern whether they could reveal their true nature to them.

As such, no one knew about these creatures until one of them, named Longana, fell in love with a mortal man. Going against the council of her peers, Longana dared to reveal herself to the man in all her goat-legged glory. He immediately fell in love with her, and without a second thought, asked for her hand in marriage. Longana agreed, but with a condition: he must never ask her name. The man agreed and she accompanied him to his estate.

There they married and lived happily. After a while, they had children who looked human, but had their mother's supernatural charm, and the couple could not be happier. The estate where they lived was particularly bountiful and fertile. In time, jealous neighbors started rumors that the mistress was a Strega or something worse. When she ignored them, they started teasing her husband, questioning how he could be married to someone whose name he did not know.

The man endured their mockery for a while, but eventually caved to the pressure. One night, drunk and weary of their malicious jokes, he returned home and asked his wife to reveal her name. With tears in her eyes, Longana shared her name and, without any more words, disappeared into the night, leaving her husband and their children behind forever and returning to her people with a broken heart.

## Nowadays

The *Longana*—as people now refer to them—are even more difficult to find since their namesake's tragedy. Some still dedicate their lives to finding them, so immense is their beauty, great their intelligence and powerful their magic.

Longana have the power to influence natural phenomena. They can, for example, prevent bad weather, preserve a crops' health and even tame the most dangerous animal. They also possess knowledge of things unknown to mortals. Some say that the fabled loving prowess and intelligence of the Vodacce courtesans are a pale imitation of the Longana's attributes. Some argue that the first courtesan was a Longana, and she passed on her knowledge and beauty to her daughters, forming the first courtesan family. Be that as it may, the company of the goat-women ranks one of the most sought after pleasures of any Vodacce noble.

In spite of numerous efforts, no one has seduced a Longana since the first. The truth is that the Logana, still curious about humans and their lives, fear suffering the same fate as that of the original Longana. They happily defy centuries of convention if they encounter an honest proposal or receive true appreciation. They pay attention to honest men and women and those who have good intentions (which they can discern thanks to their powers). To find a Longana, brave adventurers need just explore the harbors and cliffs along the coast of Vodacce with a pure heart and honest words.

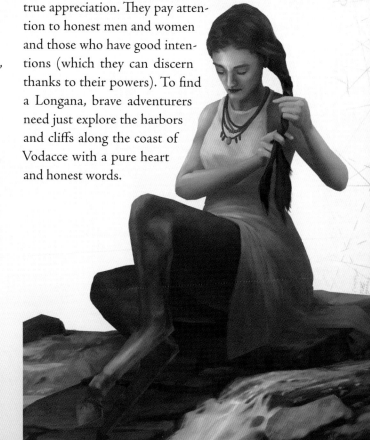

## The Monachello

The people from the deep south of the Vodacce nation have a unique legend. The abandoned abbeys and monasteries in those parts shelter the *Monachello* (Little Monk). This diminutive but thick supernatural creature dresses with long brown robes tied by a rope belt and wears a broad brimmed hat over its head (hence its name).

The creature is fond of playing tricks on people. She may pull off clothes, steal small items from bedrooms and even cause minor accidents to the most unfortunate of her victims. Some call them thieves, stealing items left out over night or money purses from inside people's pockets, the owner none the wiser until he beings searching for his belongings.

Conflicting stories tell of Monachello that appear in the dead of night, after all other hope had faded, and offer help to desperate people without expecting anything in return. In these stories, the Monachello brings food and water to the sick, and money to the poor and destitute. Sometimes, they guide their beneficiaries to hidden hoards of treasure.

Whether that treasure resulted from their tricks or other ill-gotten means no one knows. A person in this situation usually receives only as much money or help as he needs to get back on his feet and nothing more.

If someone tries to take more than she needs, she is likely to end up on the bad end of the Monachello's antics. Indeed, those who are rich or even just well-off seem to be targeted more often by the little creatures.

Since no one can come to an agreeement on whether the Monachello are beneficial or harmful, most people in the south of Vodacce prefer to avoid them at all costs—and they instruct their children and foreigners to do so as well.

## Nowadays

The legend of Monachello is particularly located to southern Vodacce because these creatures live in the underground passages that connect the many hills in the area. These hillfolk are small and humanoid with opposable digits on their hands and feet. They are suited for living underground, which makes them sensitive to light, hence the reason why they only ever come out at night.

They model their appearance after Vaticine monks, some of the first people to settle the hills the creatures call their homes. They model their ethics and way of behaving in the same fashion. In their own twisted interpretation of the Vaticine Credo, the Monachello understand that they should help "good" people, whereas "bad" people should provide that help—knowingly or not.

To ensure this, the diminutive creatures move around houses and palaces noting good and bad persons. When someone is bad, they mark her house with an invisible brand. Any Monachello who sees the mark considers it an invitation to play the most annoying pranks on its inhabitants. Especially keen on stealing items, they subsequently give to good people in need.

When seen, Monachello can be persuaded with food or coin offered freely. They appreciate these gestures and are then open to converse with whomever offered the gift. They can be influenced, in this way, to focus their efforts on a given bad person or to specifically watch over a good one. They ask for nothing in return for their services, but may, if offered, ask the benefactors to help them with certain small objects or minor tasks, usually involving theft.

The Monachello is a Strength 3 Monster with the Shadowy and Swift Monstrous Qualities.

## The Wolf d'Aggobio

There was once a walled city that feared no army nor device made by men. Some tried, though all failed to take the city. Armies broke against the walls, and even the cleverest of tacticians could not defeat them. In its hubris, the people of the city declared that nothing could hurt them behind their high walls.

And then, the Wolf appeared.

It was as big as a bear, with fur as hard as a rock, and teeth sharper than any sword. At first, the Wolf dined on the city's livestock that grazed in the land outside the walls. Its appetite was so voracious that in just a short few nights, it ate nearly all the livestock available. The people ran out of meat to eat, and had to purchase it from travelers who came to the city. Soon, news of the Wolf spread, and even travelers stopped coming to sell food.

Winter was coming, and the people of the town realized they would starve if they did not do something about the Wolf. They gathered their best warriors and sent them beyond the walls to hunt the beast, but each one fell under its immense power. Then it ate them all, and in that moment the creature tasted human flesh for the first time, and it tasted better than anything it had ever eaten.

The next night, the Wolf jumped over the walls and started dining on the city's horrified inhabitants. They cried, and they pleaded, and they tried to reason with it, but the Wolf paid no heed to their feeble attempts to stop it. Instead, the Wolf ate until full and then left the city to sleep its big dinner off in the countryside. The next day, it came back, ready to eat its fill again.

This happened for a week, until a foreign woman came to the city in the city. The people were shocked to see her, and immediately told her the horror stories of the Wolf. Ignoring the people's warning, she waited outside the city walls for the Wolf to appear. When it did, she walked fearlessly towards it. When she neared it, she extended her hand and patted the creature on its head. Without any words, they both went away as if friends from long ago.

The city, though broken, was saved from the Wolf, and they never saw the unknown woman or the creature again.

## Nowadays

Apart from being a cautionary tale about the dangers of excessive pride, the tale of the *Wolf d'Aggobio* describes one of the most dangerous creatures that roams the countryside. Indeed, this nigh undefeatable beast thankfully only appears when a population becomes prideful enough to call its attention.

No weapon can inflict any lasting injury on the Wolf, and its strength and size make it a terrible foe. It is not completely indestructible, but only the most skilled combatant has a chance at hurting the creature, much less killing it. Beyond that, the Wolf simply devours most who try to stop it or stand in its way. In this way, the creature terrorizes towns and villages for years before moving on to other locales.

What can someone do if the Wolf knocks at his door?

The best way to truly deal with the Wolf is to tame it. Only a fearless person, pure of heart and who wishes the creature no harm, can tame it. Needless to say, few people in Vodacce—even in the whole of Théah—can fulfill such requirements.

In this case, the best opportunity for any population affected by the Wolf is to send envoys far and wide to look for someone with these characteristics. Finding someone like this is the stuff of legend and a worthy task to any Heroes willing to risk an encounter with an indestructible foe. Once someone tames the Wolf, both tamer and beast leave the material world to find peace together on the Other Side.

The Wolf d'Aggobio is a Strength 10 Monster Villain with the Regenerating and Powerful Monstrous Qualities.

## The Falsoseta

Streghe appear to have ultimate power, pulling at the strands of Fate, deciding the course of history not just for one person, but entire townships. But Fate is a fickle mistress, as any Strega worth her salt could tell you, and even they must be careful about what they play around with, otherwise they might get a backlash they are incapable of dealing with.

Few other than Fate Witches themselves know the stories of the Falsoseta: the creature that feeds on the Strega's own luck, stealing her power and wreaking havoc wherever it goes.

The story goes that a Strega, at the height of her power, and who had mastered all the Tessere, got too full of herself. She claimed to have ultimate control over Fate, and for a time it seemed true. Her enemies fell before her might, and her allies grew in power and strength. She forgot that she only dabbled in fate, and was not Fate Herself. She stopped paying Fate for her use, and indeed stopped attributing her successes to Fate at all; instead, claiming she was Fate and all it embodied.

This went on for many years, Fate ever watchful of this one woman's life, waiting for the best time to enact Her revenge. A group of powerful enemies banded together in an attempt to break the power of the Strega and her husband. She laughed, saying that she would destroy all their Fates at once. Yet, when she pulled upon the strand, Fate did not obey. Instead, what came was a wretched old woman with long slender fingers.

Only the Strega could see her, as she was created by Fate. She latched onto the Fate Witch's shoulder and made off with her. When her husband came looking for her to help repel the invaders, she was nowhere to be seen. No other Fate Witch would help him, convinced the curse would get them as well.

The invades stole into his castle walls and destroyed him and his family. Now, no one speaks that Prince's name, for fear that they may bring the wrath of Falsoseta upon them. Fate Witches caution each other to avoid hubris, or Fate will snatch them away.

## Nowadays

Falsoseta may indeed be a construct of Fate, but she is not a punishment for hubris or refusing to pay Fate the correct appreciation. Fate gets back at those who refuse to accept Lashes in Her own way. The actual origins of the creature are unknown. Some postulate that the creature has always existed, but that only the Streghe are able to see her, and so they attribute it to Fate.

Falsoseta lives between this world and another, caught in between. She appears as a woman in all black, with a black veil over her face. Fate Witches say that behind that veil is nothing but a deep well of inky blackness. She has long spindly fingers that she uses to create false threads, silver and shining, between Terra and the other world, and these threads look identical to the strands of Fate that bind everything together.

One would think such an occurance a strange coincidence, but it is not a coincidence at all. Falsoseta has evolved to create webs to entrap her prized prey, Fate Witches. She even took on their appearance to blend in and hide among them.

When a Strega pulls upon a false Fate strand created by Falsoseta, she follows it back to the Witch. She then begins feeding on her power, and her luck. As she does so, waves of Fate ripple out and can affect anyone around the Strega.

Falsoseta does not feed just on Strega; anyone who accidentally runs across one of these threads and pulls it summons the creature. She may not get as much nourishment from a regular person, but any Sorcerer is as prized a catch as a Strega.

She is not invisible, nor does she snatch people away, at least not the way the story goes. Any Sorcerer can see her, through their attunement to the unnatural. She sometimes hides in the other world, which can make it seem like she has stolen her victim away. Often, before attacking, she appears as any normal Stregha, hiding in plain sight as it were.

Falsoseta is a Strength 4 Monster with the Teleporting and Chitinous Monstrous Qualities.

Appendix

# New Backgrounds

## Eisen Backgrounds

### APOSTAT

You were cast out from your homeland because of what you could do, but you won't let that stop you from doing what's right.

#### Quirk

Earn a Hero Point when you chose to ally with someone you find personally distasteful in order to accomplish something important.

| Advantages | Skills |
|---|---|
| Reputation | Athletics |
| Sorcery (Hexenwerk) | Brawl |
| Cast Iron Stomach | Empathy |
| | Notice |
| | Ride |

### BEFLECKTE SEELE

There's something inside of you that's dark and wicked, always gnawing at the edge of your mind. But power—even when it stems from evil—can be turned to good.

#### Quirk

Earn a Hero Point when you use your Monstrous nature to solve a problem and someone shuns you for it.

| Advantages | Skills |
|---|---|
| Dark Gift | Athletics |
| | Empathy |
| | Hide |
| | Ride |
| | Theft |

### EISENBLUT

There is still nobility in Eisen, and there is still iron in your blood.

#### Quirk

Earn a Hero Point when you choose to sacrifice something important to you personally for the good of Eisen or its people.

| Advantages | Skills |
|---|---|
| Imperious Glare | Empathy |
| Rich | Intimidate |
| | Ride |
| | Scholarship |
| | Warfare |

### STRATEGE

You were always excellent at chess when you were a child. Now you understand that the world itself is a chessboard, and you're still the best in the game.

#### Quirk

Earn a Hero Point when you make a critical miscalculation in your plan, and it gets you or your allies into trouble.

| Advantages | Skills |
|---|---|
| Brains of the Outfit | Aim |
| Team Player | Empathy |
| | Scholarship |
| | Warfare |
| | Weaponry |

## The Sarmatian Commonwealth Backgrounds

### MACHER

Get in, get what you're after and get out. But you make sure that EVERYONE gets out.

#### Quirk

Earn a Hero Point when you choose to reveal yourself to an enemy in order to help another character get out of trouble.

| Advantages | Skills |
|---|---|
| Specialist (Hide) | Athletics |
| Team Player | Convince |
| | Hide |
| | Notice |
| | Theft |

### MÓWCA

There's a good soul inside of everyone. Some people just need a little help in finding it.

#### Quirk

Earn a Hero Point when you successfully solve a problem by convincing another character to listen to her conscience.

| Advantages | Skills |
|---|---|
| An Honest | Convince |
| Misunderstanding | Empathy |
| Heartfelt Appeal | Hide |
| | Scholarship |
| | Tempt |

### RYCERZ LUDZI

You are a knight of the people, defending the common citizen from any threat he might face.

#### Quirk

Earn a Hero Point when you solve a problem by convincing a group of people to unite and stand up for themselves.

| Advantages | Skills |
|---|---|
| Flashing Blade | Convince |
| Leadership | Empathy |
| Linguist | Notice |
| | Ride |
| | Weaponry |

### RYCERZ SENATU

You carry the word of the Senat. You are empowered to enact their will and answer only to them.

#### Quirk

Earn a Hero Point when you choose to hide something from an authority figure for noble reasons, and it gets you into trouble.

| Advantages | Skills |
|---|---|
| Born in the Saddle | Athletics |
| Linguist | Convince |
| Patron (Senat) | Empathy |
| | Ride |
| | Weaponry |

## Ussuran Backgrounds

### BORETS

You've made a name for yourself as an exceptional Ussuran brawler.

#### Quirk

Earn a Hero Point when someone recognizes you due to your reputation, and you'd really prefer they didn't.

| Advantages | Skills |
|---|---|
| Body Blow | Athletics |
| Reputation | Brawl |
| | Hide |
| | Intimidate |
| | Perform |

### DOVERCHIVII DUSHA

You're a sucker for a good sob story, but you'd rather trust the wrong person than turn away from someone who truly needs you.

#### Quirk

Earn a Hero Point when another character gets away with lying to you or manipulating you, and it gets you into trouble.

| Advantages | Skills |
|---|---|
| Trusting | Convince |
| Valiant Spirit | Empathy |
| | Notice |
| | Scholarship |
| | Theft |

### RAZRUSHITEL

Why go around when you can go through?

#### Quirk

Earn a Hero Point when you commit to a course of action that is loud, direct and lacks any sense of subtlety.

| Advantages | Skills |
|---|---|
| Strength of Ten | Athletics |
| Wrecking Ball | Brawl |
| | Perform |
| | Ride |
| | Warfare |

### TURĂ'S CURSED

There is more than one path to power. You know this first hand.

#### Quirk

Earn a Hero Point when you convince another character to shun authority or act outside of their defined social status, and it gets you into trouble.

| Advantages | Skills |
|---|---|
| Direction Sense | Convince |
| Sorcery (Tură's Touch) | Hide |
| Sorcery (Tură's Touch) | Notice |
| | Scholarship |
| | Tempt |

## Vodacce Backgrounds

### CAPITANO

With a ship under your feet, the wind at your back and a crew singing shanties, there's nothing you can't do.

#### Quirk

Earn a Hero Point when you commit to a dangerous course of action because your bravado and ego won't let you turn away.

| Advantages | Skills |
|---|---|
| Married to the Sea | Aim |
| O Captain My Captain | Convince |
| Sea Legs | Empathy |
| | Intimidate |
| | Sailing |

### MOROSO

What's the point of romance if it doesn't come with a little—or a lot—of danger?

#### Quirk

Earn a Hero Point when you choose to let another character get away with something because you're romantically interested in him, and it gets you into trouble.

| Advantages | Skills |
|---|---|
| Flirting with Disaster | Convince |
| Time Sense | Hide |
| | Perform |
| | Tempt |
| | Theft |

### PISTOLA NASCOSTA

By the time they see the barrel of your pistol, it's already too late. You hope it doesn't come to that.

#### Quirk

Earn a Hero Point when you solve a problem with the threat of violence, but without having drawn your firearm.

| Advantages | Skills |
|---|---|
| Fast Draw | Aim |
| Staredown | Athletics |
| | Empathy |
| | Intimidate |
| | Tempt |

### WILD STREGA

Your magic is unrefined, but no less potent and no less dangerous.

#### Quirk

Earn a Hero Point when you choose to help another character using your untrained Sorte powers, and it gets you into trouble.

| Advantages | Skills |
|---|---|
| Connection | Convince |
| Foreign Born | Empathy |
| Sorcery (Sorte Untrained) | Hide |
| | Perform |
| | Theft |

# New Advantages

## 1 Point Advantages

### PENNY PINCHER

Your Hero knows how to live on the skinny in order to keep a little something squirreled away for a rainy day. For each time you purchase this Advantage, you can save one Wealth Point between game sessions. This does not create Wealth, it only allows you to save existing Wealth Points.

### PERSONAL MOTTO

Your Hero has a catchphrase, adage, or rallying cry that she uses frequently. Choose your personal motto (such as "I've got a bad feeling about this" or "We always pay our debts"). Whenever you make a Risk after saying your personal motto, and whenever your personal motto is appropriate, you gain 1 bonus die.

## 2 Point Advantages

### BORN IN THE SADDLE ⓚ

Spend a Hero Point to make a special maneuver with your horse. You can spur your mount to make an incredible leap, summon your trusted steed to your side (so long as it is physically capable of coming to you) or direct it to evade an enemy's attack or strike back with hooves and teeth (preventing or dealing Wounds equal to your Ranks in Ride).

### HEARTFELT APPEAL ⓚ

Spend a Hero Point to implore another character to follow her conscience, look the other way for the greater good or otherwise do the right thing when it isn't in her best interest to do so.

### IMPERIOUS GLARE ⓚ

Spend a Hero Point to use your authority (real or perceived) to cause another character to leave you alone, get out of your way or dismiss your actions as nothing more than a tantrum thrown by a haughty noble.

### O CAPTAIN MY CAPTAIN ⓚ

Spend a Hero Point when you make a Risk to take a bold or dangerous action on the high seas in order to inspire your crew and allies to bravery. All of your allies gain Bonus Dice equal to your Ranks in Sailing.

### WRECKING BALL ⓚ

Spend a Hero Point to break down a door, smash a barricade, knock over a carriage or otherwise destroy or disable an object using your strength and momentum.

## 3 Point Advantages

### BODY BLOW Ⓚ

When you spend a Raise to deal Wounds or perform a Maneuver during a Brawl Risk, you can spend a Hero Point to increase the amount of Wounds you deal. Each Hero Point you choose to spend in this way causes your blow to deal 2 additional Wounds.

### BRAINS OF THE OUTFIT Ⓚ

When you spend a Hero Point to give Bonus Dice to another Hero during a Risk, you may spend a second Hero Point. If you do, you grant that Hero additional Bonus Dice equal to your Ranks in Scholarship if you describe how your knowledge of academic pursuits will aid her in her Risk.

### FAST DRAW Ⓚ

When you make an Aim Risk, you can spend a Hero Point to gain an additional Raise for each pair of doubles that your dice roll. These dice can still be used for additional Raises as normal.

### FLASHING BLADE Ⓚ

When you spend a Raise to deal Wounds or perform a Maneuver to deal Wounds to a character or Brute Squad during a Weaponry Risk, you can spend a Hero Point to deal the same number of Wounds to a different character or Brute Squad in the same Scene. A Hero can only use this Advantage once per Round.

### TRUSTING

Activate this Advantage after the Game Master buys your unused dice during an Empathy Risk. You gain 2 Hero Points for each die the Game Master purchases. A Hero may only activate this Advantage once per game session.

## 4 Point Advantages

### FLIRTING WITH DISASTER

Activate this Advantage when you make a Tempt Risk. The Game Master must buy all of your unused dice. A Hero can only activate this Advantage once per game session.

### MORAL COMPASS

**Requirement:** Your Hero must have completed a Redemption story, and have no Corruption.

Your Hero knows that people are better than the worst thing they ever did—in fact, your Hero embodies this. Whenever you help another Hero complete a step in a Redemption Story, that Hero loses two Corruption Points instead of one.

## 5 Point Advantages

### DARK GIFT Ⓚ

Choose one Monster Quality. You can spend a Hero Point to gain the Villain benefits of that Monster Quality for a Round. Whenever you activate your Dark Gift, you gain 1 Corruption Point, but you do not roll Corruption. If use of this Advantage causes you to reach 10 Corruption, you immediately become a Monster—not a Villain, a *Monster*. While active, your Dark Gift's manifestation is obvious to even a casual observer—your eyes might glow brightly, leathery wings may sprout from your back or your skin might become oil-slick and black as night. Anyone who sees you knows you for what you truly are—a Monster.

A Hero can only acquire this Advantage after Hero Creation by adventuring in Eisen.